MW00652355

Lost Girl Saved by Grace

|A Memoir |

By: Chanel Dionne

Copyright © 2014 by Chanel Dionne

THE HOLY BIBLE, NEW INTERNATIONAL VERSION® NIV®
Copyright © 1973, 1978, 1984 by International Bible Society®
Used by permission. All rights reserved worldwide.

All rights reserved. This book is protected by the copyright laws of the United States of America. This book may not be copied or reprinted for commercial gain or profit. The use of short quotations or occasional page copying for personal or group study is permitted and encouraged. Permission will be granted upon request.

Some names have been changed.

ISBN-13: 978-0692396865

ISBN-10: 0692396861

Chanel Dionne can be reached at:
www.chaneldionne.com
chaneldionne@lets-breakaway.com

Cover Design: Adrion Butler/Brennen Johnson
Author photograph: Lorenzo Wallace

Dedication:

Giving all Glory and Honor to God. As I clear the clutter from my life I see more and more how you've always been on my side. Your Word is everlasting true.

To my kids and the generations to come: I pray sharing my scars will grant you the permission to always walk in freedom never allowing ANYONE to quiet your steps along the way.

To those I hurt along the way: I'm sorry I was just trying to find my way.

Introduction

Girls like me don't always make it out. Girls like me stay stuck in the cycle of dysfunction and pain. Broken. We get entangled in this big world desperately trying to find our way. Lost. Looking for love but in all the wrong places. Misunderstood. Seeking direction but somehow ending up on paths of destruction. Desperate for the truth. Crying out for something real only to receive lies dipped in half truths.

We always dream, but never wake up. We always give, but never receive. We always help others, yet steadily get crushed. After being knocked down so many times we begin to measure our worth and love for ourselves by how those closest to us treats us. When we choose to define our worth through the lenses of others we begin to hurt ourselves. Why?

Because if we hear the lies long enough and we already have an inner enemy telling us those same lies it then has the power to become your truth. That was me. Lost girl.

Growing up without an identity anchored in God, my creator, I lost my way. In an attempt to find myself I one day ignorantly handed my virtue over to the world in hopes of discovering my identity. Only to end up more lost than ever before.

*Many would say that I'm a survivor of many things. But in my reality I was just a girl **trying to find my way.** Longing to be loved, validated, and desperate to break free.*

Then one day after finally embracing God's amazing grace I finally found my treasure. All the love, hope, joy, security, worth, riches, and happiness I searched all over for was hidden inside of me all along yearning to be birthed.

This journey has taught me that hurt people truly do hurt people. Mostly importantly, healed people heal people.

4

This journey has taught me the real meaning of forgiveness. This journey has given the lost girl within me, hope. That hope is God's grace.

Because of His grace the woman in me can rise up and start to live. I don't mean waking up with roses and having this perfect life after accepting Christ. Although I wish it were so simple. Yet even under God's grace, I found myself falling short time and time again.

In the midst of it all I found out I wasn't alone. There are many just like me all over the world. Hiding behind guilt, shame, and walking in fear. Being silenced by the pain of yesterday.

I pray that as you go through the scripts of my past that you find the courage to heal the little girl or boy within you, so you too can rise up and try again.

'Failure is not the end of the road rather not getting up and trying again is.'

In the pages of this book I'm going to share with you my testimony, my story of what God has brought me from. This isn't one of those clean versions where I share with you only surface level issues I've faced. I'm taking my mask off. Join ME….

Part One

Reflections of My Past

Chapter 1

In the Beginning

Childhood.

We've all had one. Some were great. Some weren't so great. Others were short lived and you were forced into adulthood before its proper timing. No matter what your childhood was like, we've all experienced something that has laid the foundation of who we become as adults.

Many times we like to say that our childhood hasn't shaped our adult life but it's not true at all. Just sit back and think about it for a second. There may even be a habit that you're battling with right now that you can't break because the roots are too deep. Like me, you really don't want to revisit the places of where it all started.

*As adults we can either choose to be anchored in the good experiences, the bad ones, or a mixture of them both. Ultimately, the bad experiences can have the power to take the driver seat if we **ignore, mask, or hide** the pain instead of taking action to **speak up** and be* **healed.**

I grew up in a single parent household as an only child. I was the result of what I'd call two adults caught up in the moment. I was far from a love child. My mom loved me dearly but I can't say that my parents ever loved each other.

Once my dad found out that my mom was pregnant, after getting brutally cursed out by my grandma, he disappeared. Before I even entered the world, still in my mother's womb, rejection, abandonment, and fatherless love were the first battles I was forced to face. *People say quite often that you can't miss what you never had. I beg to differ. I believe you can miss what you were* **supposed** *to* **receive***. Everyone* **needs** *to know a father's love.*

My mom, 23 at the time, did what any single mother would do. Rose up to the occasion, received support and love from our family, and took on the responsibility of being a mom and dad to me.

We didn't hear from my dad again until I was about two years old. He vowed to be consistent but his actions were inconsistent and life without my dad around carried on.

By the time I was six years old, my mom had purchased our first home all alone without the help from any man or the government. Early on she taught me to **never** depend on a man financially, nor just about anything else for that matter.

We lived in the largest, one and only brick house on our street. It was in a low income area on the eastside of Fort Worth, Texas. It was an area that people considered as *"the ghetto"* but it was home for my mom and me.

Although we lived in a low income area like everyone else I knew, the kids saw the big house on the corner, the fact that I was an only child, and immediately assumed that I was a **perfect** bossy little spoiled brat who got and had all the nicest things. But it was quite the opposite.

We did live in one of the biggest houses in our neighborhood. I was blessed with a lot of things but we were still no strangers to struggle and pain. I was far from perfect.

My mom like most single parents strived to give me the best and live beyond what statistics had to say about a black single parent household. She was an amazing provider and kept me clothed, fed, and sheltered. *Still I desired something more.*

I was always so lonely as a kid growing up. *I had the only child syndrome.* I always struggled with feeling like something was missing out of my life. My journey to fill that void would start very early in life. My mom was home with me when she wasn't working but I wanted someone my age to play and explore life with.

Plus, in my household you knew not to mess with my mom when the *Lifetime Channel* was on. My mom stayed glued to the television when I was a kid. Growing up I didn't know much about personality types. My mom was an introvert.

She would ignore me a lot when we were home and I remember always feeling rejected as if my affairs or troubles I faced didn't matter to her. I didn't know back then that she was just the type of person who liked to be left alone. So we clashed a lot. I desired to be around people and interaction. My mom didn't.

I had all the latest Barbie's, easy bake oven, and game systems but none of it could fill the emptiness I felt inside. I always wanted to have a sibling in the house to play with or get on their nerves but it never happened. My mom made it clear that she wasn't having another child unless she was married.

Instead of siblings I had my cousins and childhood friends to fill the void temporarily when my mom felt like giving me a little freedom. All the way until I was about twelve it was like fighting tooth and nail at times to have company or even go outside to play.

Back then my mom always tried to keep an eye on me. I was her only baby girl and she was very protective of

9

me. Still no matter how much a parent tries to protect their child things happen. No parent is perfect and without fault. Sometimes as a parent you could be the one to make a mistake. *You turn your back for a second and you could miss a tragedy that ends up changing your child's life forever.*

A few times I'd have to cry for hours and beg to go outside and play for just thirty minutes. In those moments I used to think my mom was the meanest person I knew. When I look back I know now that was the furthest thing from the truth.

My mom had finally gotten tired of me always complaining about how lonely I was. One day she surprises me with my very own puppy that we named Chelby. She was a chow mix and I would have her to play with for a few years until she ran away.

Chelby was later picked up and returned to the pet shelter but my mom had already made up her mind that we weren't going back for Chelby and she was put to sleep. My feelings were so hurt because I really wanted to keep Chelby.

She was actually beginning to be a little expensive and I hadn't kept my part of the deal of being responsible for her. Chelby life ended and mine went on.

My grandma was a foster parent and stayed a few houses down from us so I was able to sometimes pretend like her foster children were my sisters and brothers. When we'd get the call from grandma that some new kids were coming to live with her it felt like heaven had heard my cry! For a moment I'd feel like the luckiest little girl in the world.

Those relationships were *always* bitter sweet since their time at grandmas was temporary. My grandma had adopted children before I was born but she'd never adopted anymore when I came around. As soon as we we'd start to

10

bond they'd leave and be replaced by new kids. I hated that part and I'd cry every time their case worker came and picked them up.

I'd have to start all over again with the new kids, trying to win them over and get them to trust me. Granted, some of the kids I was happy to see leave. Some of those kids were beyond bad and problematic and my grandma couldn't handle it. *Well, she could handle it but not in a way that child protective services would approve. So to avoid all of that she'd call to have the kids leave.*

I always imagined that just having a blood sibling of my own was way better than being an only child and having temporary pretend brothers and sisters.

When I wasn't at grandmas or spending time with my cousins I was home reading, playing house, and exploring my curiosity. After I got bored with playing games like Zelda or Packman on my Nintendo, you could find me standing in front of my tall sliding mirror closet doors with my music blasting pretending I was performing at a live show. I was and still am a big fan of music.

Music was my escape from my reality and became my first love. I didn't feel lonely when I had my music blasting. While some kids had imaginary friends, real friends, or siblings I had music. It brought comfort and hope to my soul.

I could close my eyes grab my hairbrush like it was a microphone and imagine that my life reflected the lyrics that blasted through my Sanyo speakers on my little boom box. I'd spend hours upon hours listening to music. I learned about **real** love and life from music, T.V., and reading.

My mom on the other hand didn't have a strong love for music like I did. When I played my songs many times she would be screaming from her room, "Chanel, turn that mess off!!"

11

I would turn it down but never off and seeds of this false sense of what love and life looked like continued to be planted in my little soul. While listening to my favorite artist like Destiny's Child, Alicia Keys, Lauryn Hill, Mariah Carey, Aaliyah and Mary J. I dreamed about what I thought family and love should really look like.

My ultimate dream as a little girl was to fall in love, get married, and have 5 kids. If for some reason I never got married or was left with a kid to raise alone I was going to be the best single mom out there. My hope was to avoid men like my dad and destructive boyfriends like the one my mom had. With some minor adjustments to what I seen at home we'd be okay.

As a kid I didn't agree with some of the family dynamics that I was raised in. There was a time that I even felt like I was adopted and just didn't fit in with my family. So my dream of having a family of my own was my way of trying to create what I always wanted for myself growing up.

My mom had been exposed to dysfunction and brokenness between a man and a woman at a very early age. She witnessed both her grandma and her mom go through abusive marriages so she vowed never to follow in their footsteps. *Like me she wanted to create a new reality.*

My grandmothers had escaped their pain by the time I entered into the world. But instead of healing they masked their pain behind work and being independent. My great grandmother had become one angry bitter woman from all the experiences and struggles she had faced and conquered in life.

My mom shared with me the horror stories of having to witness them receive beatings by their spouses. She used to ride shot gun in the car when my grandma got drunk and set out to confront her spouse with his mistress at the juke joints in town.

My mom always made sure to share with me things that my grandmothers had gone through to let me know that the concerns I had about her boyfriend were nothing to what she had witnessed.

She'd always say, "As long as he doesn't hit me."

As long as he doesn't *hit* me. As long as he doesn't hit me. Many times we always discuss physical abuse but abuse comes in many different forms other than physical.

What I didn't know was that hearing this for years and years was grooming me sub-consciously to accept abuse in other forms. Emotional. Verbal. Mental.

My mom had plans to protect me from having to witness those same dysfunctional situations. She never let a man hit her and she stayed away from alcohol other than a daiquiris every now and then. She wasn't the single black mom who partied more than parented. She hardly ever went out with friends. She never left me with strangers and family members while she did her own thing.

*Yet, no matter how hard we try sometimes if we have no healthy vision to follow and a solid foundation in **God** we somehow end up still trapped in some form of dysfunction. When our focus is more about not being like our parents verses seeking out Gods way of living we create our own unhealthy patterns.*

When we suppress our pain and don't take time to heal it has a way of still having power over us. Until we choose to break free. Patterns, like pieces to a puzzle begin to form and although they aren't shaped the same they still end up connecting to one another creating a canvas rooted from pain and dysfunction.

My grandmothers never remarried and kept a negative image in their hearts toward men. I tried rejecting what was told to me about men and I wanted to believe that all men weren't bad news.

13

Personal encounters along with stories and family patterns would make it rather difficult to create a pattern of my own that wasn't rooted from pain and dysfunction.

The example of family and love I witnessed at home between a man and woman was to be **kept a secret.** Issue number one. My mom always told me, "What goes on in this house stays in this house!" I obeyed and kept it that way, most of time.

While other kids could go to school and share openly about fun moments they shared with their family over dinner *I was told not to.* My mom had the same boyfriend from the time I was three until my junior year in high school. He never lived with us, but he did stay over a lot.

As a parent we always assume that it's okay for us to be in dysfunctional relationships around our children. We try and tell ourselves that if we speak and tell our children how to do things different they will follow what we say verses what we do. In reality we are to **train** *a child up in the way they should go with not only our words but our* **actions** *as well.*

I must not leave out the fact that in order to break old patterns and dysfunctions we are to seek God for new found freedom. Just changing your ways without God as the center will definitely recreate new unhealthy patterns and dysfunctions.

He tried to be a father figure to me but in my eyes, he had to earn the respects of being called "dad." I had a hard time believing that he had earned that privilege. Calling someone dad meant so much to me. I had never seen or known what a dad should be like but I dreamed and had visions that I held close to my heart.

I imagined a dad being someone that lived with me. Tucked me in my own bed at night. He would be the one that could make my mom smile uncontrollably. I could go

14

to him about anything and trust that he had my best interest at heart.

A dad was to be there for his family not only physically but financially and emotionally. He was to never make my mom question her place in his heart. Because he was my dad I could tell anyone in the world about him without feeling shameful about it.

That *never* became my truth. My mom's boyfriend seemed to bring more heartache and pain to the table than anything else. They worked together and to keep things professional they decided it was best to keep the relationship a *secret.*

I hated that part of their relationship because he had no problem acting as if he was totally disconnected from us in public. As if he was ashamed of the relationship. We could only see him at night. They could only go out to certain places in public to be together. *I hope you're getting the picture because as a kid I did.*

At home he wanted me to call him dad but in public he was to be known only as my mom's co-worker. I was totally confused. Between the broken promises from my dad when he came into my life and my mom's boyfriend, pain and dysfunction continued to cut deep into my soul.

I remember leaving the house with my mom in the middle of the night a couple of times and she found him with other women. Her and my adult cousin would pull up and cause a crazy scene at his apartments. I'd be lying in the back seat with the covers over my head acting like I was asleep when I really wasn't. I was in the backseat hurting for my mom and I.

Many nights I seen my mom crying over something he said, did, or failed to do. *Arguments. Broken promises. Lies. Deceit.* Still no matter the evidence that was so evident to my mom she kept staying around. I kept trying to show her that I was all that she needed.

15

He drank too. A lot. *Crown Royal* to be exact. Those nights were sometimes the worst. They'd stay up talking which in most cases led to arguments. I found myself joining into some of the arguments taking my mom's side of course. Wanting to defuse the situation but being shut out because I was just a kid.

He'd go on and on about a whole bunch of nothing trying to justify and validate his actions. Some nights were quiet and he'd come over and just fall right to sleep. Other nights he was loud and over the top in his drunk stupors.

It wasn't all bad when he was around though. We had our family outings and even game nights a few times. He let us visit his apartment maybe once or twice and cooked dinner for my mom and I. He helped us out financially from time to time but it wasn't given to us in grace. It seemed to always come with some stipulation like calling him dad when I didn't really want to.

Sometimes he'd come over a happy drunk and we'd stay up as a family. He'd come in my room and give me pointers on how to catch the right melody and stay on key with the artist I'd be singing to. He loved music like I did.

If talent wasn't a factor I probably would have considered being a singer or just someone who was in the spotlight but my mom's boyfriend made it clear that becoming a "star" wasn't in my future. So I kept that desire deep inside of me. *But I **always** idolized and looked up to celebrities as a kid.*

My other dream was to become a defense attorney and live in France. I always wanted to move far away to start my life over where no one knew me. I really liked to help people who were misunderstood. I was always very passionate about helping others. Plus, I loved to argue and could hold up in debates. *I could argue you down if it was a topic I was passionate about!*

16

My passion to become an attorney stemmed from home. I often joked with my uncle that I would one day become his attorney. My uncle stayed on the run for about fifteen years for a minor drug charge from his teen years. My uncle was a man in my life that I actually admired in-spite of the flawed lifestyle he lived.

He lived the life rap artists like the 504 boys and Cash Money crew rapped about back then. He kept stacks of cash, his friends drove the nicest cars, and he had a beautiful woman for every day of the week. He was a *hustla.* A street pharmacist.

In spite of all the luxuries his life brought part of me still hated to watch him live in fear of the cops coming one day. The money was supposed to set him free but it came with him always having to look over his shoulder. So he was more like a runaway slave.

He joined the Crip gang when he was twelve and had been living the fast life ever since then. My uncle, like everyone else has his own story to tell. I guess by the time he was 12 he felt as if he was man enough to make the decision to leave his unhealthy reality at home and create something new. *I dreamed of being the one to set my uncle free at his case one day.*

He'd always say, "Niece by the time you're an adult that case will be dropped and I won't need you."

By the time I became an adult I would find out that my uncle needed something more than an attorney to beat a little weed case.

In elementary school, I was a Girl Scout and a member of a performance cheerleading squad called, The All Stars. I made lots of friends on the cheer squad. I got the opportunity to visit different cities for competition and I went to the beach for the first time. I loved it.

Being a performance cheerleader I was able to utilize my talent of dancing. As a kid, I loved to dance. My friends and I were always the center of attention when music and dancing was involved. We were in talent shows and even participated in little dance competitions at the YMCA during summer camp.

School was fun and I had a lot of great teachers to keep me on track academically. Back then teachers still genuinely loved and cared about their students. I had friends but even as a kid it was hard to trust them because they would often reject me too.

It was like playing tug of war, one day they were my friends and the next day they weren't. I never really got to see or experience the feeling of being liked consistently in a relationship. Since I was always looking to fill a void in my life I took *everything* to heart.

Early in life it seemed like boys had it out for me too. They always found something to pick on me about. Then they'd turn around and say they actually really liked me. I never understood why liking me meant making fun of me or hitting me on the butt.

I literally had to run from this one little boy all the time because he was so aggressive but he eventually told me that it was his way of letting me know he had a crush on me. *Really?!*

It wasn't a good feeling but these destructive patterns of how people were going to treat me in relationships were beginning to form.

I grew up going to the Boys and Girls Club in my neighborhood where I got to hang with friends. I loved all the extracurricular activities like playing on the pool tables, basketball, and foosballs, to hanging out in the computer lab and art room. I participated in talent shows with my friends to show off our dance skills.

We even had sleep overs at the club. When those got of hand they stopped having them. It was rumored that the older kids were engaging in inappropriate sexual behavior that many of us wasn't at all surprised by.

I was introduced to exploring my sexuality at a very young age. I'm not even sure when it first started because it happened so much in my life. The earliest I remember is six years old. This would lead me to having an **unhealthy** foundation in regards to sex.

At home, I hardly ever slept in my own bed. I slept in bed with my mom until I was about twelve. My mom's boyfriend would be there sometimes and I was exposed to more than I should have.

The mother and daughter bond that my mom and I was supposed to share was tainted and shattered because of things witnessed during bedtime. It didn't stop there.

As kids, we would play this one game in particular called *House*. In this game each of us pretended to be either mom or dad. We did things like lay down with our clothes on and someone would get on top and start humping up and down as if we were having sex.

Back then we called it *hunching*. It was clear that we were acting out things we witnessed at home or TV but to us kids we managed to turn it into a game. It became a normalcy for my playtime with friends to turn into us playing house and doing things that only adults should have been doing. I don't ever remember feeling innocent and pure as a child.

I would continue to have these type of experiences throughout my childhood sometimes with my clothes off against my will. I had even suck my first pair of breast before I entered high school. Along with being exposed to pornography by the time I was ten and being fondled inappropriately by different individuals. There were times when I willingly engaged in doing things with others.

This is only just a few situations that laid the foundation of my unhealthy view and lifestyle of sex that would later come in my life.

Back then being so young I took it at face value and believed that it was all just another game of fun. But it wasn't so easy for me to let go. It had a hold on me and it left the door open for the enemy to embed a seed of confusion against my sexuality.

I began touching myself when I was home playing alone. As I got older touching myself turned into a secret masturbation issue. I hated it but I didn't know how to quiet the temptations I now had. It seemed natural to just give in and touch myself. Afterwards I would feel so horrible about it. A war raged on the inside of me.

I could never find total pleasure in what I was doing. Part of me knew that I needed help but I didn't have anyone to turn to about my personal issues. I wasn't sure if I was to like what was going on or not. Everyone said it fun and games while some said I needed to keep it all a secret but the daunting feelings and thoughts that ran through my mind made me feel otherwise.

I continued to struggle secretly with my sexuality alone. I felt like I had no one to trust. Even the ones who were supposed to be there to protect me often times left me feeling like they were on the opposing team.

Today I know that freedom from what I went through can only be found in Christ Jesus. My deliverance wouldn't come until I became an adult. So, imagine being a kid having to carry the burden of secret sexual issues while having to always pretend around others like everything was going well in your life?

As a kid I knew nothing about the power of the word of God or prayer. I had never seen anyone in my family pray other than over food. Even that wasn't often.

We did attend church growing up but we were more like seat fillers than actual active church members. My grandma was very religious about making sure me and the foster children went to vacation bible school at church every year. But there wasn't any ministry or volunteer involvement. In my eyes church was just part of our weekly routine.

At church my pastor always started off his sermon with a scripture. Soon after, he was yelling at the church for being in his personal business. His platform seemed to be used for rebuking the church verses teaching the good news of Jesus Christ. It was rumored that he was cheating on his wife with one of the church members and the whole church was talking about it.

My mom and grandma gossiped about it all the time when we were home. I never recall hearing much about Jesus at home other than a few gospel songs by Kirk Franklin nor did I witness my mom in her bible outside of church on Sunday.

We had a few Jesus pictures hanging up on the wall in the house. But I still didn't have a proper understanding about God and how my relationship with Him should be.

There was this one quote that my grandma had hanging up in one of her rooms that got my attention on many occasions. I carried a burden of shame and guilt because of the secrets I dealt with. The quote said, "Good girls go to heaven. Bad girls go everywhere."

I would feel so bad about what was going on I'd get on my knees in front of that quote and cry out to God telling Him that I wanted to go to heaven and I didn't want to go everywhere. "Please God help me. I don't want to go to everywhere. I want to do right. Help me to stop doing this."

It wasn't until I turned twelve that my pastor preached a sermon that moved me. My cry for help had been answered. I went down to the altar and give my life to Christ. I got baptized that same day. I wanted all my issues to go away for good. I got plugged into church to become an active member.

I started attending bible study and everything. Until, everyone in class made fun of me because I couldn't pronounce the words from the King James Version of the bible. I wasn't new to being picked on but I couldn't drop out of school. I could drop out of Sunday school and I did just that.

I tried reading the bible on my own but I had a hard time connecting the stories to my life. I would open up the bible and get totally overwhelmed. It was weird too because I actually loved to read but when it came to the bible it was a total different story. Immediately the enemy continued to come after me.

I didn't stay in church long enough to have God's Word hidden in my heart to build a foundation of faith for my life. Where I come from we're taught that you're only considered a "real" Christian if you're a faithful church member. No one ever took out the time to explain the importance of having a personal relationship with God.

From what I could tell at the time God didn't seem to care. I had been born into this dysfunction and there wasn't a way out. I continued to carry these secrets and my sexuality would continue to be attacked. I had cried out and nothing had changed. I had tried to change and stop but the temptations were too strong.

A little girl should be playing with her dolls, having fun with friends and exploring life. Instead I was fighting and playing with sexual demons, struggling with perverted thoughts, and trying to keep it all hidden to maintain some sort of a normal childhood.

The older I got I figured that I knew enough about God because I knew all about His wrath. I knew the difference between heaven and hell for sure. I always had a reverence for God, but as time progressed more situations would occur throughout my life I'd began to feel as if I wasn't worthy to honor God with my life.

I began to have a negative outlook on how I thought God saw me because of the struggles I faced as a child. I really thought he hated me. At times I would go on to feel as though I was cursed and destined to never break free.

I was ignorant to the fact that God loved and valued me before the ends of the earth was created. No one had ever told me that I needed to put God first. I had no true understanding about the Holy Spirit dwelling in me.

God was always on my list of importance but he wasn't top priority nor was it instilled in me that he needed to be. This became the mindset that I would carry about God right into my adult life. I continued to suffer secretly.

"Do you not know that your bodies are temples of the Holy Spirit, who is in you, whom you received from God? You are not your own, you were bought at a price. Therefore, honor God with your bodies." 1 Corinthians 6:19, 20 NIV

Nobody told me that my body was a temple when I was a little girl. I was being taught that my body was a playground to play house with that I had no control over. My innocence and purity had been tampered with and it seemed like there was no turning back.

In spite of what was going on behind the scenes my life continued to be rather normal. I planned to never allow what happened privately to affect my life publically. I had seemingly managed to mask my issues and I would learn to pretend very well. I had even tried to forget things that had happened to me thinking that forgetting would make it all better. But it was only the beginning.

Today my generation has been labeled as the most hypersexualized generation and culture the world has ever seen. Let's be honest for a moment can you blame us?

When I made the decision to heal wholeheartedly it was impressed upon me that I needed to take a ride down memory lane and address some issues from my childhood.

I didn't want to and honestly when I started writing this book and sharing my testimony I basically zoomed right past my childhood. Attempting to make myself believe that it played no major role in my adult life. I even had people encourage to not go there saying that it was irrelevant. What a lie that was.

I thought I had managed to bury the pain and confusion when in reality it wasn't hidden at all. It was only being revealed in other areas of my life.

Over 20% of the people reading this has been exposed to sex too soon.

How do I know?

Statistics prove it and our way of life prove it as well.

I was going to include some statistics but I changed my mind. I want to challenge you as you read my story to look over your life.

How old were you when you were introduced to sex?

Whether it was fondling to masturbation or actual intercourse.

24

Would it be acceptable for your child to have the same experiences that you had as a kid when it comes to sex?

*When I say kid I even mean being a teenager as well. Teenagers should be exploring **life** not someone else's body parts including their own. Today issues like pornography addiction starts as early as age eight.*

So by knowing these facts and desiring to live a life of truth and freedom I went back and decided to deal with things I had experienced as a kid.

Sex has become trivial to many people. Everyone is doing it. It's no longer looked upon as sacred and pure between two married individuals who love each other. At least not in the culture nor the environment in which I grew up in.

Who is the one to blame for all of this?

I don't blame parents, teachers, pastors, or even the abusers. Abusers were once victims themselves. I'm not excusing them from the damage they've done but only stating a facts by the way.

I blame the real enemy SATAN himself who has deceived the hearts and the mind of Gods people to believe that SEX is something that needs to accepted in all forms. When that is totally far from the truth.

GOD created sex to be enjoyable under marriage alone. But today it is acceptable in all forms.

Most of us was never taught how to discipline ourselves sexually. My first experience or talks about sex didn't come from a safe or healthy environment.

Many of us are afraid to go back to those places or we prefer to keep this perverted mindset about sex and sexuality that the enemy has pressed upon us.

Let's fight back. *Study and get a healthy view of what sex should look like. Talk with your kids and share with them what you've been through. You don't have to get*

25

graphic but be authentic. Kids need it.

Most importantly deal and heal from those past wounds. Your acceptance of giving your body up so easily, seeing sex as nothing more than an easy transaction could be rooted from the early childhood unhealthy experiences you had as a kid but never got addressed.

Contrary to what many say, our childhood shapes and lays the foundation of our adult life.
Were u a teen parent?
Did u lose your virginity before becoming an adult?
Have you had more than one sex partner before marriage?
Do u remember being fondled inappropriately as a child?
Were you raped and never told anyone about it?

I'm not saying that everyone has been abused or mistreated but I am saying that many of us have been exposed to soon to sex that we weren't ready for and it has shaped our adult life and left many of us confused and misinformed about the value that our sexuality holds.
Think about it... Where does your view of sex come from?

Chapter 2

My School Daze

Some kids can't wait to get up in the morning to go to school. Their eager to see their friends and learn new studies. **Not for me.** *I was ready for my childhood to be over so that I could enter into adulthood and start doing my own thing. I was having personal battles at home and then I would have to go to school and fight there.*

Fight for my image, fight to have friends, fight to keep my name clean, and fight to even keep a smile on my face. I had fun moments and I eventually made some good connections with others who tried to understand me without having to first try and tear me down. But those moments were short lived. I wanted more than anything for it to all be **OVER.**

At the boys and girls club I met my first boyfriend. He gave me a ring that had my favorite four letter word engraved on it. **LOVE.** I was flattered to be his girl. We were always so quiet and timid around each other but every time he came around I would always get the butterflies in my tummy. *Then all that changed rather quickly.*

I broke my arm playing on the monkey bars and stopped going to the club for a little while. When I came back, he had dumped me for someone else. That sucked, but I got over it and moved on. *By the time I turned seven I was already looking for love, having boyfriends, and experiencing getting my heartbroken.*

My friendships were a struggle too. One of my so called friends would have been considered a bully today because she was always picked on me. One week, she was my friend and the next, she was making me cry. In her eyes I was just another spoiled brat. I stayed on an emotional rollercoaster in this friendship. I wasn't intentionally trying to act a certain way I was just trying to find my way. But she never saw it that way.

She got rather extreme with her tactics and even put her hands on me a few times. She'd even convince the other kids not to like me. I'd come to the club the next day and no one would be my friend.

In my eyes I saw her as an older sister whose nerve I got on. I continued to get her to like me even though she treated me like crap most of the time. I was never really good at picking friends.

Being bullied was considered a normal part of childhood for me. I got bullied at school, kids on my street, and at my grandma's house by a few of the foster boys she had. With my personal issues going on and the crap I took from the kids growing up I became highly sensitive about everything. I cried about almost anything.

The older I got the more difficult it got to make friends. By the time I got to middle school, the girls favorite line was, "You think you're all that."

If the girls weren't picking on me about my hair it was my clothes to my academics. My hair was too short or I was too smart.

As a result of this, I had my first fight in the sixth grade, which got me suspended and an appearance in teen court. I always had a hard time with letting attacks go and I took a lot of things to heart instead of just being a kid and letting it all go.

Whenever I had issues at school with girls, I ended up in the counselor's office in a peer mediator session. I hated those sessions because it made issues worse between the girls and I. It would leave me friend-less and that was a place I didn't like being.

Daily I struggled with the decision of choosing to be myself or run with the crowd. Most of the time I would choose to run with the crowd. *I didn't see the value in standing alone back then.*

Finally in seventh grade, I met my best friend Shay and we started doing everything together. She was like a sister sent straight from Heaven. We dressed alike and my mom let her come over often. I even got my own phone line just like her so we could talk more.

My best friend and I sneaked boys over at each other's house and everything. We never did anything sexual with the boys though; we just talked and sometimes kissed. *Growing up I was the little girl that was labelled "fast" because I was seen trying to get attention from boys.*

Often times we're so busy trying to label little boys "bad" and girls "fast" when God is calling us to help them instead. Dig deeper. There is always a reason to why kids act out. Someone, an adult, could have challenged my behavior but instead I was thrown in the "fast girl" category and overlooked. We as a people have learned to label people things as if it takes away our responsibility of loving and respecting them as a human being. We have got to do better.

I got caught once with a boy in the house on my granny's birthday when I was in the seventh grade. We were sitting on the couch making out when my mom came home from work early. My granny was having a birthday dinner and my mom wanted to come home early and surprise me with the news. Little did she know the surprise would be on her.

I hid him in the laundry room. When my mom came in the house I tried to act like I wasn't feeling good and didn't want to go. She immediately knew something was wrong. I would never miss an opportunity to get out of the house. She grew suspicious but she wasn't expecting to discover what was found.

I went to the bathroom to calm my nerves. When I came out the bathroom she was dragging him out of the back door. She tried to whoop me after we came back from dinner but she cried harder than I did.

By middle school I had built up this inner anger toward my mom. The world saw my mom in her own mask while I saw her with it off. I knew she loved me but at times I couldn't see that she loved me the way I desired to be loved and protected. I needed more than just clothes on my back, food, and shelter. I needed to be validated. I needed to know that my voice mattered.

My mom tried her best to make sure to keep me happy even if it meant sacrificing her own happiness and falling behind on bills to do it. Her way of making me happy was through buying me things. She always told me that seeing me happy was enough for her.

After having to witness my mom sitting in bed many nights with tears streaming down her face as overdue bills lay scattered on her bed many nights, I wasn't convinced that was true. She tried her best to show me that she was content with her life but deep down inside I know that she had desired more and sacrificed it all for me.

I dreamed of one day being able to take care of my mom so we wouldn't have to live a life of struggle and robbing peter to pay paul forever. At times she didn't even like me getting the mail so I wouldn't see the pick slips.

In spite of the financial worries and disagreements we had, when my birthday came around my mom was a perfectionist. She went all out. I had the best slumber parties. We'd stay up all night playing games and the following day my mom took us to the water park.

My mom was considered the cool mom to all my friends. She was so chill often times it felt like she was more of a friend than my mom. All my friends fell in love with my mom and some would even say they wish she was their mom. She wasn't much of a disciplinary though and it would later backfire.

My mom was raised in a very strict environment and promised herself that she would be lenient towards her kids if she ever had any. *She lived up to that promise and I got away with a lot because of it when I later began to act out and rebel.*

She was raised by my grandma who known as the "mean lady" on our street. You didn't want to get on her bad side. My mom grew up around that. My mom's introvert personality probably stemmed from the way in which she grew up. But that's her story to tell.

I loved school when it came down to academics and I was always an honor roll student. I enjoyed English and Math studies more than anything. I was far from a nerd but if I stayed focus and didn't let the distractions of life get in the way my future had hope. At least my teachers thought so.

I was selected to be part of program called Sumer Bridge that was held at a local private school while in middle school. The program was in place to help students from under privileged communities stay focused on their study during the summer time while being in a fun and different environment. I had so much fun there and I made friends with many students from other schools.

I loved Summer Bridge and looked forward to it every summer. I even had a boyfriend while I was there. We ended up breaking up once the program was over because we didn't attend the same schools. I was still a virgin during this time but those kisses we shared left my heart beating for more. I had planned to hold onto the purity that hadn't yet been fully taken from me until I got married.

At Summer Bridge, I also met my long-time friend Derrick, who would become like a brother to me. Derrick and I talked all the time after school on the phone. Then one day, he shared with me that he was a homosexual. I tried to act surprised, but I wasn't. When I met him, he had a girlfriend but everyone knew the relationship was a cover up.

Derrick and I went to different middle schools, but we applied to go to the same high school. We chose the same school because of the law and government special interest program. I still wanted to be an attorney and Derrick wanted to study criminal justice.

All of the few friends I had from my middle school went to other high schools and I was back on a quest to make new friends all over again. I was shy and sort of an introvert by this time. I'd open up once I felt comfortable around you. If I didn't know you my guard would be completely up. In school they considered me to be "stuck up." I knew how the whole friend thing worked and I was really over it.

Derrick on the other hand was an extrovert and very friendly. Over half of the people I knew and became affiliated with in high school I wouldn't have known if it wasn't for Derrick. Derrick was the go to guy in school and everyone knew him. If you wanted the latest news Derrick was your dude. I didn't personally know a lot of people but Derrick kept me in the loop.

I took mostly honors and advanced learning classes. So I was hardly in class with any of the cool kids and class clowns. Most of the times my classes were boring and any fun or friend making I had was in the hallways or at lunch.

Shay didn't come to my school until after freshman year. We stayed close until our junior year. She started believing gossip and false rumors about me and we became distant. It hurt that one of the only true friends that I had believed such things about me. We would rekindle our friendship but it was never the same.

I often questioned if my new friends were truly my friends, or if they just tolerated me for Derrick's sake. So, I decided to try and make my own friends. I was on three-way call once with friends and I was supposed to hang up, but my line didn't disconnect.

I ended up muting my line and staying on. They began to talk about how ugly I looked, yet how nice of a person, I was. It hurt to know that they talked about me behind my back.

I never wore make-up because I always believed in looking natural. I didn't want people saying that I was wearing make-up because I believed I was ugly. Instead, I did what I knew best and continued to stay on top of the latest trends and fashion.

I tried not to let how others talked about me change how I say myself but that became another battle within myself. People took my kindness for weakness and it became a norm for me accept that in my relationships.

There were times where it felt as though the friendships were based more on competition than on the qualities of what I thought friendship stood for. I desired sisterhood and connection while the others girls seemed to only want to compete about something.

Kids always joked about me having a big sized head then it was my fat face and long chin. When I was in the seventh grade I fell off of a bike riding down a hill. The fall left a scar under my chin that I became very self-conscience about. People would make fun of it a lot.

It wasn't the first time I had been called ugly. After hearing it so many times and being criticized about my traits I began to believe that it may have been some truth to it.

I stayed trying to defend myself outwardly but no matter how hard I fought outwardly I had already lost the battle because secretly because I believed inwardly, that I was u-g-l-y.

Bad hair days or the wrong outfit were the worst and added fuel to the fire. So I started to over compensate in keeping my hair and dressing nice to keep the pressure off of being talked about.

When that didn't work, I talked about others and hurt people with my words since it had been done to me.

I had my mom and other people try and tell me I was beautiful but even they slipped sometimes out of anger and jokingly said I was ugly too. It gets hard trying to believe the good people have to say when they say not so good things too.

I always thought that if I had siblings I could have bypassed all of this. *I eventually learned that even siblings can turn into adversaries.*

I continually tried to fit in and hang with these girls. I knew that if they really gave me a chance, they genuinely like me. It never worked. I really didn't need them to like me. *The real problem was that I needed to like and love myself.*

One of my childhood friends attended high school with me and I thought we could start hanging out more. We had a different circle of friends and didn't get to hang as much as I'd liked to. Our friendship got tested a lot but through it all we managed to stay close.

When I look back many of these friends are what I'd call convenient strangers today. In reality none of us genuinely enjoyed one another.

34

*Real friends don't tolerate you they actually enjoy
you. Real friends don't talk about you behind your back
they defend you. You are a mirror image to the company
you keep. If you're always complaining about your friends
to other people I would suggest looking in the mirror or
changing circles. Ask God to send you the right friends. He
won't let you down. It's taken me a lot of wrong turns to
understand that.*

My mom worked hard to keep me in the latest
trends, and I constantly begged for new stuff. If Jordan's
came out, I got them. When everyone started wearing
stilettos and pumps, I had them. I made sure that everything
I wore matched to the *T*. I continued to over compensate to
help fill the voids I had. I continued to find ways to keep
busy so I could disassociate myself from the battle going on
within myself.

My mom worked a salary job and she got a part-
time job to help keep bills afloat and afford my fashion
habit. That was a bill all by itself. Fashion gave me life.
When I put my foot in a pair of Jordans my confidence
came and my self-image issues temporarily went away.

All in the midst of this I ended up becoming quite
popular in high school. Keeping up with the latest trends
became an escape for me. At home, I continued secretly
struggling with my sexuality.

At school my friends openly discussed their issues
with me and my friend Derrick even opened up to me about
some horrific childhood experiences he had. I wanted to
confide in someone but I was afraid of being looked at
differently. It was clear my issues would have become the
latest gossip at school if ever revealed. Gossip wasn't a
stranger in the circles I ran with.

I didn't really want people to know that I had
struggles especially the struggles that included my

sexuality. I felt nasty as if I had done something wrong to cause this confusion to come upon me. Whenever I got the courage to speak they would either keep the conversation about themselves or end it.

Back then I was everyone's confidante but I had no one to dump my issues upon. Through the eyes of others I had it ALL together anyway. I was an only child, my mom loved me, and I got all the cool stuff people assumed if they were in my shoes life would be great. Although I knew it was far from the truth I continued to let people view me that way.

The façade was much better than what lied underneath. Underneath it all, I hated being an only child. I would have given up all my materials stuff for a friend. I even questioned whether or not my mom really loved me.

My mom and I were close but she never liked to discuss "deep issues." When I did she always say, "You'll be alright don't worry about it."

She didn't even prepare me for my menstruation. I was in the 7th grade when it first happened. It took about two hours and four trips to the restroom later to discover that it was that time of the month. That was only because I went to the principal and tried to explain to him what was going on and he immediately sent me to the nurses office.

My life as a teenager continued to unfold. I continued to anticipate on the day I would finally enter adulthood so I could leave everything behind.

To get a head start I got my first job at Six Flags when I turned fourteen. I continued working all during high school from fast food restaurants, catering food, to working at a gas station. I picked up my strong work ethic and independent spirit from both of my parents.

I didn't know much about my dad but one thing I find out was that he managed to always keep a decent job just like my mom.

At my school instead of gangs we had different cliques. I joined one called Most Hated Females. There was cliques for everybody. The kids who liked to fight, pretty girls, the criminals, the freaks, and nerds. MHF consisted of mostly upperclassmen, juniors and seniors.

We had monthly meetings and threw parties regularly. I finally felt like I belonged to something of importance once I got accepted into the clique. MHF was built on sisterhood values like college sororities. If something went down at school they were there to have my back.

A majority of us had a lot in common and we got along rather well. It all came to a bitter sweet end when the seniors graduated. The rest of the clique went their separate ways and I was right back where I started.

Academically, I continued to excel in school. My only setback was *my attitude.* It was bad. *Hidden pain and confusion has a way of revealing itself in an unattractive way if left untouched.*

I stayed in the office for being outspoken. I didn't even get to cheer much in school because I was always in trouble. Teachers changed after elementary school and I felt boxed in to what they thought of "us." The black ghetto kids. So many students were uninterested in what school had to offer and I looked to fit that description so I always had to defend myself and prove otherwise.

I was very passionate person and to the teachers it came off as disrespect. Every teacher I had in high school wrote me up at least once for being outspoken. I didn't care and I continued to stand up for myself and others vocally.

While my image to the world seemed well put together, I was considered one of the popular kids and I was on top of my academics, my private issues continued to spiral.

Relationships would become my outlet and they kept me away from dealing with the issues I had going on within. My secret struggle with my sexuality didn't come by itself. It left me more insecure and very self-conscience. I struggled with self-value and having a healthy self-image. There were times I didn't even like me.

Relationships helped me to feel good about myself. They became a piece to my puzzle that I yearned for to validate and make me feel worthy. I would place my value on the material possessions I had, the good grades I made, and the money I had. Maybe I did have some value other than my cool Jordan's, if so I was oblivious to it.

From this point on I was the girl who was book smart but heart dumb. Give me a school test and I'll pass it. When it came to a relationship and discerning a person's true motive it was a total different story. I only paid attention to the fact that they were interested in me. I'd dive right into the relationship.

I never took out the time to discover if they had any ulterior motives. It would be too late and I'd already be in too deep once the ugly truth surfaced. I'd be in and out of verbal and emotional abusive relationships from this point on. Brokenness attracts brokenness. Like most teens, I thought I knew what I wanted. Boy was I wrong...

I once heard that a girl's first love should be her dad. Your dad should be the one to sit you on his lap as a kid and confirm with his actions how a guy should treat you and love you.

A girl is to discover her identity and learn how the opposite sex should treat you from the love and teachings from her dad. What fathers fail to realize is that their absence still paints the picture and lays the foundation for their daughters. And sons.

Neglected and rejected is the foundation that was laid before me. When I finally got to know my dad, he came in and out of my life every few years. He would make promises to come around more but never followed through.

He'd pick me up and take me around his friends or someone he was dating at the time but he was never consistent on his promises to be more involved in my life.

My dad was very big on appearance and I remember on many occasions he made it his business to take me shopping for better quality clothes. He was into designer labels like me. My mom was never been into fashion unlike my dad. I thought our interest in fashion would bring us closer but I was wrong.

He had friends who owned urban clothing stores and we'd go there to get the hook up on the latest fashions. He insisted on always focusing on my appearance critiquing me. Whenever we got together he always had something to say about my appearance. Just being around him was never enough. He would make suggestions that I wear authentic ear rings instead of cubic zirconia.

I never got those diamond earrings but I did get a tennis bracelet once that I ended up losing at school. Not only did I have to face focusing on my appearance from the kids at school my dad was just the same.

By the time I made it to high school he started dating a lady whose kids went to high school with me. My dad came up to my school many times and didn't even acknowledge or speak to me. I often wondered just what was so wrong with me that made my dad want to keep me a secret and not acknowledge me in front of his new family.

I knew it wasn't my mom causing him to be that way. My mom never spoke ill of my dad and she made it clear to that she wanted me come up with my own conclusion about who he was. I did just that.

At first, it hurt to witness my dad with his family. Then, it turned to hate and bitterness. It wasn't just the fact that he was absent that affected me but it was the fact that he acted as if he wanted to be around but he never followed through on it. In private he was my dad but in public we were total strangers.

Then coming up to my school and I tell my friends, "there goes my dad", and he walks past me like I'm a stranger. Being angry about the situation helped to hide the pain and confusion that I felt inside. I was more motivated to one day have a family of my own to break this pattern. *After that, every person I dated I would make them try to do and become what my dad never was to me.*

I couldn't stand men who denied their own flesh and blood. I hoped that my kids' father wouldn't be that way. Even if he was, I would handle him just how my mom handled my dad. My mom never argued with him or chased him down in an effort to force him to be part of my life.

She always left the communication open for him to step up at any time but he never did. To a man who is used to being chased it probably seemed like my mom didn't

40

care or she was letting my dad off scot-free. But that wasn't the case my dad knew what he was supposed to be doing as a dad.

It wasn't just his presence that was inconsistent. My parents opened up a savings account when I was about eight and my dad only deposited fifty dollars in it the whole time it was open. Things began to get rougher for us financially and my mom started collecting child support when I was thirteen years old, but there was no retroactive pay.

She received approximately 400 dollars a month for me. But in all honesty a kid needs much more than financial support from a dad. *At least I did.* I made a promise to myself that my babies would never have to partake in being neglected like I did. I was going to love and provide all that they needed.

I didn't know, the energy you feed is the energy you will receive. If you're hurting from daddy wounds seek out healing. Don't harbor those feelings or focus all your attention on what not to do. Most times you will end up creating the same pattern instead of creating a new one.

*My desire to be loved and validated by someone never left. I wouldn't discover until later that true validation and love can **only** come from my Creator, God, not people and in most cases not even your earthly father.*

I started going to a new Boys and Girls Club while in high school and met a guy named Trent. He was a junior, seventeen, and went to a different school. He played football and ran track and was very well known in our city.

In the beginning, it was all innocent. We just talked on the phone all the time and hung out at the Club shooting hoops. I eventually fell head over heels in love for Trent and pleasing him became top priority for me. We made things official and he became my boyfriend.

You couldn't tell me that Trent and I weren't going to spend the rest of our lives together. We talked about it often. He took me on my first date. Trent didn't deny our relationship in public and he really made me feel special.

He never called me out my name unless it was to call me his baby. He seemed to have so much love and respect for me and the feeling was mutual.

I always wanted to wait until I got married before I had sex. I had somewhat of a belief system. I believed that I was going to wait until I got married to have sex. I wanted to keep my good girl image. *No one knew about the issues I faced in private. I was determined to keep it that way.*

My decision to wait until I got married to have sex wasn't because I had some deep relationship with God or saw how waiting until I was married honored God. I just didn't want to be part of the latest gossip at school or be seen as a promiscuous girl by my peers.

The closer I got to Trent, I became more concerned with pleasing him than keeping a promise to myself. Trent was cool with my decision and told me that he was willing to wait. My friends knew how I felt about waiting until I got married.

I would come back to school and listen to all their fun stories and miss the wild parties. Part of me was curious and wanted to partake in the fun my friends claimed to be having. But that's one thing about my friends that I can honestly say, they never tempted me with peer pressure.

At school, Derrick and I only took law classes together. In class Derrick and other students began to openly share their sexual encounters often. I just listened with curiosity.

Apparently everyone was doing *it* and I was missing out. There was no more playing house by this time. Everyone was going all the way. Derrick figured, rather assured me Trent was probably doing it with someone else since I wasn't willing to give it up.

Once I mentioned it to Trent, our relationship shifted rather quickly. I let him know that I didn't want him sneaking around with anyone else. He promised he wasn't and I believed him.

Then, after leaving a basketball game one night, he fingered me while we were in the van on the way back to the boys and girls club. Touching myself at home never made me feel the way Trent did. If sex felt anything like that then maybe it wasn't so bad to try it out.

I lost my virginity to Trent my freshman year. I struggled with feeling guilty about us having sex. We planned out our special day and even had to change it a couple of times because I was so nervous about really going through with it.

Trent reassured me it was okay to have sex before marriage as long as you loved the person you were doing it with. Our special day happened on Halloween.

Sex was quite the opposite of being fingered. It was painful and I wanted to end it all but he insisted we had to finish what we started. I remember my first time quite vividly. I even shed some tears that evening because it hurt so badly. It was nothing close to the intimate love making scenes from TV.

Trent made sure to be as gentle as he could but it was impossible to be gentle under those circumstances. It felt as if he was trying to create his own entry way into my body. I left his moms house in pain but feeling closer to him than ever before. It was my very first *soul tie*.

A soul tie is that invisible feeling you get when you've allowed yourself to connect to a person physically, mentally, and even emotionally. You can't really explain it but even when you're not around this person you long for them.

A scent reminds you of them. You find yourself reflecting their attitude and saying things that you'd normally hear them say. Many times we confuse this feeling and connection with love but sometimes love isn't even in the equation. Lust is.

He never tried to use a condom and when I asked him about it, he told me that since he would be my first and my only, we didn't need to use any. Condoms were for people who slept around with multiple partners.

Since we wouldn't be sleeping around outside of the relationship I had no reason to worry about diseases. We knew that condoms were to prevent pregnancy too but Trent told me "pulling out" worked just as good to avoid getting pregnant. I didn't know any better so I took his word for it.

Trent always said that condoms took away the true feeling. Since he was my first and I didn't have any diseases, we were safe. I trusted Trent. Even though he wasn't a virgin, Trent claimed he had only been with one other person before me and they were each other's first, so we had nothing to worry about.

I was naïve, what fourteen year-old isn't to some degree? Especially when no one has prepared them for the journey. I never had the sex talk with my mom or any healthy adult. My mom didn't see the need to discuss those

44

types of things with me. We later had what we thought was a pregnancy scare, but my period was just late. I ended up having to tell my mom that I was sexually active but she still never intervened.

In the beginning, Trent and I couldn't stay away from each other. Everywhere we went, we held hands and locked lips. We snuck off from the club often to go and make love at the local college library and many other random places.

The pain I once felt from sex turned to pleasure. Trent was happy and so was I. My battles seemed to be over. I had someone to remind me how beautiful I was more often. I no longer had to battle with my sexuality. Trent's love for me was my fix and he gave me much hope. Since we began to have sex more often my secret issues had just about ceased.

Then all of a sudden the relationship started to drift away. The calls came less and less. We didn't hang at the club much anymore. Conversations between us turned to arguments. I began to accuse him of cheating and my suspicions began to bore him.

Trent had an anger problem that I had only seen him take out on other people in the beginning of our relationship. Once things started changing in the relationship I was now the one in which he took his anger issues out on.

I stayed up many nights listening to Alicia Keys' *How Come You Don't Call Me*, crying my eyes out. I was often late for school because I was tired from either staying up waiting on him to call or crying to him all night pleading for the relationship to continue. My little fairy tale was coming to an end.

A guy from my school named James took interest in me and wrote me letters to cheer me up. He noticed the redness in my eyes and the sadness on my face. My spirit had changed and those thoughts begin to surface again, "What's wrong with me?" The letters from James really put a smile on my face but underneath the smile still laid pain.

I eventually gave in to James, we exchanged numbers and became good friends. He had just ended a relationship with another girl from our school. To keep the peace, and since Trent and I hadn't officially broken it off yet, we kept our friendship between the two of us.

James was a very affectionate guy and he was determined to convince me to end my relationship with Trent. One day, he kissed me with his soft, juicy pink lips and I could no longer resist the passion we shared for one another.

I wasn't ready to end it with Trent, so I would go see him after school and be with James at school. Although I kissed James a couple of times, we never went beyond lip locking. James knew I was still in a relationship with Trent but he was trying to do everything possible to make me his girl.

Then one day, Trent, James, and I were all at the same place and I was forced to choose. I honestly didn't want to end it because I still felt like Trent and I were meant to be. I still wanted to fight for the relationship but it was clear Trent was done. He had gotten what he wanted and was eager to throw me away. Trent and I broke up for good that day.

Trent had moved on and it was quite disappointing, but James still wanted to make it work. So, we started dating and made it official. Since we had already built a friendship it seemed like the next best thing to do. I didn't want to be alone and wallow in the residue left from the relationship with Trent and me. So I covered it up and moved on.

Suppressing my pain became a cycle of my own that would later build up into a self-destructive cycle.

James was determined to have sex, but I was really skeptical about it. I didn't love James like that. He was convinced otherwise and every time he tried, I cried. Saying, "No" and "let's wait" wasn't enough either. I liked kissing him but I didn't want it to go any further than that.

I felt guilty about being with someone other than Trent. It just didn't seem right sharing that part of me with someone else. After many failed attempts, he realized I was serious about not wanting to have sex and he stopped.

I didn't see it as James trying to rape because outside of those moments, he was a gentleman. He never became violent to the point of hitting or choking me in those moments. A little forceful but once he saw I was fearful he would kiss me and apologize.

Back then I blamed myself for misleading him with the passionate kisses we shared that may have confused him into thinking that I wanted more when I didn't. James didn't reject me in front of others. That alone made up for what went on privately between us, not to mention how handsome and popular he was.

Once we became exclusive, I acquired more haters at school. Girls picked on me in class and even whispered to me that they were having sex with him. I asked James about the accusations, but he always denied them and said the girls were just jealous and trying to break us up. I didn't believe him.

The accusations made it even more difficult for us to explore sex. I made every effort to make sure that I didn't put myself in that predicament for him to even ask for it. I stopped going over his house and I stopped going out alone with him.

I had my second fight in high school with one of his girl fans who hated me. She was a year older than me and she was much heavier than me. In my eyes, I always thought she picked on me because she knew the closest she'd ever be to James was a friend. Her excuse was that she didn't like me. I had a hard time believing that because she didn't even know me to like or dislike me.

I was never a fighter at heart but I found myself having to adjust and compromise to be somewhat comfortable in my environment. Since I didn't have siblings or close friends that's where my clique MHF came in at.

I had cousins attending school with me but by this time we rarely even spoke. I often begged my mom to let me transfer to another school because I just didn't like the atmosphere nor the kids at my school.

Since I begged to attend for the law program she suggested I suck it up and stick it out. From her perspective we were just kids so it couldn't be that bad.

James later admitted to me that the accusations were true. He had sex with one of the girls who was giving me a hard time. I ended the relationship shortly after I found out about him and Mary.

James and his friends got into trouble and he went to jail for a little while and I didn't see or talk to him for a long time. I decided to take a break from dating. I had guy's friends but I was done with trying to be all exclusive.

At my school, it was normal to see lesbians and it was rumored that some of the girls were being forced into the restroom stalls to be "turned out". The faculty, teachers, and staff seemed oblivious to the issues going on at school or they just didn't seem to care.

I made sure not to make any contact with the girls who dressed like boys or be caught in the restroom. They were just studs but a lot of them looked really mean and scary. At my school you were exposed to a lot of things like drugs, homosexuality, sex, and a host of other things.

Boys and girls were very open about their sexuality in school. If I told anyone I went to Eastern Hills the first thing they wanted to know was my sexual preference. Some schools are known for having a great football team while my high school was known for "turning" girls out in the restroom and boys giving girls oral sex at parties.

My school was called "Eat 'em Hills" or "Eat em' up Hills." After joining MHF my sophomore year I got to know a lot of upperclassmen and I went to a couple of those crazy parties.

One of my close friends confessed to me that after her break-up with her boyfriend, she was now dating a girl secretly. I never looked at her any differently and I confessed to her about my early childhood games of house and how we had explored our curiosity.

I had been touched by a girl before. Thoughts of attraction had ran through my mind a time or two but I ignored them. I liked boys not girls. My dream of a family with five kids didn't include me being with the same sex.

I wasn't expecting a door to open up for those ignored thoughts to come back and be tested. Then one night at the skating rink, this mixed girl with long black hair with a big red bow on her head started flirting with me. She didn't look mean and scary like the other girls at school. I smiled back at her and kept it moving.

A couple of weeks later while my friend was over my house talking on the phone with her girlfriend, the short girl from the skating rink came on the phone wanting to get more details about who I was. My friend let her know that I didn't get down like that but she was persistent about getting to know me. She asked if I could get on the phone to introduce myself but I declined.

We didn't attend the same school so the only time I got to see her was at the staking rink and one night she gave me her number. Toni wanted me to make the first step.

It took a few weeks for me to gather up the courage to call Toni. I had never talked to a girl before who liked me outside of the friend zone. I couldn't even believe that I was contemplating it. It felt weird and the one friend I confided in encouraged me to try it out. In her eyes it was harmless. *When curiosity and confusion intertwine anything is possible.*

I called and we ended up talking until the sun came up. We talked about everything from family issues to personal aspirations and dreams. In our first conversation we both shared that we wanted children and a family one day. We were both merely acting out of confusion.

After that night, it was pretty much history. Toni would become my first girlfriend but I definitely wasn't her first. She had done this before and was convinced that she had surpassed the confusion phase of dating girls and was sure that she was a true lesbian.

We dated off and on the rest of my high school years. I was crazy in love with Toni. She forced me to tell my mom that I was a lesbian or she would break up with me. I felt special that she didn't want to keep me a secret so I told my mom. My mom was so disappointed and disturbed by the news. After revealing to my mom that I had a girlfriend, she felt the need to start paying more attention to my personal life.

A boy from my church started crushing on me and invited me over for dinner one evening. Without hesitation, she let me go over there.

We had been attending the same church for years and he was handsome so I didn't see any harm in going over there just for dinner and to talk. He had just recently lost his grandmother.

When I got there, it was clear that he wanted to do more than talk. Apparently the word "no" didn't matter to him and there I lay in a situation I didn't want to be part of.

I saw him again at church and he apologized for his behavior. I never spoke to him again after the apology and I didn't tell my mom what happened. I continued blaming myself for other people actions.

I told Toni about what happened and she was there for me. She was pissed and wanted to go and hurt the boy for hurting me. After that I was certain that I had made the right decision.

Toni was my lover, sister, and friend all in one so I didn't need to try and fit in anymore at school or date boys anymore. After that incident I decided to date girls only.

I never liked labels and I didn't like being called lesbian or bi sexual. I was just Chanel who happened to have a girlfriend. Being labelled made life complicated. People always wanted to question me and debate over my choice for choosing to date girls. *I just wanted to be loved and accepted even if it was complicated.*

Chapter 3

Is this love. Or is this...

Love is Patient, love is kind. It does not envy, it does not boast, it is not proud. It does not dishonor others, it is not self-seeking, it is not easily angered, it keeps no record of wrongs. Love does not delight in evil but rejoices with the truth. It always protects, always trusts, always hopes, always perseveres. 1 Corinthians 13: 4-7 NIV

Lust hurts. Lust divides a family. Lust has no conscience. Lust is selfish. Lust dishonors God and self. Lust breaks the heart. Lust never protects. Lust bears false hope. Lust is the byproduct of confusion.

Now u decide...

There were plenty of signs that she wasn't the greatest person to be with. Most of our nightly phone conversations consisted of her belittling me about something. I'd just cry and try to convince her otherwise.

Initially Toni was nice and charming. She was a great listener and she seemed to really care about me. We could talk about anything. The longer we dated things continued to fall apart between us. She was a manipulator and a cheater. She had no remorse in regards to her actions. It hurt because I had put myself on the line for her.

I even dated other girls with the intentions of getting Toni's attention. But, no matter what we went through, we always ended up back together.

When I made the decision to have sex with my boyfriend for the first time I told myself he was worth the consequences that came with what we had done. When I started dating Toni I told myself the same thing. If I gave my love to a person I was putting my life on the line for the sake of the relationship.

Growing up I was told about homosexuality. In my eyes God said to love all people. I couldn't help who I had fallen in love with and in my opinion loving someone wasn't based on gender. *This became my justification to ease the confusion and guilt I felt for becoming a lesbian.*

If God didn't love me because I dated girls I figured he probably stopped loving me long before I began dating girls. My issue with sexuality didn't start there the only difference was that it was now public.

It didn't take me long to start embracing my newfound freedom wearing rainbow belts and Care Bear t-shirts to let the world know.

I became rebellious and stayed out late to be with Toni. My mom tried to become strict about curfew and monitoring who I talked to and spent time with. But by this time I wasn't trying to listen to her. She hadn't listened to me all this time.

People from her job began to see me out at games with Toni and it was getting back to her. I thought she was just trying to save face from her friends rather than genuinely caring about what I was facing.

Since I was working I felt in control of my life and it didn't help when I got my first car at sixteen. I skipped school to be with Toni. My attendance dropped drastically but my grades stayed on point.

Toni never really liked school and she had already been held back a couple of times but I didn't care. Her mom was cool most of the time and we chilled over her house often. I started smoking weed with her and her

53

friends. *Before I turned eighteen already had my experience with sex, weed, drinking, clubbing, and hydrocodone pills.*

Toni loved to embarrass me just for laughs. She'd invite me somewhere and when I'd get there, she'd be with someone else. Overcoming her rejection and trying to keep her attention became something like an addiction for me.

While normal teenagers were involved in sports, finding themselves, playing video games, or at the mall hanging with friends on their spare time I was home depressed behind my girlfriend or out partying with friends.

My mom would say, *"You're only get to be a kid once Chanel, you better slow down and just enjoy this time while you still can."*

I was always thinking about becoming an adult and I was ready for that part of my life to start. I wanted my life to matter and as a kid it was like no one took me serious. I thought being an adult would give me more control of my life. I thought becoming an adult would be my escape and I could start fresh. But I was wrong.

The foundation of what my adult life would become was being laid out for me in these moments.

Toni knew my personal insecurities that I struggled with and anytime we got into an argument she would use it all against me. With anyone else I could stand up for myself but when it came to her my only weapon I fought with was *my tears.* She called me ugly and cursed me out whenever she was ready to date other people.

Lies always easily drowned truth in my life. The truth didn't have a foundation to stand on in my life but lies did. Seeds of insecurity continued to be planted deep within my soul.

One month we seemed fine then all of a sudden she'd flip out on me and I knew it meant she was interested in someone new. It became a regular cycle in our relationship. *Breaking up then making up.*

Toni even used to threaten to fight me. She not only verbally abused me, it got physical. She slapped me once for talking back to her in front of our friends. Somewhere in all that chaos, ***I still saw love.*** I set out to prove my love for her time and time again.

As long as I maintained looking nice every day and kept my grades up everyone continued to think that all was well with me.

I got into a relationship with one of my assistant managers at my job and she introduced me to hydrocodone pills. I would go out to the club with her and her friends using her old ID or a fake one. The relationship was just as toxic and I eventually ended it and got back with Toni.

I got really upset one evening and decided that I was going to run away from home. I was just tired of everything and everybody. It always seemed as though those closet to me were out to hurt me and I couldn't deal any longer.

I left my cell phone at home to let my mom know that I meant business. She would know something was strange because I never went anywhere without it.

I left the house walking with some money in my pocket. I had no idea where I was going so I got on the city bus unaware of how far I could really go. I had never been on the bus and everyone on it looked so strange and it made me nervous. I sat at the front close to the driver.

There was this one guy in particular that came up to me while on the bus and said that he wanted to give me some street advice. He started asking me all these questions to try and find out where I was headed but I never said a word.

I gave the driver a look to let him know I was uncomfortable and he told the man to leave me alone. I made it downtown and walked around a little before going to Barnes and Noble. After sitting around in Barnes and Nobles browsing through all the books I went to the movies and watched the latest Tyler Perry film.

I thought I had wanted to runaway but when I really left home and got a small glimpse of what it looked like to be out in the world alone I knew I was in over my head. I couldn't do it.

When the film was over I called my mom to pick me up. I could hear the sound of release in her voice when we spoke and it was obvious that she had been crying. She immediately came downtown to pick me up and we rode home in silence and never talked about it again.

My life went right back to its regular scheduled program. Some insecure and lost girls strive to fit in with the cool kids for validation and approval. I was already part of the in crowd. Others join gangs. I had my clique for that. I strived for validation through relationships.

Toni and I shared our dreams of one day being mothers. I had gotten so caught up in this homosexual love that I had even came to peace about not being a mom if it meant spending my days with Toni.

She was so detailed and sure that her dream would become a reality that she had already had a guy in mind. He was her old boyfriend. Even though she had planned who her child's father would be, she always stressed how she didn't like guys sexually and that he was the only guy she had relations with in the past.

Things seemed much different when Toni and I started dating this last time. She made me promise her that no matter what, I would stay with her. I thought she had finally got the picture and was beginning to see just how much I loved her. Before all of this one of her guy friends had even tried to tell me to end things with Toni but I just wouldn't listen.

"Chanel you're too good to be all mixed up with Toni. Get out now while you can. She's not any good for you. Trust me on this one. You honestly deserve so much more." Toni's friend expressed to me. I still wasn't trying to hear it. I wanted to believe that Toni had really changed this time.

One day, I'm at work one day just minding my business when one of my co-workers from another school tells me that she heard Toni was pregnant. I just knew this was a rumor and she clearly had some wrong information.

I was used to hearing rumors and people coming up to me to gossip about Toni. She was very popular and well known in the community. I refused to believe her. We argued back and forth all day about it at work.

57

Toni and I had been spending more time together and I just couldn't imagine how I could miss a baby bump. The rumor was that Toni was past her first trimester. She still wore kids' sized shoes and clothes. She was short and petite. If she was pregnant, I thought it would show for sure.

I asked Toni anyway because the more my coworker talked about it, the more I began to believe that there could be some truth to the accusations. I called Toni every chance I got that day at work and she wouldn't pick up. I grew more and more anxious about getting to the truth.

I left her voicemails and texted her threatening messages. By this time I'm heated because the change in Toni was quite drastic and I assumed it was for good. I kept asking and she finally confessed through a text message that she was pregnant. *'I don't need you. All I need is my mama and my baby.'*

Not only was she pregnant-- she was six months pregnant. Toni always wore boy clothes and big shirts so when they got bigger, it never dawned on me that she was hiding something like this from me.

I sped over there as soon as I got off from work and it was true. She came out the back door and walked up to my car wobbling with a baby inside of her. All I could do was scream and cry. I was devastated.

The following week I scheduled a visit to the doctor. We had been sexually active and I didn't know at the time who her child's father was or how diseases get passed by same sex partners but I needed to make sure I wasn't walking away with more bad news. Everything came back negative.

As bad as the situation seemed I still couldn't just let it go. I found myself shopping for my girlfriend's daughter first outfits and pampers. We continued to date but it didn't last very long. The interference with family and her ex-girlfriend became too much to handle so I broke it off the day she gave birth to her little baby girl.

My heart was crushed that day. I had sacrificed so much to be with her. I didn't have anyone to confide in that I could trust nor was I going to pray to God for help. I didn't want to hear Derricks mouth because he had already told me time and time again to let Toni go.

The one person I thought I could trust to talk about my issue would later betray me and start dating Toni. I had heard that being in same sex relationships was the worst thing in the world to God.

A substitute teacher had heard that I was dating girls and she brought a bible to school one day and told me that it was an abomination and that I needed to end the relationship. *I figured this pain was payback from God.*

Shortly thereafter, a guy I went to high school with got shot. Senseless violence was another normal in my environment. I went to his funeral and a guy started flirting with me after the service. We exchanged numbers because he claimed he wanted to talk to me about helping him get a job where I worked.

It was my senior year and I had left the local zoo to work at Quik Trip. At first, Michael and I didn't talk much. I had my guard up about guys. It seemed like all they wanted was sex whether I wanted it or not. I didn't want to go there with Michael I just wanted to get to know him and get my mind off of Toni.

A couple of weeks later we started dating. I was hesitant about dating him because he already had a child on the way by someone who went to school with me. He told me they were over for good and that he wanted to be with me. He called me from the hospital when she had the baby so I really believed they were done.

I honestly didn't even care I just didn't want to feel the pain I felt anymore. *Filling the void with someone else seemed like it was going to do the job. Even if it hurt others along the way.*

He had already graduated from high school a couple of years earlier, but he still came up to our school with his younger brother. He even invited me over to his parents' house which back then I thought was kind of special. *I was so wrong about that too.*

On Thanksgiving, he came over to my grandmother's house for dinner. We even discussed moving to Atlanta so I could attend a historically black college and he could pursue his music career. I was falling for Michael and he gave me the impression that the feeling was mutual.

He had even exposed me to his hustle of being a stick up kid. He and his friends robbed people for a living. My uncle sold dope for a living. My mom and I had even went with my uncle a few times to make runs for extra money. So I didn't have a problem accepting Michael's way of life.

I always encouraged him to try and do more with his life. I went to go see him a few times before he went out do his dirty work and I could see the fear in his eyes. He didn't want to be that person but there was no man around to expose him to a more positive way of providing and instill his true identity within him.

Like most kids from the ghetto he became a product of his environment. I was a product of the circumstances I found myself in. I envisioned that putting my broken pieces with someone would make it all better. I still wanted love, but I was sure I didn't want it from a girl anymore.

We started having unprotected sex but I made sure to show him my STD test results to assure him I didn't have anything. Having a disease was always a great fear of mine but the possibility of it happening to me never stopped me from putting myself at risk.

I asked Michael for his results, but he said that he knew he was good since his baby mama hadn't come back to him with any bad news. I took his word for it. Come to think of it, he didn't give me a choice not to.

When we had sex the first time, it was at his moms' house in pitch black darkness. It started and ended so fast I hadn't even realized that we had done anything. In less than two minutes it was over. He said that he hadn't ejaculated yet, but when I went to the bathroom it was clear that he had lied.

I didn't get the chance to think things through and initially he claimed that we were going up to his room to "talk." I was okay with having sex with him because I was beginning to really like him so I laid there. I wasn't on birth control at the time nor did I think I would end up pregnant.

We joked around about me becoming pregnant just like my ex Toni, as if we were protecting ourselves from the possibility of it ever happening.

All of the jokes turned serious. After only a couple of months of dating, I broke the news to him that I was pregnant. I was really nervous about sharing the news with him. Although we had talked about building a future together one of my greatest fears was that he'd change his mind and leave me like my dad left my mom. Just like that, he stopped talking to me and got involved with another girl from my school.

When the news came out that I was pregnant things got crazy at school. Everyone was shocked to find out that I was pregnant. Teachers were disappointed that someone *like me* would end up pregnant.

My teachers got to see the Chanel who excelled academically and challenged them to take their jobs seriously. They didn't know the broken and lost Chanel hidden behind the good grades and outspokenness.

I got expelled from school because I had a fight with a mutual friend for spreading my business. I wasn't even really mad at her I was more disappointed in myself. When his baby's mama returned back to school, she never even looked my way. *I was hurt and embarrassed, but I refused to let it show or get me down.* I just wanted to erase the pain from the break up with Toni but my plan to move on broke more pieces of my heart.

I even went to prom pregnant. Even though my son's father attended the prom, he didn't with me—he went with his first child's mom. My friend Faith decided to wear the exact same dress as me and she was my date for the evening. In spite of all the chaos going on in my life I still ended up having a great time at prom.

I graduated in the top 10% of my class with honors. I accepted a scholarship to Texas A & M for four years to enter their ROTC program. I visited the campus for a weekend and everything my junior year. But because I was now walking across the stage pregnant, I had to decline the scholarship. I was disappointed, but I didn't have time to weep about it. I still had a life to live. Now I had a baby to raise.

I was strongly against abortions but after much convincing from my mom and her boyfriend she took me to the clinic anyway. Going to college seemed like the only way out of the toxic environment and she wanted me to take a chance and fulfill my dreams of becoming an attorney.

I cried so hard that the lady at the clinic wouldn't even continue the process and we never made it pass the sonogram. Other ladies that were there to get an abortion left too.

In my eyes being blessed with a child was the closest thing to God. It was like God's way of letting me know he cared about me if no one else did. It may sound weird but that's the one thing I was sure about.

Children, no matter how their conceived are a gift from God and if he doesn't want the baby here God was big enough to make that happen without my help.

I was determined to show my mom and everyone else that I wasn't going to fail in life just because I had a child. My baby was a blessing, not a burden. I was going to love him and be the best mom I could be, no matter what storms came my way. Everyone was doing it this way, so I was certain I would be okay. My mom did it.

I continued to work and I planned to attend college after I had my son and find me a better job. I convinced myself and others around me that I was ready for life and motherhood. *Underneath all the boasting I was scared as hell.*

I was seventeen and pregnant without a clue in the world of how to be a parent. I had an idea of the basics but I wasn't all sure that was even right. Inside I was so scared but I managed to hide it very well like I did most of my real issues. I cried many nights, but I always wiped my tears away and got up the next morning to do my best.

Depression and pity parties weren't anything that I wanted to partake in. Instead of feeling sorry for myself, I placed it in my jar of pain covered it up and tried not to dwell on it.

If anyone brought up someone from my past, I got angrier about it than I did sad. That was how I coped with it all. I didn't blame anyone but myself for my outcome.

I was just pissed that my son's father didn't stick around to help raise our son. Aside from all the joking we talked about the "what ifs" of our actions. I shared with him

63

the issues I had with my dad and he claimed to be different. His actions proved otherwise.

Growing up I assumed I would be capable of handling a man turning his back on me and my child but it often kept the question drifting in my mind, "what's wrong with me?" He knew how I felt about men who didn't raise their kids, and he assured me that he was nothing like those guys.

His dad wasn't around either growing up and he said that he wanted to be different than his dad. Instead Michael was just like my dad, absent. I was hurt.

My mom took me on all my doctors' visits so I didn't have to go alone. In spite of my mom being disappointed that I got pregnant, she never stopped being there for me. I would need her more than anything at this point. My mom became my ride or die. I was her baby girl and now I was having a baby of my own.

My granny was upset and she cried just about every time she saw me. She graduated high school pregnant with my mom. My mom didn't have me until she was twenty-three years old. My grandma figured the cycle had been broken but now she saw herself all over again.

Once I got pregnant, I promised myself that I wasn't going to let having a child stop me from living. I still planned to attend college and fulfill my dreams. I was more determined because now I had someone looking up to me and I didn't want to let my son down.

I refused to give up. I was going to be independent and not use government assistance or depend on a man to help me. *I wanted a man for love not what he had in his pockets.*

My mom never used it nor did she receive any income tax when all my others friends' moms did at the beginning of each year. I wasn't going to rob Peter to pay Paul either. I watched my mom live in financial bondage because she tried to give me all that I wanted and needed and keep all the bills afloat. I was going to find a job that paid well even if I didn't have a degree. If I needed two or three jobs to make it I was all in.

I had it all planned out. Little did I know life would have different plans for me.

Not only did Michael leave me pregnant with a child, but I walked away from the doctor's office with an abnormal Pap smear and medication for an STD.
It was hard to be left alone to deal with all of this and be pregnant. My dream of being a mother of 5, gone. My dream of being a wife. Dead. Just like that.

When I left the Doctors office that day I just knew that was confirmation that God had truly created me to live a cursed life. Who would want me after this? How could I share this deep dark secret with someone? All the judgements I was going to receive. It was embarrassing enough to be pregnant at such a young age now my life was being taken away.

We always hear about the consequences of having unprotected sex but I'm convinced that a lot of times we think we're untouchable. In my mind if I took a risk like that I thought the person was worth it and I believed the feeling was mutual. Sometimes I was just afraid to stand up for myself in those moments. I cared more about trying to subdue the pain of my insecurities than I did my health, morals, and integrity.

I didn't really think I would contract any disease and I believed the person I gave myself to was clean. I took his word and I was stuck with those consequences. I thought letting him have unprotected sex with me qualified me as someone "special" to him. But I was only just another girl for him to say he had sex with. I had placed my life on the line just to be placed on some guys smash list.

Ladies, we are worth more than that. From the beginning my first led me to believe that having unprotected sex meant that I was special. I held on to that lie as truth. By this time I had picked up the mentality that everyone "is doing it so maybe it's not that bad." Dating is *deadly. Protect yourself always. Know your status and his status first BEFORE you lay down.*

My heart was crushed. I remember feeling so discouraged about life. I was supposed to be preparing for graduation and getting ready for college. Instead I was sitting in a doctor's office drowning in tears of frustration.

Even though it was all curable in that moment it felt as though it would last forever. What hurt even more is that I had to walk it out alone. I was too ashamed to share it with anyone. The only person I told was my mom.

That day our relationship was restored. The anger and frustration I carried towards my mom I decided to try and let go. She was the only one there for me. While I had lived most of my life carrying her secret she now carried mine. I had promised myself that I had learned my lesson this time.

I was going to take my time and not give myself sexually to another person. I vowed to never take my life for granted like that again. It was easier said than done. Sooner than later I would be back to comprising my body for that four letter word. **Love.**

It would take many wrong turns before I realized that males are just as broken as females. Those who hurt others are on a journey to find a cure to ease their own hidden pain. Hurt people hurt people. Broken people attract broken people and the cycle continues until someone steps up to break the cycle with change.

One of my friends told me that a guy named Jason was interested in me, even though I was pregnant. I was shocked to hear that a guy could still be interested in a girl even while she was pregnant. Jason and I had took classes together and I had never saw him as nothing more than a classmate. It wasn't until one of our senior outings that I noticed that he saw me differently. We exchanged numbers before graduation and started talking.

He was different from anybody I had met. I liked him

67

more than I should have. He told me in the beginning that he was only interested in sex. We talked about other girls currently in his life, he made it clear to me that he would remain honest with me, he wouldn't hurt me and he wouldn't mislead me in any way.

He also told me that a relationship wasn't completely out of the picture for us, but at this particular time, all he wanted was sex. While I was disappointed, I appreciated his honesty.

I could share personal stuff with Jason and he didn't judge me. Jason reassured me that I wasn't alone and hadn't been the only person on the planet that had experienced contracting an STD, although it felt that way.

By the time I started talking to Jason I had already finished my meds and been retested. Jason trusted that I was clean. I was just grateful that I had finally met someone who could just be real about their intentions with me.

When I noticed us getting close and comfortable with one another I stopped calling him. I didn't want to fall in love especially since he had made his intentions clear to me. I wasn't ready to start having sex again. I wasn't interested in having sex anymore. Although I had been retested I was afraid of taking another risk with a man and I still hadn't seen any of Jason's test results.

Although I wanted love I wanted it *without* sex. I had almost been scared straight after my experience with my son's dad. But Jason was determined to have things his way and I was desperate to be loved. *Our brokenness would soon intertwine.*

I told him that I wanted a relationship and that I didn't want to be a part of any fling just because I was pregnant. My heart couldn't take another piece being broken and I didn't want to witness another person turning their back on me.

I wanted my son to have a father figure in his life. Someone who was consistent. I wanted a family or nothing at all. He didn't want the new friendship to end so quickly. Neither did I.

I still let him come over and he tried his best to have sex, but I just wouldn't let up. I tried to finally set boundaries and stick to the promise I had made to myself.

We continued talking and the time came where we eventually had sex. He came over one night just to talk and it was too late for him to come in the house so we stood outside to talk.

The passion between us both was too strong to avoid. Next thing you know we pull off in his Tahoe and the rest is history. We were inseparable and couldn't get enough of each other's company.

He met my mother and we even had our favorite shows that we watched together. But, our relationship was short-lived. Other women became an issue and we broke up. That playing second fiddle stuff was not cool in anyway and I wasn't about to put up with it.

If I had to play those games it wasn't real from the start. I wanted to be his one and only. Since we had shared such deep things with one another and he was accepting of me having a child I believed that he was the special guy I had always been looking for.

The day before my son DeAnthony was born, he called and we talked until it was time for me to go to the hospital. I hadn't talk to him for about a month and we missed each other and more importantly, we missed the friendship.

We were honest and open about everything with one another, even about the difficulties that we both faced in our lives. I was on my way to being a single mom and he was dealing with financial trouble.

The time we spent together always made whatever problems we had bearable. And for that moment, it actually

felt like everything would be alright.
I had finally found love.

Chapter 4

Shattered Dreams

I honestly hate the stigma associated with the term "baby mama". I was determined to not carry the weight of that stigma with me. In my mind, I told myself that I was going to surpass that stigma by any means necessary. Unhealed. Fearful. Broken. Lost. My plan would soon take a turn that I truly wasn't equipped to handle. But with what I knew I tried my best.

The day had come and it was time for me to transition into motherhood. The morning at the hospital while preparing for the cesarean delivery was the first breakdown I had in public about my pregnancy.

I admitted to my family that I wasn't ready to be a mom. Tears were running down my face and I was shaking uncontrollably. My family tried to calm me down but I wasn't trying to hear it.

I tried snatching out my IV's and everything. I asked the doctor if my son could stay in my stomach a little while longer. My doctor threatened to strap me to the bed and put me to sleep to deliver my son if I didn't calm down. A million and one thoughts ran through my mind that day. Everything just felt so surreal.

On August 17th, I had a healthy baby boy my cesarean. Once I seen and held my son DeAnthony for the first time I was sure that I could actually do this. His life depended on it.

Michael never made it to the hospital but Jason did.

Jason and I got back together soon after and it was like we had never missed a beat. Michael came to see our son once when he was about a month old and we never heard from him for a long while.

Jason immediately stepped in like it was a natural instinct of his to be a dad. I hoped I could one day bless him with another child. I never forced or pressed him to take on the role he was just the kind of guy who accepted all that you came with. I loved that about him.

After I came home from the hospital Jason started staying the night. My mom initially didn't agree with him staying over but as their relationship grew she stopped complaining to me about it. She enjoyed having him around just as much as I did.

I was an adult and could make my own decisions, but she still wanted me to follow her rules. That was pretty difficult to do since I had never been disciplined by my mom. I always struggled with that and I let Jason know that I was thinking about moving out on my own. I wanted Jason to come with my son and me. In my eyes we were a family now.

Having Jason around brought me hope again and I was determined to show him my appreciation. I wanted my son to have what I didn't. Although I didn't have a father figure in the home deep down I felt and knew it was important. I wanted Jason to adopt DeAnthony as his own one day if we ever got married. I had it all planned out. I was sure *this time* that Jason was the one.

My brokenness would often times blur my vision and I would make poor choices that would cost me greatly. I now know that obedience to God was always for my protection.

72

I started working as a bank teller when my son was only two weeks old. I was exhausted from the training and testing I had to do to keep the job. I didn't get the six-week break most mothers take. My body hadn't fully recovered from the cesarean and I was still experiencing pain from the scar that was left behind. I was breastfeeding too and leaking all over the place.

My mom and Jason always joked with me about being lazy because I slept so heavily. I hardly ever got up during the night, but I knew it didn't bother Jason or my mom to help me out.

Sometimes I would turn over in the middle of night and see my son sleeping peacefully on Jason's chest and I would feel like the luckiest girl in the world. It seemed we were one big happy family.

At the time, Jason wasn't working a normal job, but he was hustling. He preferred hustling because he always said it was in his bloodline. He was a street pharmacist like my uncle. I had witnessed the lucrative amount of money that could be made being a street pharmacist.

Jason had a mind of his own and no one could convince him otherwise at the time. We knew all about the consequences but like anyone else from where we had come from we were just simply trying to make it.

Jason dad was a big time hustler back in his younger days. He became a real business man and had established himself as a tax paying citizen. His dad went legit and after serving time and had an established business in our community. Jason admired his dad.

My uncle had even helped Jason score from time to time. I assumed from all the money I saw as a kid growing up that my uncle did well so I figured Jason would eventually get there too. I was cool with being his ride or die chick. Jason made sure I never had to partake in any of the dealings other than making a phone call to my uncle.

Jason promised to be careful and never bring his dirty business home. He did just that. During that time I was the breadwinner in the relationship and I was okay with that. My job as a bank teller was going really well.

Jason had high hopes that things would pop off sooner than later for him. *When you're in love you look out for one another*. That was my motto.

I was confident that once Jason got his clientele up he would help out at home more. Having him around was truly enough for me.

We were in for a rude awakening. Although the rappers glorified hustling as this easy way of getting paid and my uncle bragged a lot it was much more difficult than we both expected. Things were slow for a while and there were times when came home empty handed.

I had a family now and I was determined to get out of my mom's house. I now had a better job to support us and a few months later, we got our first apartment. Jason decided it was best that he not be included on the lease since he didn't have consistent income.

Aside from my job as a bank teller I still worked part time at Quik trip from time to time and I picked up a seasonal job at Macy's. I loved working at Macy's for the great employee discount so I could shop for my family.

Jason always warned me saying that if we ever broke up to never treat any other man the way I treated him because I would lose in the end. Jason called it being gullible and naïve. I called it being in love and taking care of my family. *Jason saw my brokenness and tried to warn me.*

When Jason and I first dated, he didn't have any swag. I loved him totally for who he was and how he was there for us. I took it upon myself to start filling up his closet space. Keeping up with the latest trends was always something I did and I now wanted Jason to be part of that with my son and me.

It was the least I could do since he had taken in my son as his own. He had it a little rough as a kid growing up in a single-parent household. Wearing the latest fashion and name brand clothing was the last thing on his mind.

Jason was always thinking ahead while I stayed concerned with the present. We clashed on things like my spending habit on materials because he wanted to save while I would prefer we spend.

Although I promised to not pick up the habit of robbing peter to pay paul, I eventually did. Jason wanted to show me a different way on how to handle money. I wanted to show him that he wasn't living with his mama anymore and that I had his back. He had a woman, a girlfriend and hopefully a future wife.

We talked about marriage a lot. Like most young men Jason wasn't in a rush. I was. I didn't want to just be known or seen only as a baby mama or girlfriend forever. We had our moments of separation and our disagreements like any other couple but we always found our way back.

On holidays, he took my son and me over to his family's house. He was so down for me that he helped take my micro braids down. Any woman will tell you that is hard to find!

When I was sick, he was there for me and vice versa. When my son's father walked away, he was there for me. I was certain this time Jason was the one.

Jason was a very smart guy and his parents, more so his dad, continually tried to get him to attend college. He refused because, in his eyes, college wasn't for him. We struggled financially and his hustling money wasn't much help. Neither were all three of my jobs, but we continued to work at it. I continued looking for better work and I got an offer at a call center for a home alarm company as a monitoring operator. I was able to quit all three of my jobs to work as a full time operator.

Jason stayed home with DeAnthony and when he needed to make runs, he took DeAnthony to my granny's house. To have more money, we moved into a cheaper apartment after about six months of being on our own. Jason still refused to get a decent job. He was determined to make the street thing happen.

It didn't take long for me to be over it once the bills started rolling in and I started to see the dope game for what it was. Jason liked to gamble with his friends and that was another issue that played on our money issues. He still didn't have a solid clientele and I assumed it was a sign that hustling just wasn't for him. I thought hustle money was made quick and easy.

My granny and I agreed to co-sign on a car for me and Jason. I felt that if we both had reliable transportation, it would help us out and even push him to get a job and leave the streets. It didn't work.

We did end up attending community college together. My dream of becoming an attorney had been pushed in the back of my mind. My focus became keeping my family together. I still wanted to become an attorney but I figured it would take much longer to finish college and I wasn't sure I had the time for all that. So we decided to go to community college to pick up a couple of classes.

We agreed that the least he could do was attend college to make his parents proud. The refunds checks were a plus too. Everything seemed to be going alright, other than our typical arguments.

Then one night when I was working overtime, I got a disturbing phone call from my brother Derrick. He asked me if Jason and I were still together and if I knew where he was. I assumed he was home or out hustling, but I was wrong.

76

He was out having drinks with his cousin and some chicks. One of the chicks was his ex. Before me, Jason had a girl who he had dated off and on since they were kids. She always managed to stick around and for a while, she wasn't an issue. Jason always felt torn between the two of us.

I didn't come into his life to take anyone's place. I only wanted to make room for myself, but I couldn't be with a man who didn't want to be with *only* me. After all, at this point we had our own place, a new car and a great bond. I couldn't understand why Jason would want to jeopardize it all.

I was heated. I headed right to the location when I got off work. I wasn't sure of what I was going to say or do. His cousin didn't care too much for me. I always felt it was because he didn't have Jason around to chase girls with anymore and I had taken his friend away from him.

I was well aware that at the age of eighteen, Jason had taken on a great responsibility by taking DeAnthony in as his own. I felt guilty about it all the time. So I made sure to do whatever it took to keep Jason satisfied. I understood his sacrifice and commitment but cheating was that one thing I couldn't and refused to deal with. I really didn't want to lose him again.

He was my future husband and a wonderful dad for my son. There were even times when I thought he loved DeAnthony more than he loved me.

I made it to the restaurant and his cousin threatened me that if I set foot inside, he was going to hurt me. Jason came outside and we talked. He said that he just needed to go out and clear his mind. *Here I was working overtime, paying the majority of the bills, and he needed to clear his mind.*

I tried to make things comfortable for him so that we didn't have to reach this place. I always tried to take care of

77

my man in every way, including financially. In my eyes his helping me out with my son made up for what his finances didn't cover. Deep down, I felt that if I did everything he wanted and needed that I would never have to be neglected and rejected again. But it still wasn't enough to keep the relationship afloat.

My feelings were so hurt. I felt so stupid. Jason always warned me about how the next guy would mistreat me but he ended up being the guy that he warned me about. I took my car back and ended the relationship that night because his actions proved that he didn't appreciate the kind of love I had to offer.

He called often to see DeAnthony. Being silly, I told him, "If you can't be with me, then you can't see my son!"

It crushed Jason but he respected my decision. DeAnthony and I had never lived alone and although I had talked a good game about being single and on my own, this journey was something that I hadn't really planned for.

Chapter 5
Destructive Dating

"But mark this: There will be terrible times in the last days. People will be lovers of themselves, lovers of money, boastful, proud, abusive, disobedient to their parents, ungrateful, unholy, without love, unforgiving, slanderous, without self-control, brutal, not lovers of the good, treacherous, rash, conceited, lovers of pleasure rather than lovers of God- having a form of godliness but denying its power. Have nothing to do with such people. They are the kind who worm their way into homes and gain control over **gullible women who are loaded down with sins and are swayed by all kinds of evil desires, always learning but never able to come to a knowledge of the truth."***
2 Timothy 3:1-7

I should have taken out time to heal from past wounds. Reflect over how I ended up in certain predicaments I found myself in and created a plan to avoid going down the same path. But my longing for love and the fear of being left alone to deal with the reality of being a young parent I instead ended up on the path of destructive dating.
Commitment has become a thing of the past nowadays. Dating and getting to know someone has become nothing more than friends with benefits. Meaningless sexual relations. People fail to mention that when you partake in such activities something on the inside of you is broken. While we have been subject to believe that it's normal. It's really not. It's destructive.

I thought it would be easy to go to work, come home and take care of the bills. For a while, it was all too easy. It was routine survival of the fittest type of living. Wake up, get dressed, dropped my son off at daycare, go to work, then school, pick my son up, and go back home. No excitement. Once DeAnthony went to sleep, I was lonely and bored.

I was attending Remington Technical College for medical coding and billing at the time. This was never in my plan but since I had a family to take care of, the seven months of class and the possibility of having a career in less than a year worked for me.

I had stopped by the campus to tour the building and the next thing you know I was walking out of the doors with a welcome packet. Back then I was always in a hurry to get things done. As if I had some deadline to reach.

Although I had promised myself that I wasn't going to stop pursuing my dream of a family and being an attorney somewhere along the way I lost sight. *Once my plans of a family and being an attorney didn't go as I expected I began to just try things to find my way again.*

One of my instructors was from California and she was one of few people who saw better for me. She was heaven sent and was one of those people that God sent my way to encourage me to keep going in the right direction. She reminded me I should never let having a child and living in the ghetto make me think that I couldn't be more and give my son more.

In her eyes, I was wasting away at Remington. She was right. At Remington I wasn't being challenged. The classes were so easy that I was able to do most of my homework at school. She pushed me to apply to an actual accredited university.

I took her advice and got accepted into Texas Women's University in Denton to study nursing once I completed my studies at Remington. She encouraged me to stay in the medical field for the money.

Apparently nurses made more money than medical coders and had a flexible schedule that would offer me more time with my son. I went along with it thinking it could be just what my son and I needed. *Whatever seemed to get me there quickest I was down.*

While I attended Remington I got my scheduled changed at work so I could attend evening classes. My son and I were always getting home really late at night and I was beginning to miss having a male companion around. I was ready to see if someone was out there for me. Jason and I weren't talking anymore and I was sure that he had gotten back with his ex.

I started going out with friends to the local clubs. Guys were showing interest in me and I was enjoying the attention. I wasn't used to getting all that attention. I also didn't know that the attention wasn't really about me but about what I had to offer. *My body.*

I was nineteen years old, had my own place, two nice cars, and was attending college. I looked at myself as being a good woman that a guy would be lucky to have. I was looking forward to dating and I assumed it was going to be fun and innocent.

Not many of the guys wanted to go out on an actual dates like movies, miniature golf, or dinner. Instead they wanted to come by my place and *"see me."* Their request seemed harmless. I went to night school and didn't make it home until after eleven so to me it made sense. *"How about if I just come over to your place and we just chill?"*

My dating life consisted more of sexual relations than actually getting to know anyone. I knew and had experienced the consequences of what sexual sin could do to me in the past. Although I knew God had spared me I continued to put my life at risk time and time again for the sake of what I used to call my *quest for love.*

I couldn't see that my quest for love was turning me into someone I didn't want to be. A Promiscuous girl.

Love was somewhere in the midst but the real root of my actions wasn't love it was my brokenness. So many times in life we confuse the two.

Guys always wanted to do more than just "chill." I had missed the memo that accepting a guy's offer to come over and chill meant having sex. It was as if I couldn't get around not having sex with a guy.

I had no sexual discipline, boundaries, or voice. Back then it seemed like an automatic thing to do to avoid things getting out of hand. So I compromised and learned to disconnect during those moments in an attempt to get what I wanted.

Even though I tried to say, "No" a number of times, they'd simply say things like,

"Don't you want to be with me?"

"I'm not going to hurt you like the last one. You can trust me I'm not like the rest."

"You're not a slut. We're grown and feeling each other so there's no harm."

Little did we know it was harming our souls.

In an attempt to take control of the situation I began to ask the guy's upfront if they just wanted sex. I wanted the choice to choose before they even came over but they still would lie.

These guys were nothing like Jason. I found myself missing Jason and his authenticity. Jason allowed me to choose and he never hid his initial intentions from me.

These guys were much different. Once I gave it up they disappeared like clockwork. I tried to act as if it didn't bother me but it did. I often lived in fear that my consequences of still engaging in sex were going to catch up with me one day.

Living in that fear was the only thing that kept me calling out to a God that I thought had turned his back on me. I stayed praying for myself and every person I had a sexual encounter with. I would even make promises saying that each encounter would be my last one but the stronghold was just too powerful. ***I needed to be delivered.***

No matter how much I tried to stay away from love and avoid taking these empty moments serious I couldn't help it. I desired to be in a long-term relationship. Every guy I met back then made it clear that if sex wasn't in the relationship I couldn't have their time or attention.

My friends would often encourage me that having *meaningless* sex with people was harmless but *internally* it felt otherwise. It just didn't sit well with me. The rejection I received after spending time with a guy was one of the worst feelings in the world. Especially if I thought he was cool enough to meet my son.

DeAnthonys dad even acted as though he wanted to come and be a part of his life. That turned out to be a lie. All he wanted was sex and a free place to sleep like the other guys. I had even finally confronted him about leaving me alone with a son to raise and contracting an STD. His response was only a smirk and an empty apology.

Soon after all this meaningless dating my promiscuous ways backfired and I got pregnant again. I told two guys that were possibly the father and one of them gave me $600 to get rid of the baby. I took the money, but I wasn't going to abort my baby. Once he understood that he took his money back and let me know that if I had the baby he wasn't going to be around.

I got a call from a high school friend who had went off to college. She basically called to try and convince me to abort my baby. She was friends with one of the guys I had dated and she didn't feel it was a good idea to ruin his reputation with a baby. I was so pissed with her.

After the conversation thoughts begin to race through my mind that maybe I had ruined my life. She was right I wasn't ready to be a mom to another baby but I didn't want to hear it from someone who took the opportunity for a better chance at life. I envied her because she had actually got away.

I immediately overrode those thoughts telling myself that babies were from God. If God didn't want me to have another child God would end the pregnancy without the help of an abortion clinic.

Two weeks later I ended up having a miscarriage. It was painful yet peaceful at the same time. I wasn't ready to raise two kids. I didn't want to have two kids with two absent fathers. I didn't want to be known as someone who was selfish to take another humans life. God had given me another chance.

DeAnthony and I stayed at my mom's house to recover. Jason saw my car parked at my mom's and contacted me to check on us. I shared with him what had been going on since our break up including the miscarriage. Just like that, Jason and I got back together and things picked up right where we left off.

He moved back in with us and my family was back together just where I wanted it. My son had even began to act out because of Jason no longer being in the picture. Inpsite of my terrible actions my heart still longed for Jason. Jason and I both decided that we were going to fight to keep our family together at all cost.

Jason decided to get a decent job. I got promoted on my job and things were going really smooth. I even treated myself to a new car. It didn't take long for things at home to get sour between us. Jason craved more sex than usual and I craved love, more stability, and real intimacy.

Things continued to get out of hand. Even when I didn't

want to have sex Jason would pressure me to have sex anyway. We clashed because of it and his escape became watching porn more. In the beginning I even tried to join him in his porn interest to help fulfill the fantasy he seemed to so desperately desire. I knew what it felt like to struggle with issues regarding sex because of my own private issues I had as a kid.

My attempts to help him didn't work though. It got so bad that he crashed our laptop and depleted all of his bank accounts. Jason ate, slept, and breathed porn. It didn't matter what time of the day it was it wouldn't be a surprise to walk up on Jason and the laptop. It was almost worse than Jason having another woman.

We tried to fight through it but his porn issues brought out more of my insecurities. I became the crazy girlfriend. I started checking his phone and popping up at his friend's house. I began to think that he was cheating on me with other women.

I was always questioning whether or not I was good enough for him anymore. I hated the strain it put on our relationship but we were determined to not give up.

In the midst of all this we moved out of the ghetto and into a really nice two-bedroom luxury apartment. It was all my idea to move.

Instead of finding a way to deal with our real issues I continued focus on changing the outer image everyone could see. When we actually needed some real help not an apartment we could barely afford.

Friends were jealous of us. None of our friends had it "together" like we did and some even made it known that they envied our relationship.

No one had a clue about what went on behind the four walls of our home. *Arguments. Yelling. Rage. His porn addiction. Total dysfunction. Financial hardships.* For the sake of the love, we agreed to try and make it work.

85

Whereas Jason used to tolerate, or even embrace my flaws, he began to magnify them. We both started playing dirty. I hung out with my friends more to avoid having sex with him.

For the last six months of our relationship, we didn't have any sex. Jason was fed up and gave me an ultimatum to have sex with him or he was going to leave. We ended up doing both. Jason left and it was just my son and me again.

Jason was the closest thing to a good man that I ever knew and I hated to see him go. We continued as friends and he even helped me pay the bills at our place since we were both on the lease. It became ever so clear to us that our relationship was really over this time.

He remained faithful to his relationship with my son until I couldn't take it anymore. While I wasn't good at letting go, I was much better at cutting off. So, that's what I did. I cut him out of my life and my son's life.

I took no time to heal. My insecurities and ignorance wouldn't allow me to. Instead, I jumped right back into the dating scene. I got involved with a girl from my past. She became violent and my son didn't like her and I broke off the relationship. Less than a couple of weeks later my place got broken into.

I rekindled another old flame. Since I knew him already from previous encounters, I was cool with him coming over to my place. He'd cut my son's hair a few times in the past.

Randy had a son too. He told me that I would be a great woman to have by his side. We started off all wrong instead of really getting to know one another. It seemed as if there was potential for us to get serious. He was attracted to the *image* I portrayed.

Randy claimed that he wanted to take things slow since he had just gotten out of a relationship too. Taking it slow didn't mean that he didn't want to have sex, though. Randy only wanted to take it slow when it came to being exclusive.

As soon as he came by to chill he let his demands be known that he wanted sex with no attachments. Even after swearing that he wasn't coming over my house for that. He'd promise that one day things were going to change and our rendezvous would become something more *but it never happened.*

Dear sis,
He may say all the right things in the beginning. He may even do all the right things. After many trials and error I learned later to guard my own heart. Just because the traps are set doesn't mean you have to get caught up in them. Be sure to guard your heart.
"Do not arouse or awaken love until it so desires." Song of Songs 2:7
I was too busy trying to give my heart away. Change your story and make better choices than I did. Wait for the right one.

Randy never mentioned using a condom and neither did I. Part of me was afraid. Whenever I turned guys down in the past, it never ended well for me. I assumed Randy would be the same way. Since he was already aggressive and overbearing when he came around I just went along with it instead of standing up for myself.

In a way I seen it as an even exchange. He'd get sex and I'd get affection.

I tried telling myself when a guy didn't mention using a condom, I was "special" to him. I didn't think that men slept around with a lot of women and didn't use protection. *Little did I know, in the same way women struggle with*

seeing value in their bodies men were just the same.
Randy was always telling me things like,
"I want you to have my baby."
"We're going to be a family one day."
"I want to come home to you."
Part of me believed it.

I knew the possibilities and the consequences of the risk I was taking but I felt he was worth it. The need to fill my void of loneliness continued to be more important. I wasn't on any contraceptives at the time and I ended up pregnant. Randy turned on me.

One second he was happy I was pregnant with his child. Next thing you know he'd be calling me a bitch and telling me that I needed to terminate the pregnancy. He continued to give me mixed signals and I'd fall for his sympathetic apology and give in. Then all of a sudden, his visits stopped. It was truly devastating.

I didn't want to be known as a slut or someone who got around. Did I sleep around a few times, yes but it wasn't to be slandered by the men I trusted my body to. I was under the impression that they wanted to date me. *I went from feeling like his special somebody to a dirty, dumb chick who got played for a lousy lay over and over again.*

Now I was bringing another innocent child into my chaos. Randy even began to deny our son. It was the worst pregnancy ever. I had been in tough relationships but Randy made no apology about his plans to ruin my life.

DeAnthonys dad just left but Randy was determined to make my life a living hell. I shed a lot of tears. We argued all the time whether I was at work, school or at home. I never thought I would be on someone's hit list. Then one day, Randy tells me, **"I got you pregnant on purpose."** We had talked about having a child one day but when he said he got me pregnant on purpose it was during an argument as if he had done it out of spite.

Initially, I thought a man wanting a woman to have his baby was a beautiful thing. If she wasn't his wife yet, she would be one day. If not his wife they could still be cordial and he could still be an active father.

I wanted to believe that the man was going to be active in his child's life. Even if the man chose not to stay, that was easier than staying around just to confuse the mother and the child.

I had let DeAnthonys dad off easy because we were young and I had only got with him because I wanted to get over Toni.

Randy was supposed to be different. I never looked at children as a burden, neither did I want to believe that people used children as leverage. I never thought having a child by a man meant that he could control you.

Since Randy was active in his first son's life I had high hopes he would an active dad towards our son. It seemed to be of extreme importance to Randy. But not all things are what they seem.

I had our son on May 19th 2009, just a month before I turned twenty-one. Randy came to the hospital with his mom and demanded to name our son. Tired of fighting I let Randy have his way.

Randy made promises to be active in our sons life but under certain conditions. He only came around if I agreed to have sex with him. He harassed me for money, demanded to drive my car, and even thought it was a good idea for us to move together when I got my own place again. I declined all of his propositions.

Randy would tell me often, "This is what *baby mama's* are supposed to do."

I hadn't read any baby mama manual. Apparently having a baby by Randy meant that I was to support him even if he treated my son and I like dirt. I refused to go out like that. If that was his idea of love I didn't want it. I would rather be alone or try love with someone else instead of being made a fool by child's father.

We moved back with my mom for a few months when I was pregnant because I was drowning in debt. I could no longer support my family financially. I felt so powerless.

I grew up always having more than enough when it came to material stuff. I didn't necessarily consider myself to be better than anybody else, but I was aware that I had more than most.

As an adult I prided myself on being independent. I wasn't financially ready to support another baby but I was determined to show Randy I could continue to make it on my own. I wanted to prove to him and myself that I could do this without him.

Jason even came back around. Once I shared the news with him it was clear that he only wanted to see DeAnthony or have sex. He had come to my rescue once but he wasn't about to be with me after having two children apart from him.

My mom started dating her now husband, to give them their space the kids and I moved out after I returned back to work from maternity leave. Not only that, I hated feeling like I was going backwards. I felt like such a failure being back home. I wasn't ready or willing to give up just yet. I knew if I picked up more hours at my job or got a second job things would turn around for us.

Randy continued on with his antics after I moved from my mom's place. He'd pop up at my place and demanded his way inside often, claiming he wanted to spend time with his son.

Then to make matters worse, I found out that he had another girl pregnant during the same time that I was pregnant. My life was full of drama and I was sick of it. I couldn't wait until I hit the big twenty-one. I was ready for a hard, stiff drink.

I had been wearing the "S" on my chest, acting as though I could balance everything just fine. On the outside things seemed normal, internally, I was losing it. I never wanted to ask for help, especially from those who had hurt me. I knew how to seek God for mercy but not guidance nor wait in faith for Him to move.

I never stopped believing that God existed, but I was sure now that I was on his hit list, too. I wasn't even going to try to get in good standing with him. It just seemed impossible at that point. I was better at being bad than I was at trying to be good. It was the only way. I always believed that children were a gift from God, but now it was feeling as though he had made a mistake by blessing me with children because it was getting harder by the minute to keep it together. I had let myself down.

Chapter 6

When it ALL FALLS DOWN

*After all the crap between Randy and I was over I decided to stop focusing on finding love. My financial situation was getting out of hand and I was totally losing grip. I was tired of the cards I was dealt and I felt **powerless** to change it. The changes I did make continued to put me in a deeper hole financially, mentally, physically, and emotionally. I was breaking down every chance I got. I could never really explain just what the root of my issue was. I remember my mom telling me that I had some form of post-partum depression but I wasn't trying to hear that. I just wanted to **find my way.***

Instead of being home with my boys I got my first shot of Patron for my 21st birthday. My uncle, his lady friend, and I went to a strip club to celebrate.

My uncle was one of the coolest guys I had in my life. He was only twelve years older than me. When I was a kid, he always had money. He never wanted for anything. *At least it looked that way.*

He always told me that when I got older, I could hang with him and his friends. I finally got what I always wanted. My uncle, his lady friend, and I partied until the sun came up. I had never gotten that drunk before. This night began the start of a habit that I wasn't willing to break. *Drinking became an outlet for me.*

I had often began to entertain thoughts of even making money **with** my uncle but he never let me in on that. Until one night after borrowing money from my uncle he asked me to go and dance for a man at a club to pay him back. Instead of making money with my uncle he wanted me to make money *for him*. I didn't go through with it but I began to see more and more that no one really cared about me. *Not even my own family.*

The dream of a better life seemed impossible to accomplish and I was barely making ends meet. My 9 to 5 wasn't cutting it and no part time mall job was going to help either. I wasn't eighteen anymore and life was becoming more real by the day. We needed some real *stability.*

Once I turned twenty-one, I couldn't keep liquor out of my hands. One of my friends gave me an ecstasy pill one night at the club. She explained to me how the pill made her feel. *Free. No Worries.* For the first time in a long time she had fun and danced all night.

I wanted to feel like that. Normally when we went out we just stood around listening to the music and walking around the club peeping the scene. We hardly ever had fun and I wasn't even sure why we felt the need to go so much. I guess it was just something to do. But once drugs and alcohol came into the mix it was a different story.

I demanded that she hook me up. She insisted that I only take half of the pill since it was my first time, but I needed and wanted the *whole* pill. She didn't think I could handle it, but I reassured her that I was a woman now and could handle my own. I had kids like a woman. I paid bills like a woman *but inside I was still a lost little girl.*

In high school, we attended house parties and went to dance at the skating rink to have fun. We didn't need drugs or alcohol. As an adult, we now needed to smoke weed and drink just to enjoy the moment and escape our everyday worries. The goal was to be happy, but we were only getting high. *Getting high was our new happy.*

Many times in life when we should be picking up a **BOOK** *we pick up a drink or a drug instead.*

My life was changing. I was angry, frustrated and downright fed up. As time went on, I turned to excessive partying and my priorities were rapidly getting out of order.

My mom would hardly ever say no to watch my boys so I could go out with my friends. This was a norm for her. She often times struggled with guilt of how my life had become. Since I had never really had a chance to be just be a young adult who was able to explore life and discover myself my mom would give me a pass to party with my friends a lot.

"Chanel you've always been the responsible one and you've never really had a break. I understand. Just go have fun." My mom would say.

She grew up around my grandparents excessive partying. In her eyes I would overcome this and slow down just like they eventually did. She called it a **part of life.** She stood by me no matter what.

But the partying would backfire and turn into a lifestyle for me. Instead of just the weekends I was now going out during the week. Like any responsible adult, I maintained my job and was actually one of the best employees on my team at work.

My bosses at work admired my work ethic and my drive to succeed and they would often sit me down and encourage me whenever I seemed to be ***drifting*** off.

By this time I had worked my way into a position that required little supervision so I had no one at work anymore to be the *beacon of light* to help me out when I started drifting away this time.

I always thought about paying bills, taking care of my family and maintaining the expectation of who *Chanel* was. People looked up to me because in their eyes, I had made it. Deep down inside it was never enough for me.

94

I had the decent job but I was still **broke and broken.** I had my own place and the decent cars but I was still **unfulfilled and without true purpose.** I had my boys to love and to love me but I still felt like my family was **incomplete and not whole.**

My mask that covered my pain was cracking and it was cracking fast. It was no longer bringing me satisfaction.

At work, I did all I knew how to do. I moved from one position to another at work, thinking it would ease my frustration and make me happy. With each promotion, I received a dollar or more raise. I was promoted four times within two years of being at the company. School was alright, but I needed a financial breakthrough in my life right then, not four or five years down the line.

I paid the price for the cards that were dealt to me. I was trying to adapt and fit in, but it was slowly beginning to feel like I had missed the mark. *This just couldn't be all that life had to offer.*

I reached that place in my life where I begin to ask myself, *"Why am I here?"*

I wanted to know my **purpose.** Back then no one talked about living a life of **TRUE** fulfillment. Everyone was out for themselves only seeking to survive for the next day. Fulfillment in their eyes was hitting up the club and buying a few drinks. Satisfaction came from making sure the image you portrayed to the world was one of **vain perfection.**

I just knew it had to be more for my boys and me in this world. I wanted to give my boys the best life that they **deserved.** I wanted to show them that life had meaning.

My cycle and way of doing things were only making it worse for us. If there was any hope left for me, I couldn't tell anymore. I had let them down. *I could see the unhealthy pattern I was continuing in my life. I just didn't know how to break it.*

I felt so lost and unsure of what my next turn would be. I needed and desired direction. *The bible says, if any man lack wisdom let him ask God. I didn't ask God instead I would ask a man.* ***Bad move.***

When we should be on our knees praying to God for help but instead we turn to frenemies.

Ecstasy gave me a false sense of power. When I went out, I had a hard time enjoying myself because my mind was always somewhere other than in that moment in time. The pills brought out a part of me that I didn't even know I had.

It was like an ***alter ego.*** Like Beyoncé turns into to Sasha Fierce. I had this newfound confidence and I was ***loving it.*** I became extremely vulnerable to the point that it was dangerous most of the time.

I started hanging out with my uncle more, getting high drinking, and kicking it with his friends. Many would assume that an uncle would be more of a protector over his own niece. *He didn't have the strength to even take care of himself in a healthy way. So how could he help his lost niece???*

I was still settling into my new position at my job. It was only four of us working in the department, so it didn't take long for us to get acquainted with each other. I began to have a change of heart towards my current friends at the time.

We got into a really big argument and ended our friendship on very bad terms. Even though we had our differences, I never thought we would end our friendship. Instead of seeing me as a generous, caring person, my friends saw me as ***weak.***

The argument pushed me closer to the edge. I felt betrayed by everyone around me. I was trying to handle the fact that I had a son by someone who was actually more of my enemy than a lover. Now I had to hear that my friends didn't hate my actions--they hated me. They exposed how much they hated me as a person and even threatened to kill me.

I would have given my last to them. We partied together. We dressed alike and went on double dates together as teens. We shared secrets. These were the friends who were there with me when I had my kids. I knew their families and ate Sunday dinner at their house.

I attended church with them growing up. When one of my friends had no water and food in her home, without question, I helped.

I thought I had weaned out the bad seeds of friendship once I left high school but clearly my worst enemies were sitting at my round table. Although part of me knew they weren't the greatest bunch of people to hang with they were all that I knew and who I grew *accustomed to.*

*I dusted myself off from the situation and tried to not let it bother me. I was going to **start fresh.** Change my surroundings. Make new friends. Create new memories.*

I started hanging out with a girl named Olivia after I found out that we stayed in the same apartment complex. We had a few things in common besides our children being related. We partied together a few times and she popped pills just like me, so we got along great.

She was a beautiful young lady and from the outside looking in, you would think she had this perfect happy life. Many times the image we portray to the world is not the reality that lies underneath.

Getting all dressed up continued to be our escape from the everyday troubles we faced. Although I believed in my heart that there was more to life I didn't know just where to start to look for it. I didn't have anyone around to confide in who would understand.

Even when I tried they thought that I should be satisfied with what I had. A job. A car. My own place. Taking care of my kids on my own. A mom who cared about me. That's all life is really about right?

To me life was so mundane and something was still missing.

I stopped dating once I had my 2nd son. It seemed like every guy that seemed interested in me walked away leaving a scar on my heart. I was tired of the love games.

I befriended a lady from my job named Amber. I started kicking it with her and she introduced me to a new party scene. They attended swinger parties where couples met single women to join them in the bedroom.

Some of these couples even had full blown relationships with other people outside of their marriage that went beyond the bedroom. *It was crazy.*

The new club looked just like a scene from the movie Pandora's Box where only people who were on this *"special list"* were allowed inside. Outsiders unaware that it was a swingers club still managed to get through the door if they paid the right price.

At first, it caught me off guard because one minute, people would be dancing and the next minute, someone to the right of me would be having sex on the couch like no one else was in the room. I was so dumbfounded and amused all at the same time. I saw stuff like this on T.V. but I didn't think it was really going on in the real world.

*When I should have been around **positive influences** or seeking out a healthy better way to discovering the answer to my question I was here. In the wrong environments that were causing my **pure** question of "why am I here" to be contaminated by the things of this world.*

A year ago I wouldn't have been caught dead in a club like that. Things had changed but I figured as long as I stayed to myself and didn't exchange numbers with anyone there I was good.

I initially just wanted to hang out with my new friends

and have fun. This was their thing and I planned to keep it *that way.*

One night, I met the 'pill man' and it was over from there. Once my pill *took over,* I stopped worrying about what was going on around me. Since we had a reserved table, I danced near the table and sometimes I went the dance floor.

When I did made it to the dance floor, I didn't make eye contact with anyone because I didn't want them to think I was there to *"play"* as they called it. I just wanted to have fun dancing.

I rather quickly started enjoying the new club scene because I didn't have to worry about people just standing around looking at me, checking out my wardrobe or looking at me funny, like people did at a normal club.

They even had a stripper pole and I sometimes danced around the pole just for fun. I never took off any of my clothes, though. I joked sometimes about becoming an exotic dancer one day just for laughs amongst my friends.

During that time we listened to music that glamourized stripping and even normalized erotic sexual behavior and fantasies. *No one tells us that the environments and the information we allow to reign in our ear and eye gate can plant seeds in us that will **one day grow and uproot themselves.***

When you already have unresolved issues going on in you like I did the wrong environments often times push you closer to destruction.

Being high just gave me confidence to step out of my comfort zone and try new things. I said a lot and did a lot whenever I was high.

I used to sometimes wish that I could have the same confidence I had high all the time without the need to pop a pill to get me there. I would always tell myself that I would *never* let my life get to a place where I needed to get high to bring satisfaction into my life. *There I was doing just that.*

I was invited to a private party called *The Chocolate Swirl,* which was a swingers' event that was held once a month at an unlisted spot in Dallas. My friend took me around the club to show me the VIP areas. I normally stood by myself while my friend enjoyed herself.

I told Olivia about the club and she admitted to me that she had been once. She was well aware of what went down in the club. She was a part of a modeling agency in Dallas where they did photo shoots and worked different events in the Dallas night life.

Olivia told me that sometimes, other things went on after the parties they worked and she met many different guys who offered her money to do certain things.

I shut her down right there. I had **NEVER** slept with a man for money. That was actually part of the reason my old friends and I got into our disagreement. They had started sleeping with men for petty money like going to the club and getting their hair done. It *infuriated* me because they were fully capable of working a decent job but refused to.

I begin to think that maybe this whole "new party scene" wasn't new at all and I was just late. Initially, I was glad that I had missed that train but that was all about to change.

I was much different from my friends. They could snap out of it and go back to their normal lives like nothing crazy happened the next night.

I couldn't do that and I found myself struggling quite often. I was questioning everything including myself and my own beliefs.

What I had believed about life and love was proving to be a lie. Husbands and wives living double lives? Going to church on Sunday after being in a swingers club the night before? Partying and having fun but behind closed doors

orgies and other outrageous things were going on? There I
stood falling prey to the twisted lies.

I still hadn't done anything sexual with anybody in the
club but I started having conversations with ladies in the
restroom. I even came across other co-workers at the club.
It was a total mind boggling experience and I kept going
back because it kept my mind off of the issues within
myself and in my life that I didn't know how to face.

Olivia and I talked about dancing at a strip club one
night for fun, so we visited a spot in Dallas. We chose the
place because we wouldn't run into anybody we knew. We
danced **once.** It wasn't fun at all. There wasn't even five
guys in the building. We danced for a couple of hours got
dressed, laughed about it, and never thought anything more
about it.

My friends and influences had changed. My mindset
and perspective on life was rapidly changing. I guess you
could say that I was **unknowingly** being groomed for
the next season of my life. As I started hanging more and
more at these swingers' parties, I begin wandering through
the club by myself.

One night in particular at the Chocolate Swirl party I
made my way upstairs and things took off from there.

A couple asked me to join them. Then a guy came up
from behind and grabbed me away quickly. He told me that
I didn't need to join them when I could have him.

I gave him a hard time and told him that he was no
different from anybody else in the club. All he wanted was
sex. He said he had been watching me for a while. *I was
becoming a regular at the spots just like my friends.*

He noticed that when I normally came to the club, I
never *"played"* with anybody and I rarely left the table.
This time was different and he decided to come and find
me. I guess he wanted to be the first guy I had any relations
with in the club. I was high and horny that night and *I*

didn't care anymore.

We sat down on the couch and I was able to get a better look at him. He was so attractive to me—swag on point, light-skinned, short, stocky and had tattoos. He was also very young.

Most men in the club were well over thirty. To see someone near my age was rare. He explained to me that his cousin owned the club and that he only worked the door. I had never seen him before. At least I couldn't remember.

He told me that he'd never engaged in any of the club activities until that night. I believed him, but I didn't care if he was lying.

He asked me if I was high and I told him that I had taken an ecstasy pill and I was feeling myself. I asked him if he was on anything and he told me that he didn't pop pills, smoke, or drink. I had a hard time believing that anybody could handle being in a spot like this and remain sober, but he had made it clear that he was sober.

Next thing you know we're in VIP on a floor mattress. He put on a condom and we begin to have sex. A couple of people stopped to watch us but we kept going. The sex between us was short, but it was so intense. We both wanted more. When it was over he told me I was going to be his new ***"bitch."***

Where I'm from it's not seen as a derogatory word and women even called their friends "bitch". I never really liked being called that but I was too high to care and clearly I had set the standard on how he could treat me.

When you add drugs and alcohol to your life it has a way of eliminating any sense of standard you may have. Even to the point of killing your conscience mind causing a spiritual death inside of you. Then to add sex to the equation it takes you to a whole new level of destruction.

He asked me to leave with him and I agreed to. He introduced himself to my friend as ***Fatt*** and told her that I

102

was in *good hands*. They exchanged numbers just in case my friend Amber got worried and wanted to check on me.

I waited for him in his car until he got done closing down the club. I was so anxious and nervous that I kept gritting my teeth and moving around. I was trying to stay calm, but I couldn't control myself. I was too high from the ecstasy pill.

We got a room and finished what we started at the club until the sun came up. He took me home after we were done because he said that he had to attend church.

My high was gone and my eyes were really low because the sun was hurting them. I was also embarrassed and I didn't want to make eye contact with him. My pill had worn off and my conscience was waking back up.

I had done some crazy stuff before but I had never had sex with a man inside of a club.

I had a one-night stand when I nineteen years old, which went horribly bad. It wasn't that weird because I went to school with him. Most guys I dealt with in the past I knew because we either grew up in the same community or I met them through a friend. I didn't even know this guy at all.

We talked the whole way back to my house. That's when I found out he was a barber, he had a son and he was currently in the process of breaking up with his child's mom, that he currently lived with until their lease expired.

I told him about my boys, my job and that I was single. I moved back home with my parents a few months before I gave birth and I let my cousin move into my apartment until after I had the baby.

I moved back into my apartment after finding out that my cousin that lived there hadn't been paying the rent and my apartment was up for eviction. I withdrew the funds from my 401k to catch up on my rent payments and moved back in.

When I got out of his car, I told myself that it would be the last time I would hear from him again. I figured he only asked for my number out of sympathy so I wouldn't feel like a ***total slut.***

He surprised me and we ended up hanging out all the time. We went out to eat, to the club, and I even introduced him to my boys and he introduced me to his son. I introduced him to my uncle and he came over to my parents' house to meet them.

He was like a breath of fresh air--honest, outgoing, spontaneous and nonjudgmental. I loved every bit of it because he didn't seem care about how we first met or the fact that I already had two boys. Even though it seemed as if he saw me as more than just a baby mama and a slut I continued to question his true motives.

I really liked him and he stressed to me that once his lease was up and his money was right, we would become more than friends. I wanted to believe we could really have something more but all along I was just playing his ***fun side chick.***

I tried proving to him that although he met me in a swingers club high, that wasn't who I really was. The more I dated him and the more I kept going out with my new friends you couldn't tell a difference in who I was.

Fatt did his best to reassure me that we had possibility but I didn't believe him and based on what I had been through in the past, it seemed that I only attracted men who always had something going on with someone else and just wanted to trail me ***along at their convenience.***

I tried to end things with Fatt because I was tired of him not being able to come home with me every day. Once I moved back into my own place he was coming over a lot. I hated feeling like and being a side chick. ***To ease my mind*** he would do things like call me while she home to try and prove to me that they weren't together but just cohabituating for the sake of their son.

He'd promise me that they weren't sexually active and that I was the only one he was having sex at the time. He told me many times that he'd move in with me and the boys. Then he'd turn back on his word and just ask me to patiently wait. We continued kicking it in ***total dysfunction.***

His barber shop had a tattoo artist inside and I got a tattoo of his name on my hand. I had started popping pills in the daytime. I ended up getting four tattoos in one day because I was so numb from the high. I couldn't feel the pain. Just in case we ever parted ways, I wanted to have something to always remember him by.

On my back I got the scripture 1 Corinthians 13: 5-8, Love is patient. Love is kind written out. *In the midst of the chaos my ultimate goal was still to find love. I had tried to act as if I was over my quest for **seeking** love but I wasn't. Loved seemed so far away from me at this point in my life I got the tattoo as remembrance of how I once knew it.*

Tattoos had always been a way for me to express myself and each tattoo I had told a story. My love for tattoos started when I got my first one at fifteen. Japanese symbol that stood for the word ***HOPE.*** I could have just written my memories in a journal back then instead of marking up my body but writing was the last thing on mind back then.

We talked about spending our life together and one day having a daughter. I never got pregnant when I was with him, though. We used protection most of the time, but surely not all the time.

After his attempt to sleep with my friend Olivia I decided to cut tides with Fatt. I was tired of him sending me mixed signals and deep down I knew he never really wanted to be with me. *I was the one he went to when he* *needed a **cheap thrill.***

My financial situation continued looking more like my romance situation. ***Dysfunctional and out of control.*** I went to my mom for advice about my financial issues because I had always been taught to keep my issues *private.*

She had been the only person that I went to about my issues. She didn't have good money management skills and in her eyes as long as they got paid she was good regardless of how late it was.

Her advice to me was, "Let some things go and in seven years it will be wiped from your credit anyway."

When I became an adult I was adamant about keeping good credit and paying my bills on time. Although I lived paycheck to paycheck and maintained a lifestyle that was really above my means I made sure to keep my bills in order. ***That had changed.***

Asking outsiders for help was just something out of my vocabulary. Then that changed too. I started asking my new party friends if they knew of ways I could make some *fast cash.*

Back then, I didn't have God fearing friends like I do today. *We were either our **own gods** or the habits and things that brought us pleasure became **our idols.***

I didn't have someone around to tell me, "Just pray about it and wait on the Lord." It was more like, "We gotta do what we gotta do, ya know?"

Even if I did I probably would have thought they were crazy. I had never waited on God for a financial breakthrough. *I had always seen the blessing in having a job but what happens when you start to believing and seeing that the job isn't enough??*

No one knew I was living above my means and I never had the best money management skills. If I had it I spent it. I paid my bills first and spent the rest every two weeks like

106

clockwork.

I started dressing sexier and trying to keep up with the *new me I was quickly becoming*, all the while I was accumulating more bills. More money was going out than what was coming in. I had maxed out all my credit cards.

I was no strangers to payday loans either. My mom had used them a few times when I was growing up. It got so bad for me that I had to close my bank accounts because I couldn't afford to make the payments on the payday loans any longer and pay my bills. I did still have my 401k savings plan from my job but I needed more *now.*

I was trying my best with all that was coming up against me to still try and do the best I could for my family. I returned to college after I had my second son.

I really didn't know what I wanted to do with my life anymore. I just knew that I wanted to make money and be happy. Obtaining a degree no longer looked promising, the refund checks were the only convenience. I would get my refund pay a few bills and blow the rest. *My money habits were horrible.*

A lot of people I worked with held degrees and sat right across from me making the same amount of money I did. They often complained about being in debt and school being a dead-end. *Like me they didn't know their God given purpose for living.*

My dream career as a kid to become an attorney was long gone at this point and my focus now was to make money to provide for my family.

Apparently, if you didn't have experience already in the area that you held your degree in, it was difficult to get a job. I continued to ponder over what life was really all about. I didn't know many legit entrepreneurs and the one's I did know was involved in shady side hustles. *In what looked to be my freedom to the world I still felt trapped.*

I tried new positions at work. Even applied to other companies but nothing was coming through. I tried changing shifts at work at one point to spend more time with my kids but none of it worked. I didn't want the one or two dollar raises anymore *I desired a real promotion.*

I planned to study nursing instead of law since the job demand was much greater. I was told the money would be great once I received my degree. I took my old instructors' advice that nursing was better than trying to pursue my old dream of becoming an attorney.

Questions like, *What if I didn't even like being a nurse? What if it's too hard or boring?*

I didn't have a *real passion* for it. The only passion I had at this point was to provide for my family while suppressing the brokenness within me.

I liked helping people, but I never thought of helping them in that way. Being a nurse just sounded boring and like a cop out to me. I remember thinking, *"Is that all there is?"*

My old instructor pressed it because of the money and the fact that I had kids. I needed more than an average call center job to survive. I had no other experience to seek other opportunities, so I continued working at Brinks and attending school.

One of the ladies I befriended at my job, Carma, was a part-time model. She was the typical model type—tall, nice complexion, beautiful smile, and skinny. I was more average sized but I figured that with a pill in my body and some sexy clothes on, I could hide the baby fat, and be an urban model like the ones I seen in the black entertainment magazines.

I idolized celebrities and being in the spotlight all my life. It had always been something that interested me. That was one of those fantasies I'd never share with anyone. Growing up I loved watching America's Next Top Model.

I asked her for help to get me a gig so I could try it out but she blew me off initially. I hadn't went into to details with my friends about the things I was facing internally. I only let her know that I was looking to make some money. I didn't want my mom's advice anymore.

At work, I expressed to my boss that I was ready for a different role that offered more pay and responsibility. We talked about me transferring to another department and applying for a supervisor position when one became available.

However, that option was down the road and I needed some extra cash ***now along with the notion that was searching for something new.*** One of my classmates had started his own income tax business and I asked to work for him but that was a dead-end too. I continued running into to people who would offer me fast ways to make money but they were all dead ends. ***Unbeknownst to me, my life was about to take a turn for the worst.***

One of the hardest things to do is to admit you're lost in a world that pressures you to have it all together. You'll never get clarity until you face your *truth.*

Instead of healing from our pain we cover it up. Instead of surrendering to God we end up *enslaved.*

Don't miss grace like I almost did.
Seek God. Seek Godly counsel. Don't be afraid to admit that you need *help.*

Part Two

Lost in Traffick

My Life in the game

Part Two
Introduction

In spite of all that was going on I still didn't see this coming. Me, being sexually exploited? Me, having a **pimp?** *Handing* over my independence to someone? Exchanging sex for money? Leaving my children to follow a false promise of a better future only to come back empty-handed and more lost and broken than before? I **never** woke up one day and declared, *"I want to become a stripper, have a pimp, and sell my body!"*

Yet all the pieces of my past would be the very tool that was used against me to convince me that this **new business proposition** that was to be offered to me was the key to unlock the doors to my freedom. *I was in need. I was broken. I was lost.* **I fell.** *Hard.*

I didn't grow up with an anchor in God my creator. My anchor was the pain and brokenness I had experienced. I always thought that I had a pretty good grip on my life. As you've read that so wasn't the case. I thought that I had managed to overcome things that had happened to me but I was wrong. *In reality they were* **defining** *me.*

For a long time I was able to mask my issues under my smile, education, jobs, fashion, and relationships. Until I met a man who desired to look past my image and façade I portrayed to the world. A man that would take away all that I once knew as my identity and security in exchange for another identity and foundation to stand on.

My new identity: A hoe. My new foundation: The game. You may know the game as the life of pimping and hoeing. The game is a glamourized lifestyle in which pimps/traffickers uses a system of rules, coercive tactics, and manipulation to force women and girls into being sexually exploited.

That man would in fact become my very first pimp. I had engaged in and done some crazy things but never did I think that I fit the description of becoming someone's commodity to make a profit from.

Little did I know *any* vulnerable person could fit the description of being sexually exploited if the pimp and or trafficker decided that he wanted you.

Most pimps/traffickers seek someone who is vulnerable and longing for something that seems out of reach. They look for someone who is hungry for love and attention. They want the ones who feel like outcast and have been marginalized and mislabeled by society as **nobodies.** They want the ones who are longing for security and stability.

They're looking for someone who already engages in promiscuous activities or has an unhealthy view and knowledge about sex. It's easier to transition someone who meets that criteria into the sex industry.

But if they want you bad enough your background really doesn't matter. No one would assume that someone like me could ever end up entangled in the hands of a pimp. *No one also talks about the realities and the depths pimps/traffickers alike go to have a woman/girl under their control.*

I thank God that today I am a free woman. Today my dreams and my life are finally in the right hands. *God's hands.* But, before becoming the woman that I am today this is the dark crooked path on which God has made straight.

Sex trafficking is defined as the recruitment, harboring, transportation, provision, or obtaining of a person for the purpose of a commercial sex act where such an act is induced by force, fraud, or coercion.

I would have never considered myself to be a victim of sex trafficking. I mean, I wasn't chained to a bed. I wasn't being beaten to have sex with strangers for money. I wasn't an underage runaway. I wasn't from a poverty stricken foreign country.

Unfortunately the media and movies portray sex trafficking in this light. So for a while it was very hard for me to identify myself as someone who fell under the category of being trafficked.

In those instances it's very easy to see that one is being victimized. Since my story didn't fit into the cut and dry definition that I had seen of sex trafficking, I didn't think I could in any way had been victimized. *My situation was different.*

My *willingness* to share my current crisis and my past hurts played right into the web of manipulation my first pimp had already laid out. The manipulation used on me would in fact make me feel like I brought all this on myself. I don't negate the fact that to some degree that may even be true.

The discussion that we would have about fulfilling dreams and financial stability were *false promises* he would use to lure me into sticking around. In fact it didn't take long for me to eventually *embrace* this new identity I had. It **complimented** my brokenness. The game and the sex industry, would become my new normal.

I didn't need to be beaten to be sexually exploited. *The mind games, the dangling promise of a better future, the lie to want to help me instead of hurt me, the twist on words, and the shame I carried for falling prey to empty words were enough for me.*

I was willing and ready to do whatever it took to gain financial and personal security, as long as I didn't have to kill anyone, and it would not kill me. I *never* imagined that my passion for a better life and my desire for love would lead me here but unfortunately it did.

I didn't learn about what sex trafficking was until two years after I left the sex industry. Before that I always described this period of my life as my ***"mid-life crisis"*** that I survived.

In my eyes, I was just a dumb girl who got caught up in the game and managed to get away. Although I had met hundreds of girls along my journey who shared similar experiences and worse, I never knew that there were people fighting for *girls like us.* I never saw what was done to me *as a crime. I was too busy drowning in the guilt and shame that I carried for falling for it all.*

Sex trafficking is the legal term that describes "the game". Sex trafficking can also take on *many different forms.* My story isn't to take away or add to anyone else's experience on how they were trafficked. My only hope is to challenge everyone to see that this is an issue in ALL of our backyards.

I decided to share my story of how I entered the sex industry through the manipulation of a pimp and prostituted to help raise awareness and to show you how one *CAN be a victim of sex trafficking simply by being manipulated with the use of lies and false promises of a better future.* I pray you will read it with an open mind, and an open heart.

Mostly, I pray this will bring light to the far-reaching dangers we face in our world and the importance of sharing the *True Gospel* with people. It is only by the *GRACE* of *GOD* that I was able to break free from that dark lifestyle that I once lived. Everyone has their own story to tell. This is mine.

Chapter 7

When Brokenness meets Fraud

"You will not certainly die," the serpent said to the woman. "For God knows that when you eat from it your eyes will be opened, and you will be like God, knowing good and evil."

When the woman saw that the fruit of the tree was good for food and pleasing to the eye, and also __desirable__ for __gaining wisdom,__ she took some and ate it." Genesis 3:4-6

It doesn't take long for deception to come and change the course of someone's life. In just a matter of a few moments Eve disowned God. Conversation along with our own desires has ruled ever since then causing us to go in the right direction or leading us to fall into sin.

With just a twist of a few words like Eve we bite right into the forbidden fruit. **Well at least I did.**

Although I knew people who hustled illegally to make fast cash, I *always* prided myself on being one who did things the right way. I had been working since the age of 14, by collecting a *legit check.* No side hustle and no shady business.

I had always envisioned that life would remain the same in that regard. I wasn't oblivious or ignorant to what was out there in the world. *The fast life. By this time I had been introduced to many different types of ways to make fast money. In the past it would have never even been a consideration of mine. Then life threw me a curve ball.*

116

I never thought that any side hustle would be done by me. I had dated hustlers who sold drugs and been around my uncle but that was as far as I had ever gone. Growing up I had seen somethings too.

My life was shifting in a direction that I had no plan or way to handle it all. I owed almost every payday loan store in town. *It was getting to a place where I had to decide if I would pay my bills or feed my children.*

I had never saved for a rainy day nor did I ever learn any money management skills. As long as I had a check coming in every two weeks I saw that as my security. I could barely afford the rent at my place. *I was sticking to my plan of never needing any government's assistance or calling on a man for financial help.*

Reaching out to my son's fathers was out of the question. They didn't have any money and the little money they had come with ultimatums that I wasn't willing to partake in. Child support was pointless. I believed that if they wanted to help I shouldn't have never had to ask for it.

I was very independent minded and was too prideful to ask people who had hurt me for help. My mom was always the exception. Times were changing. My family and I were in need.

I had two past-due car loans. It was only a matter of time before for the repo man would be knocking at my door. Collection agencies were constantly ringing my phone – aggressive ones, too. One company got so pushy *my mom* had to get an attorney to get them to back down.

I was still entertaining the thought that everyone expected me to have it all together. In my mind somewhere along the way I had even fallen for the facade everyone had about me knowing privately that *I desperately* needed help.

What would I think of me if everything somehow fell apart?

What would they think of me if they knew I didn't have it all together?

I couldn't go down like that. Not me. I was supposed to be the one making it. But I wasn't. I couldn't give up now and I was tired of going back to my mom's house. I thought I had all the answers. ***But I didn't. Along with all this I was still wrestling with the thought of discovering who I was.***

Hanging out with the wrong crowd. Priorities were all out of order. Financially and relationally I was losing. The only good I had going for me were ***my kids*** and my job. Even work was beginning to bother me.

I've always been the type to get easily bored at work. Once I had finally mastered the new position, it turned out to be equally tedious as the last. I was right back to being bored.

Carma was finally about to come through with this possible new gig. She was going to introduce me to her friend, Kenny, who could help me make some extra money.

Carma claimed she had known Kenny on an intimate level. She also knew him to be a businessman ***and a pimp. I was just desperate enough to meet him and find out what he had to offer. I didn't care anymore.***

Whatever it was I had already made up my mind that it was going to be part time so it wasn't going to affect my day job. *I was going to be smart about it all.*

A couple of weeks later I met Kenny at a club in Dallas. He pulled up in a pearl white Cadillac Escalade that was sitting on 26 inch rims. I was impressed. I remember being so nervous walking up to the vehicle, yet exhilarated at the same time. The window rolled down, and this guy was sizing me up – like he was buying a new car.

"Step back and turn around." He said, while getting a good luck at the future product that would be on the market. *My body.*

He complimented me on my beauty and my smile. Then he asked me what I needed, and I told him. I was very forward with him. I needed to make some extra money for my family. Point. Blank. *Period.*

He asked me several more questions and I answered them all him without hesitation. I let him know that I was only interested in modelling part time. That's when he told me that he couldn't help me and that what he had to offer required full-time availability.

Kenny then added that he was skeptical about bringing someone *like me* into his circle. His words were, "I don't ever want to be the one responsible for introducing someone like you into this. *You're too green,*" Meaning I was inexperienced and gullible.

He was right. I had no idea of what I was about to get myself into. All I knew was that I desperately needed some help. I was lost and in need.

I went back inside the club but I was perplexed by what he said. I was confused. I was curious. And a part of me was indignant. *Was I not good enough for his little 'job'?*

He sent me a text later that night asking me to send him a few pictures, just in case he knew of anyone else who could help me. I jumped right on the opportunity and sent a couple of my best selfie shots I had taken with my phone.

A couple of weeks went by. As my usual custom, I wanted to go out to release some stress of my day-to-day worries. I put on one of my favorite black skin tight club wear dresses and called Olivia up. She was always down to get out of the house.

We called the pill man, popped an ecstasy, and rode around Dallas trying to find a 21 and under club for us to party at. Olivia wasn't 21 just yet.

That same night a friend of mine named *Faith* called asking me to come get her from work. She was a dancer at a popular strip club in Dallas and was feeling too sick to drive home. I had known her for years, and as far back as I can remember – even as far back as high school – she had been dancing.

We didn't talk often because we were running in different circles. But I still had love for her and we talked from time to time. *I had even encouraged her to make some changes in her life at one point.*

As we were sitting in the parking lot of the club where Faith worked, she came to the car and she kept telling me she was done. She was tired of the stripping scene. She made a decision that night that she wasn't going to dance anymore.

I had always known her to brag about all the money she made and the ***freedom*** it brought her. Even when I ran into her on rough days she always ***defended*** the lifestyle of being a stripper. Seeing this side of Faith was a first.

I had no idea that I needed to take heed to the words that dripped from her mouth that night.

My phone rang and it was Kenny calling to meet up again. I told him where we were and within five minutes he was cruising into the parking lot. Pulling up next to Kenny's escalade was a ***gold Lincoln Navigator.***

This tall, handsome man wearing blinged out jewelry, hair to his shoulders, and snake-skin Prada shoes stepped out of the Navigator and made his way to my side of the car. He came over and introduced himself as

Smooth.

He never did look at any of my friends. It was clear that Kenny must have shown him my pictures because I had never seen Smooth a day in my life. He carried himself in a way that was unforgettable. *Very over the top.* I was high as a kite that night. Smooth already had my attention right from his first impression.

My friends were agitated and ready to head out but I was not in the mood to end the night just yet. I was beginning to peak on the ecstasy I had taken. Plus I knew that Smooth wanted to talk business since Kenny had called.

He told me to go sit in his *SUV* so we could talk. I obeyed, after saying goodnight to my two friends. Olivia had already made it clear to Faith that she would keep my car since we stayed in the same apartment complex.

Kenny came over to the truck and told me that Smooth was his friend, and that he could help me with my money issues. *Faith was hesitant about letting me go, but I insisted.* I knew that if I had told her I was high she would have never let me leave. I wasn't going to miss out on this opportunity.

Everyone knew that I got out of hand when I was high. My alter ego came out and I was a totally different person. I'd done stuff in the past without thinking clearly or at all. Olivia knew I was high, but she wasn't going to tell Faith. Smooth assured Faith I was in good hands and she relented, and told me to call her if I needed anything.

*Seems fateful that my friend was walking away from the industry on the same night I was meeting with the man who would become my first pimp. I was headed down a path of **self-destruction**. My life would never be the same after I pulled out of the parking lot.*

Smooth and I drove off and headed toward *Walnut Hill off I-35 in Dallas.* Immediately he exposed me to a totally different scene that I wasn't used to. It was like I had stepped into a whole new world. We drove down side streets near the night clubs in Dallas and girls were posted up everywhere. *I couldn't believe my eyes.*

I had never seen anything like it before. Being high, I summed it up in my head that they were either waiting on a ride or leaving the club. As he pulled up to the girls, they

121

all ran off with their heads down. *I didn't have a clue back then, but I was witnessing real-life street prostitution.*

He pulled the truck into a store and parked. The parking lot was packed with men and women standing around their luxury cars blasting their music just chilling.

It was normal for people to leave the club to either hang out at an after hour spot, go eat breakfast, or post up at a nearby gas station to show off their cool cars. *Smooth on the other hand was taking me up there to show his patnas his new hoe. **Me.***

"I got me a new bitch."

Smooth started bragging to his homeboys. *"Beautiful Intelligent Talented Charismatic **Hoe.***"

He said I was beautiful! And intelligent, and talented!

I was so high that I completely ignored the fact that he called me a hoe.

Smooth was what you could call a finesse pimp. Most finesse pimps are really persuasive with their words. Instead of using physical force they choose mind manipulation to force women and girls into the sex industry. Since I was high I couldn't understand none of which was being laid out before me.

*Kenny introduced me to Smooth because he knew that Smooth would be willing to do whatever it took to persuade any woman/girl to be down with him. I would have been too much work for Kenny but for Smooth I was a perfect piece of art. **Naïve.** On the edge of life crying out, seeking **HELP** on my own, and **WILLING** to receive direction.*

We pulled out of the parking lot and continued our conversation. Smooth had been asking me about my dreams, and my goals. I don't know if it was Smooth's demeanor, or if it was the ecstasy, but beyond the thoughts of this being a business meet up I was attracted to him. Without him touching me he had already *touched* me.

Not once had we discussed the reason on which I presumed I was there. I tried letting him know that I was only looking to make **some extra money.** He ignored me and urged me to share my 'crazy' fantasies with him.

"Not the one where you want to be married and have a lot of kids. The one without any limits – the one you could never let anyone know you had. You know the dream or fantasy your friends and family would laugh about if you ever shared with them." Smooth said.

"I'm over that whole love thang. Trust me. It ain't for me. All I want right now is to get my money and my life together." I responded.

Being probed in this way, encouraged to reveal my deepest desires, I started to remember...

I always admired women who had high-profile jobs and were able to sustain a seemingly-healthy family life. Back when I was 19 I had taken a speech class at a local community college and we made a vision board as a class project. I'd never made a vision board before but she let us know that we could dream without limits. So I did.

*I had pictures of big stacks of cash to represent wealth and riches. Along with a picture of a brand new Bentley Coupe. There were pictures of my family right in the middle because they were center of my vision. A picture of Oprah was on my vision board. Along with the words respect, independence, power, fashion, strong mother, and determined. **I desired influence and I wanted to make a difference.** I had pictures of an airplane, a future salon of my own, and pictures of high end fashion **clothes for me to model and own.***

*In my crazy dream I was unstoppable. I conjured up images of **being a celebrity**, and a person of strong influence – like Beyoncé but singing wasn't my gift or talent.*

*But this was just a fantasy. **A very special person rises up to the top. Not me.*** I wanted to believe in that hope of being successful, but that voice inside my head quickly shot the idea down.

Let's be honest, girl. You ain't gonna be able to get out of the ghetto. You're setting yourself up for disappointment if you start dreaming now, the voice prevailed.

"Let's just keep this about what I need right now and that's some money." I told Smooth.

He agreed that keeping my job wouldn't interfere with the possible gigs he had for me. I made it clear that I needed the cash right away to get me out of the hole I was in.

From the beginning I explained how important my boys were to me. Smooth made it clear that the family would always come ***first*** no matter what. Smooth listened so attentively, and seemed genuinely interested in me. This was something I hadn't experienced before from any man before.

His interest in my intellect was an incredible force, drawing out of me anything I kept guarded from others. He was not perusing my body, instead he was mentally undressing me.

It wasn't about how sexy I was, or how big my butt was. He wasn't impressed by my mediocre job like guys were in the past. I could tell that he wasn't trying to befriend me just to ride in my car. I remember feeling so comfortable around him that night.

Smooth had charm, and charisma. He actually wanted to converse, and I was like a piece of putty in his hands. He was quite strategic in his approach and just like that I was ***hooked.*** *It seemed so harmless.*

We continued to talk and he told me a little bit about himself. He was an up and coming rapper from Memphis. He had no biological children, but he was taking care of a

124

little boy which he raised as his own. *'How sweet I thought. A man that takes care of someone else's child.'*

Smooth claimed he was currently living in New Orleans and he was just visiting his friends in Dallas on **business. *The true story: He was in Dallas to recruit women.***

He showed me videos of him performing and he played his music while we rode around talking. At the time he had his own entertainment company. Before that he had previously own printing and graphic design company, and tax service. He was a college graduate. He was in a fraternity, Q-Dawgs. When he was 21, he bought his first home – *with cash!*

He seemed well established, and perfectly capable of helping me out. Truthfully, I had never been with a man of his **caliber.** I wasn't even thinking that I needed to go and check to see if he was telling the truth or not. *Who was I for him to need to make all that stuff up?*

He was a hard worker, a true go-getter. I admired that about him. He showed me pictures of other women he had previously helped financially. I cannot explain why this was not setting off alarm bells in my head. For one, they looked like regular women, and he used these pictures to reassure me that I was in good hands. It could have been the drugs in my system or the desperation. Maybe a mixture of it all.

I felt such relief as if I had finally done something right. Smooth told me he wanted to do more, though. He wanted to help me achieve my dreams. He already seen a plan to get me there. He believed in me. *It was surprising because by this time I had lost all hope in me. I was at my wits end.*

All along, I would find out later, this plan of his *was not* altruistic in the least. He had aspirations that ultimately *only* included him rising to the top and he had found the perfect stepping stone in ***me.***

Smooth continued to lay down his web, very craftily, and intentionally. He began the mind control and manipulation by telling me I would have to change the way I did things, and the way I thought about things.

He confirmed this sense of urgency in me, and he added an air of exhilaration to his dialogue. He had a way with words and could charm his way into anyone woman's heart who would listen. ***Especially, one who is already vulnerable and on the edge.***

"This is your one and only chance", he said.

I remember thinking, *opportunities like this didn't just come every day for girls like me.* Meeting someone who actually wanted to just help me. No sex. No games. ***Just getting money.*** He would be leaving town soon, and we had to get our game rolling, fast.

He took me to his friend's condo so we could go chill and talk more. I am not going to deny that there was a physical attraction, but mostly he *finessed* me that night, just by listening to me. We talked all night until the sun came up. Not once did he lay a hand on me.

He totally seemed to get me. He explained to me why I was having a hard time with men. *He told me I was square, someone who is ignorant to the real facts of life, and I needed to learn the value of the treasure that I held inside.*

He explained how no man would take me serious because I already had two kids of my own by two different men. Instead these men really viewed me as a slut, rather than someone desperately longing to be loved.

"Most niggas today are still boys, and aren't ready to raise kids, especially kids that aren't theirs. In their eyes you're damaged goods. Square niggas are so lame and

126

nasty, they'll lie to you and say they love you, while having unprotected sex with other bitches all behind your back."

"Not me I have dreams to pursue, I see the potential in you and if you stick with me I got you and I'm going to hold you down. You need a man in your life to help you and I'm the real one you've been waiting for." Smooth said.

He was right. I wanted to be loved so badly, I had allowed the men in my past to portray me in a negative way.

*All the while purposely negating the fact that my real issue was **NEVER** just about the men from my past but more about the need for me to heal and deal with what I had been through. He needed to make me focus on what they had done wrong in order to keep me from focusing on what I really needed to deal with. **ME**.*

All I ever wanted was someone who would love my boys and me. I wanted a happy family under one roof – something I never had as a kid. As much as I had tried to tell myself that I was done with love it would never fully leave me.

In his eyes I had better things to worry about than love. This plan he had to help me fulfill my dream was the piece I was missing from life. It was the answer to my question of "why am I here."

He declared that I deserved better. He declared that the men that broke my hearts were cowards for *misusing* me. He declared that I was a prized possession with so much **potential.**

"You just need some guidance and direction." Smooth said. He declared that I shouldn't have to carry all the weight of raising my boys alone. And finally, he declared that my boys and I would have a new family, if I would take a ***leap of faith with him.***

No other man or person had spoken to me like he did. I thought he was so honest and real that night. I had finally met someone who understood that there was really more to life. Men I had known before Smooth were only concerned that I had a job, my own place, and that they could have sex with me without any commitment to a meaningful relationship.

Not Smooth, he didn't take advantage of my brokenness like the others. He was in fact going to help me get back the power I had lost. At least that's what I thought. **Oh how naïve I had become.**

I had a tendency to reveal too much anytime I was high on a pill. The pill had me in a very vulnerable state. I remember feeling like a little girl again finally breaking free from all her troubles. That night I was easily persuaded by the passion in his voice, and the conviction of his words.

Believing a man's words and promises before seeing his actions was nothing new to me. The only difference was that this man's intent went so much deeper than a one night stand. Smooth had plans to exploit my insecurities and my desperate financial state for his own personal gain by, pimpin' on a b.i.t.c.h.

Smooth told me that the temporary gig would include me modelling and dancing part time. Modeling like the girls in the black entertainment magazines. Dancing like the girls I seen in rap videos. The way he described it made it all sound glamorous.

I'm thinking, *the same girl who always got talked about for being ugly? The same girl who had gotten played by men was now being told that I had potential to make money off the looks that everyone else including myself had talked about or mistreated? I was all ears.*

He encouraged me to not only consider taking modeling seriously, but to stop speaking negatively about myself.

*"I'm going to give you your confidence back. A woman like you is **too beautiful** to be insecure," Smooth said. "With the money you're about to start making you can easily buy bigger breast and have surgery to get those stretch marks removed. That's nothing." He continued.*

All of my life, I thought I was ugly. Beautiful, to me, was light-skinned girls with long, curly hair--or a light-skinned girl period. I didn't fit that description. I even had 'friends' tell me I was ugly. I believed I was ugly. The only time a man called me pretty was when he wanted something from me. *Little did I know Smooth was doing the exact same thing.*

I couldn't recognize the game he was playing and at that time, I wasn't even trying to. I was more interested in this opportunity to finally get a financial breakthrough and receive the direction I needed. Along with the reality that the deception in his words was complimenting the **brokenness** *inside of me. I didn't want to leave him that night and the feeling seemed mutual.*

As the night continued on into the morning Smooth would add that aside from him being an up and coming rap artist and entrepreneur that he was a ***pimp.*** Smooth explained that he would be managing the money I made from the gigs since I wasn't good at it. *I had shared my lack of money management skills with him too.*

He told me I wasn't to worry about him being a pimp. We were simply doing business. *I had a need and he knew the way to fulfilling my need. He claimed I would be investing in my dreams and the future of my boys instead of the* **"white man's dream" of keeping me trapped in a dead end corporate job.**

"No more wasting your potential man. I'm going to teach you everything you need to know to make it. You won't have to struggle anymore. We're a team now," he said.

I liked the idea of having someone who wanted to stick around. *Someone who wanted to see me make the most of my life. Someone who had direction and knew what they wanted from life. He had real goals and dreams unlike most men I dated in past.*

It all sounded too good to be true. And it was. Sadly enough, I was too blind to see. I remember going to the bathroom and not even recognizing the woman I saw in the mirror. *I made a deal with the devil that night. His presentation and conversation had me sold.*

Chapter 8

Right Light, Wrong Stage

Do you know that before you were born that God already had a plan for your life?

I mean a specific plan and purpose perfectly fit for you?

One that doesn't involve having to engage in illegal activity to gain real success?

*During these times I didn't know that. I didn't know that **imperfect** people like me could still honor God with their lives.*

Now that I know the truth I can look back and see that my desires to be loved, financially stable, walking in freedom, having influence, and etc. are valid and okay.

The trouble with those desires back then is that they were on the wrong stage. Wrong environment. With the wrong people.

*What happens when we have **right** desires but wrong motives? Wrong environments or influences? Lies dipped in half-truths?*

*"The eye is the lamp of the body. If your eyes are healthy, your whole body will be full of light. But if your eyes are unhealthy, your whole body will be full of darkness. If then the light within you is darkness, how great is that **darkness**!" Matthew 6: 22, 23*

*If there is one lesson to learn from reading my story is that the enemy has only one plan for us **all**: **To make a mockery of God. He can only be a perverted carbon copy though.** Back then I had a strong zeal for life and I was very passionate about discovering the reason for my being. I had been chasing and doing life the enemy's way even before I had met Smooth.*

Smooth was only going to give me a purpose for my zeal instead of living life aimlessly.

If no one has told you before God has a good purpose for your zeal and passion for life. If like me you've misused your zeal for ungodly ways of living God is waiting to restore and redeem you. Seek Him. Only God knows the ultimate plan for your life.

One of the popular songs being played around that time in the club and on the radio was Kandi Burrus and Big Bank Black called, "Try it out." The song basically tells the listener to try out pimping. In my everyday world the word pimp was used rather loosely.

Strangely, that song would later become our anthem song to motivate me into thinking I had made the right choice to trust him. He painted a picture of our future together as one of ***luxury,*** like the celebrities we saw on TV and in the hip hop culture– as long as I stayed with him and obeyed what he said.

Rappers used the term pimp in *their music.* Television paraded the word around as though there was nothing negative about it to be on guard about. I had already conjured up in my mind that Smooth was harmless too.

I had even met guys in the past who claimed to be pimps once I started hanging with my new circle of friends.

I had seen movies that involved men who called themselves pimp but the word still didn't have a negative connotation attached to it like the words ***rapist, murderer***, or ***pedophile.***

I found out this was part of the reason Kenny and Smooth referred to me as 'green'. Smooth explained that because I had never been with a pimp, I didn't really know the truth, and squares like me had it all wrong.

In his defense, he argued that I was already being pimped by the *white man* living by the *white man's* rules, always struggling to make ends meet, while the *white man* lived in his big suburban home.

"You're a slave to their system working your *little* 9 to 5 j.o.b., *just over broke*, getting paid the minimum while doing the most work. Never having time or enough money to invest your kids' future or even take them out on a vacation. I bet you the CEO and your manager at work takes vacation unlike you and your family." *He said.*

Smooth was challenging my belief system by using **the old plantation mentality structure and I didn't have an argument.**

He had an answer prepared and ready for all of my concerns about this subject of pimping. *He continued talking with confidence reassuring me that he was the answer to my cries for help.*

The next morning, I texted my mom to check on the boys. I could tell she was agitated by the short responses. I told her I had had a long night, and that I would be by to get the boys soon.

Smooth had already informed me not to tell anyone about things we had discussed- especially my mom.

He said she wouldn't understand because she was too much of a *"square."* He had told me I was a square too, but he was going to change that sooner than later. One of his favorite sayings was, **"I turn lost bitches into boss bitches."**

133

Instead of calling my mom that whole weekend I continued to respond only by text. I could tell she was upset that I had left my babies all weekend with her. I had carried out this lie that I was partying all weekend with the girls and hungover.

Whenever I went out I would let my babies stay the night with my mom if I got too drunk or high. My mom went right along with it as if this was just like one of our normal weekend parties.

Since I still had on the clothes from the night before, Smooth drove me to my apartment to shower and to get my car. I went over to Olivia's to tell her what was going on with me. I told her that Smooth was going to get me some gigs to start modeling and dancing part time.

"Chanel, please don't quit your job or do anything crazy. You're one of the few women I know who has made something of herself and hasn't got caught up in any bullshit. **Don't** let him bring you down." Olivia tried warning me. I was too prideful and desperate to listen at the time.

Olivia had already been through somethings and been in trouble with the law. Things seemed so bad for her back then she could never even find work. I could have taken her advice but honestly I didn't respect her advice.

She hadn't even managed to find a better way for her and her family. At times it seemed as if she had already given up. She seemed content with only having to pay $50 a month for rent because of the governments' assistance she had. I wasn't about to go out like that.

*It was already happening like Smooth said it would: **no square** was really going to understand. She couldn't see what I could see – or perhaps it was the other way around. Pride and arrogance always comes before the **FALL**.*

I promised her that it was only going to be part time and it wouldn't interfere with my current job. Smooth had already made it clear that family came first and working part time wasn't going to be an issue. Olivia's friend, Dasha, was there, and she had overheard us talking. *Dasha wanted to be down.*

She had modeled before with Olivia, so she saw Smooth as just someone who could help her get more gigs too. She was crashing at Olivia's with no place or job of her own so to her it was just what she needed. She had nothing to lose.

I took her over to my place to meet Smooth, and he instantly said that he could help her out too. He wanted her on the team. *"What business works without team effort?" Smooth said.*

He claimed that he wanted to help Dasha too. It made things better that I wasn't going at it alone too. She went back over to Olivia's to get her things and asked if she could crash at my place since we would be working together. Dasha said she would watch my boys for free when I went to my day job if needed. It sounded like a great plan, so I agreed to let her crash at my place.

Smooth took us to eat later that evening and we went back to Dallas with him to chill. He wanted to speak more with Dasha. When he took us back to my place he asked to borrow my car while he left his truck at my place.

This was quickly beginning to feel like something more than a business opportunity, which I was cool with. He was already texting me little *'sweet nothings'* and telling me he missed me and couldn't wait to see how much better life was going to be for me and my boys.

Since I struggled with rejection my whole life, I typically gave myself quickly to men in an attempt to avoid even more rejection. Smooth would be no exception to that rule. **This time I would be giving away much more than my body.**

After the weekend was over, I got up to get ready for work as usual. Smooth came in the bathroom and told me that I wasn't going back to my job anymore. He instructed me to call and quit. *I wasn't having it.* I reminded him what I had said about this only being part time, and how I was going to keep my job. He startled me by shouting back at me in rage.

*"**Bitch,** I changed my mind! I need you with me all the times. I'll take care of you and show the real way to make it out here. What you're making now every two weeks at that piece of shit job you can make with me in one night. You'll even have more time with your boys.

Let me show you how to really be a **boss.** It's time to start working toward your own dreams. Forget making the white man rich. **We** need to get rich. Make the phone call now! You're tired of your bullshit life you been living anyway, right?"

He gave me all sorts of reasons why I needed to leave my job and **step out on faith** with him. He had taken everything I shared with him and twisted it. I remember being more confused than anything else. I couldn't tell if he was pissed at me or just really passionate about wanting to **help me.** Out of my confusion I asked him not to hit me and I started dialing the number to my job.

*What he was saying was right. I had previously expressed to him that I was bored at my job and that I wanted more out of life. I tired of how men had been mistreating me and I was drowning financially without a plan to fix any of my issues. As I quickly weighed my options, stepping into the unknown seemed like the only option. **Smooth was offering me keys to what I thought was my freedom. A new life. A better way.***

In reality, I had been caught by the warden and was on my way to solitary confinement. My solitary confinement

136

didn't include being trapped behind four walls. It meant being trapped mentally. Smooth presented himself to me as someone I could make money with. I would later find out that I hadn't escaped anything but entered into another hell. **THE SEX INDUSTRY.**

I should have cut ties with him that day. I should have told him, "It was nice to meet you," and gone back to my reality. But something in me ***wanted*** to take a chance at something different. I was tired of living paycheck to paycheck. *I was tired of robbing Peter to pay Paul.* I told myself that I didn't want to follow in my mother's footsteps financially, I was doing just that just.

I wanted to be a better parent and make my babies proud. I was failing at that too. There was no way that I was going to instill in my kids that being an adult only meant going to a dead-end job and attending college with no real purpose. If I was financially stable my kids could bypass *ALL* the crap I had went through and I could invest in their future.

I was always the one out of my friends who was determined to keep pushing no matter the obstacles that came my way. Now I was only existing in the world and not actually living. My past relationships with men, my unwillingness to deal with my pain, and trying to find love had created this destructive pattern in my life.

I tried to just call in sick the first time. I wasn't high anymore like the initial night Smooth and I had met. *Anything sounded good when I was high.* Now Smooth had totally flipped the script by demanding that I quit my job. Although Smooth had said a lot of things that first night I hadn't seen any of it but pictures and videos.

I figured I could call into to work, try out the modelling and dancing a few days. If it didn't work out I could just go back to my regular job. Smooth overheard me say I was calling in sick and told me to call back and *quit.*

"When you want to fulfill a dream you gotta go ALL in. You can't be half stepping and if you really want something different for your boys you gotta really trust me. I got you." He said.

I called my manager at work and gave him the excuse of a family crisis. I could hear the disappointment in his voice, but he said I could call him if I ever needed anything. We hung up and I could tell my supervisor was very appalled by my phone call. He called right back and asked me to come in and sign a letter of resignation.

Before disconnecting he kept asking me over and over if everything was okay. With Smooth standing right in front of me motioning me to hurry and hang up, all I could say was, *"Yes, I'm okay."*

My manager insisted I cover my tracks in case I ever wanted to return to the job. He could see potential in me too. We had been talking about my next role within the company. I reassured him I was fine and I would be in later to sign the resignation letter.

Smooth made it clear that he was coming with me to sign my resignation letter. *I thought it was to be supportive but he only wanted to make sure that no one would interfere with the decision I had just made.*

He didn't come inside with me but all I kept thinking about was the fact that he was sitting in the car and that I didn't want to see him get upset again.

As we drove out to my job he had me rehearse the things I was to tell my boss. Most importantly, I was to *not* mention anything about what was going on between him and I.

When someone introduces you to a new ideology or way of thinking they need to isolate you from people who can challenge what's being imbedded in your mind.

138

My mom had been calling frequently, and Smooth told me to ignore her calls because she wouldn't understand what was going on. He said *nobody* from my old life would. *I went along with it because I believed that everyone simply just wouldn't understand that I wanted to try something new.*

Smooth kept calling it *faith,* and promising me that I wouldn't regret it. I definitely wasn't going to talk to my mom now that I just quit my job. I had *never* let a man invade my financial security – my heart, yes; my body, yes. *NEVER* my means of supporting my family. I had never left a job without having another one in line. An offer letter that detailed my hourly pay and schedule.

*Leaving my job was **supposed** to be the start of a new journey for me to make some real money and reach my dreams. Smooth insisted I was just stepping out of my comfort zone and walking in faith. But truthfully, I was walking deeper into the **wilderness**. One that I wasn't at all prepared for.*

Dasha and I had promised each other that we would stay close together on this journey. She wanted to believe that Smooth had a way out for her, too. After Smooth and I returned from signing the resignation letter, he told us that we were going to start dancing at a strip club that night – temporarily.

Smooth said it was the fastest and easiest way to make a lot of money while we saved our money for the top modeling jobs.

I didn't think twice about it. I was now jobless. I had no choice. Some pimps take their time with girls and others move really quickly when the girl or woman is already vulnerable and ready to make a change like I was.

I had mentioned to Smooth that I liked to dance, stripping was supposedly not much different.

My friend Olivia and I had tried it once before just for fun. Never was it supposed to be part of my resume of jobs I've had. I knew I would need a pill for the night, but Smooth made it clear that I wouldn't need a pill to work. I needed to stay focus but more than anything I desperately needed something to clear my mind and kill my nerves.

He drove us to a local strip club in Arlington. While in route to the club he went over stage names. He gave me the name Charisma. Dasha had already picked out her own name. Smooth claimed that I had the characteristics of a charismatic person. I wanted to use my real name, Chanel, but he insisted that when I performed I was to always have a stage name.

Smooth dropped us off and never came inside of the club. He gave us clear instructions on what to do once we made it inside. It was clear that we weren't the first girls that he had taken down this road.

As told, we spoke with the manager for the night and filled out an application. We paid our club dues, tip out, upfront. No one danced in the club for free. After filling out paperwork and getting a drink from the bar we made our way to the dressing where the other girls were.

The women at the club were friendly for the most part, but it was vividly clear that this was all about *competition.* We were there to make money, not friends. It was early in the evening and girls were already arguing with one another.

At the strip club every new girl had to audition on their first night. Dasha and I were no exception. Smooth had given us stripper outfits and shoes, but it was clear that the items were used. He promised we would get new clothes later. *That would never happen.*

Dasha and I stayed close together, changed into our dance outfits and made our way back out to the club. As we waited for our names to be called we must have walked back and forth from the dressing room over five times. I kept looking in the mirror and asking Dasha and the other girls their opinion of my stretch marks showing.

"Girl, these dudes don't care about that."

"They're really not bad you're tripping."

"No one can see them unless you point them out."

"Relax. You're not the only one here with stretch marks."

"You don't even have to take off your clothes unless you want to."

They were really trying to encourage me but it wasn't helping my nerves in any way.

*"**Charisma** you're up next."* The DJ yelled through the mic.

The time had finally come for me to be on center stage. As I downed the last bit of my drink I anxiously awaited behind stage for the music to start. It was like time had stopped just for me and the whole world was on the other side of the curtains waiting on me.

*This wasn't the idea that I had in mind when I thought about me being on a stage or fulfilling my dream. My vision included people like Oprah not thirsty men who wanted to undress me. But this stage and this audience was all I had and the closet I had ever been to my dream of **influence**.*

When the music started playing again I stepped out onto the stage looking straight-ahead eager to not make any eye contact with anyone. I had never paraded my body around for that many people at one time. All eyes were on me.

I turned around and started giving them view of what I figured would be my best asset at that time, my backside. It wasn't my smile or my slow seductive dance moves. Six stages. Three songs on each stage later, it was finally over.

After my first stage performance I knew that although I had claimed to be on this new journey for financial stability and freedom to pursue my dreams, *it was clear I was there for something much more.*

Part of me had always known that there was some pieces in me that were broken and hurting. Now, I had been proven to be beyond repair. I was in fact a broken and clearly **lost my way.**

I was now a product, like being examined on a shelf at a store. My shelf was in fact now a stage. The audience could touch me wherever and whenever they wanted.

Like little kids in a candy store men wandered around the club moving from stage to stage deciding on which product was worth their money and time. It hadn't took long for the alcohol to wear off and I found myself sitting at a table with Dasha asking her, *"What the hell are we doing here?"*

We made money that night, but it wasn't as much as a two-week paycheck, like Smooth promised it would be. A couple of hundred dollars. That wasn't at all close to the **breakthrough** I was expecting. Weekdays were supposedly really slow. It looked and felt like a packed house to me that first night.

Smooth wasn't upset that we didn't make much money that night. I was more upset than he was. He was more satisfied with the fact that we had enough courage to get up there and do it. The promise of making two-weeks' worth of money in one night drifted out of the window.

Smooth was now telling me, "Relax, you gotta to stay down to come up. Don't worry I got you. Look at it this way you worked 5 hours today. If you did that four or five days a week for a whole year that's well over 50,000 a year. The better you get at it the more money you'll start to see. Trust me, I know you can do this."

Smooth paid extra attention to me that night. It was obvious I was beginning to feel strange about everything, so he knew he needed to reassure me. That's the night we became intimate for the first time. *He held me real close that night.*

As we lay there he began to explain how he believed I could handle the darker days, the ones you have to go through to get to the sunny days. He bolstered my courage to stick it out, and promised I would see the benefits and reward of taking this leap of faith one day. Under his *spell,* I placed my hope on his every word.

He finally said it was cool to call my mom back instead of texting her about my boys. I really missed them. She brought them over for a little while, and they even all met Smooth. He introduced himself as someone I had befriended.

He already given me a new lie to tell my mom. The story was, I would be picking up later shifts at work, so she would need to watch the boys again. I had never given my mom a reason not to trust me as an adult, so she took my word for it. I could tell that my mom wanted to ask me more questions but she would never overstep the boundaries she lived by, *"What goes on in this house stays in this house."*

The house could be on fire and my mom would still be hesitate about calling firemen to the rescue. My mom has always been the secret bearer and she never wants anyone to interfere or know what's going on behind closed doors. There were red flags everywhere but my mom wasn't going to dare speak up and question what was going on.

I had let the boys spend the night with my mom before but *NEVER* four days in a row. Life had shifted a total 180 degrees. I was a party girl but I had always made sure that my babies were good.

I felt horrible about leaving my babies so suddenly without explanation. *Just like the ones who had hurt me in my past, I was now hurting the ones I loved most.*

143

The way Smooth saw it, I was finally taking care of my family, and it required a little time away from them for now. But this was only *temporary*. It wasn't neglect at all, according to him. "You gotta stay down in order to come up." He'd always say.

Each night he collected our money all the while reassuring me he was holding it to go towards investing in my dreams and my kids' future.

We went back to the club for the next few nights. The stripper scene was really cut throat and it didn't take Dasha and I long to see that there was a lot we needed to learn if we were going to make some real money.

Being a stripper wasn't just about getting on stage and dancing on tables. Like any job, being a stripper came with rules and strategy. While we were trying to figure things out this was working all in Smooth's favor.

Most of the customers were regulars to the more seasoned girls. To avoid any drama, I waited on a guy to approach me. That really didn't work out for me because in the club you almost have to be like an aggressive salesperson. I wasn't confident in me, *the product*, and I've never really been much of a sales person.

Fighting amongst the girls was normal. It felt like high school all over again. Instead of fighting over boys, gossip, friendships, and competing in fashion everyone was fighting over every dollar that hit the stage floor.

Survival.

Some girls were fighting to pay for school. Some girls were fighting for their child's next meal. Some fought over a place to lay their head. Some had quotas, amount given by a pimp, to meet. Others were simply just fighting for their lives.

Contrary to what a lot of people may think being a stripper requires more courage and self-confidence than any other job I ever had. People often times assume that

144

one must have *low self- esteem* in order to take off one's clothing for money. I beg to differ. It was in the darkest place of my life that I'd go on to meet some of the most strong and determined women.

At least that's the impression I got initially. Eventually I would learn that the smiling faces and seemingly high self-esteem that the dancers were only a cover-up for many just to get them through the night. *They had good intentions but were just in the wrong environment. Many like me had it in their mind that this was only temporary.*

Dasha and I were becoming closer by the minute. The more we shared our past hurts, the more we understood each other. We continued dancing, but things weren't getting any better for us. Neither one of us wanted to be there. Yet, every time we went to Smooth with our concerns he always said something to keep us hanging on another day.

The word was getting out around town that I was stripper. Everyone was coming out to see me. Like a brand new item that was hot on the market everyone wanted to touch and test me. *It was literally driving me insane.*

My old friends had come by to laugh and make fun of me. Guys that I had once dated and knew wanted to see this new Chanel, *Charisma,* in action. The more people came the more I began to hurt inside.

I had become a total mockery of everything that I ever stood for. It wasn't private like most of our hypocritical moments mine were made public for all to see.

As the atmosphere continued to push me further into this new lifestyle, God would still intervene and plant little seeds of hope in the midst of my darkest days.

A guy that I went to school with would find himself sitting next to the stage on which I was dancing on. It was clear that unlike the others he was there to actually have a good time instead of coming to make fun of me. He was startled when he recognized it was me.

"Chanel is that you?" He said.

I smiled and shook my head. I assumed like the others he wanted his touch of the latest product but instead he wanted to just talk.

"I would have never thought someone like you would end up in a place like this. I see you being a model, a high-end one, before I'd see you being a stripper."

I explained to him that eventually that was the plan. Yet he was still disappointed that my detour would lead me to this stage.

"Can I ask you something?" He said.

I nodded yes not wanting to scream over the music.

"Do you know why my friends and I never approached you in high-school?"

I nodded. Thinking to myself. Because I was ugly of course.

"I don't think you really know. But we always thought you were too good for us to approach. You were different from the other girls. Beautiful. Intelligent. You knew what you wanted out of life. I know I never really got to know you but I know for a fact that this isn't you."

Right there I wanted to break down in tears but he was right, he didn't know me. He didn't know my story. Like the rest of the world he knew my image that I portrayed to the world. *That night, he met the broken girl, behind that image.*

146

Chapter 9

Mental Shackles

Have you ever found yourself in a complicated situation?

A relationship? Maybe he promised you he's not going to hit you again.

A job? At the job, your boss has promised that next year the promotion you've waited five years to get is coming.

Maybe a traditional church? You grew up at this church and although you feel led to leave your family convinces you to stay. Even condemns you for considering leaving the family church.

While it's obvious that you need to leave you find yourself unable to move? ***You've attached yourself to a lie that you believe as truth and it now has you bound.***

No one is holding you hostage physically. Yet you complain, ponder, and contemplate leaving but never get around to it.

Mental shackles is what I call that...

When a woman or girl is being trafficked or under the control of a pimp she won't always be strapped to a bed or physically forced. She won't always have a gun to her head forcing her to stay with a pimp.

Instead, it's those mental shackles that keeps her staying around under this illusion that things will get better. Even when the option to leave may be within arm's reach. EVERY pimp/traffickers main goal is to break you down mentally so physical force won't have to happen. A pimp once told me, "I'm not at all concerned about how

147

*much money you make. I want your mind. Once I get your mind I got you **forever**."*

A couple of weeks had passed and things were still the same for Dasha and I. *There was no modelling.* No dancing that didn't involve me having to undress myself and expose parts of me that one would only see behind closed doors. Still hanging on to every word from Smooth, *'This was all only temporary'* Dasha and I continued to go to the strip club.

One night while I was dancing, a customer followed me from stage to stage, throwing bulks of cash at me. He was handsome, a little heavy-set, and clean shaven. It was obvious that he took very good care of himself. When I got off the last stage, he signaled for me to come over to his table. He ordered us a couple of drinks and asked me my name.

He liked what he had seen on stage. He leaned over and spoke right into my ear saying that he wanted to get to know me outside of the club. He came closer to me and asked, *"How much is it going to cost for me to have your time outside of the club?"*

I giggled, smiled, and excused myself acting as if I needed to go freshen up a bit. I called Smooth right away and told him what was going on. I had been calling Smooth about everything. *He wanted it that way.* I had never had a guy ask me to leave the club with him. He gave me the vibe that it wasn't a private dance he wanted either.

Smooth explained to me that the man wanted sex for money. I was surprised at the lack of concern in his voice. I declared I would have nothing to do with *that*. Stripping was as far as I was going to go. His tone became much more authoritative.

Stripping is actually the gateway to prostitution. Not all strippers are involved in prostitution but I know that all

148

strippers have been approached by men in the club who desire more than just a private dance.

Most pimps today start their girls and women off in a strip club because it often times helps to eliminate or diminish their concerns about the sex industry. I had already been in environments where erotic sexually behavior was acceptable. My past endeavors had paved the way to make my transition easy.

The strip club helps to glamourize the sex industry. While some women are there to truly pay for school, they love to dance, or feed their children *pimps are using the strip club as their training and recruiting grounds.*

"You ain't missing out on *any* money Bitch!" Smooth shouted through the phone.

He quickly reminded me of my past, telling me I had no problem sleeping with square niggas for absolutely *NO* money. After tonight that was about to all change. I had given my body over freely for the purpose of love and pleasure but *never* as a transaction.

Smooth knew I didn't have a healthy view of sex and had sex with men easily. He was sure this wasn't going to be a hard transition for me.

"I don't normally deal with bitches like you, but I see the potential in you. I want to turn you into a boss bitch but you gotta trust me. I know you can do this." He said.
"Okay." I said.

What did I have to lose? I was already stripping now. I couldn't believe that the exact same things that I had encouraged others *not to do* I myself was now about to engage in it. Smooth's justification for it all, *"At least you making some real money and you doing it for your kids."*

"This is what you're gonna do: Go back and tell him that you're down to see him after work. Get the details of where he is staying and how much money he is willing to spend. I'm on my way to follow you as protection in case you need me."

When Smooth and I talked the first night, I ***never*** mentioned any dreams of becoming a stripper or a prostitute. Mentally he was breaking me down, ***challenging*** my old way of thinking and presenting me a new way of thinking. A way of thinking that continued to compliment the brokenness within me.

Since Smooth and I had been together he talked a lot about how he despised square bitches ***like me.*** Women who gave too much of themselves too soon. Women who had sex or gave their time to men without getting paid for it. *Looking for love but in all the wrong places.*

He talked about women who had been down the path I had come from so badly. I was beginning to *feel special* that he had considered helping someone like me. After talking with him about it something in me was beginning to agree with Smooth. *It was as if I began to see him as my false savior and I became his faithful follower and servant. My little g **god.***

He was right. I had given my body up so easily for the false hope of love. Getting money for it shouldn't be that bad. Smooth broke it all down to me on what I was to do. It felt like I was being trained for a new job.

Rule #1 GET MY MONEY first before I did anything.

Rule #2 ALWAYS use protection when dealing with customer's even oral sex.

 Rule #3 ALWAYS send him the address of my location and the price of the services I perform.

Dasha and Smooth followed us over to the guys place. Smooth sent me text messages of encouragement letting me know that it was going to be fast and easy. ***With his word, my babies on my heart and my bills on my mind, I was all in.***

I turned my very first trick, the act of exchanging sex for money, that night. It was fast and easy, just like Smooth said it would be.

I was always the type who allowed men to have their way with me out of fear of never getting what I truly desired from a man. His love and his constant presence.

Although I felt uncomfortable initially once I went in the room with my first john I zoned out and let him have his way. I'd had sex and been misled before, this time I was finally in control. It was solely **about the money.** At least for the moment it felt that way. The trick walked away satisfied and I walked away **paid.**

When I made it home, we counted up our cash from the night, showered and smoked a few blunts. I was expecting it to bother me afterwards but I wasn't really bothered. **Smooth was right I could handle this.** Suddenly it became easier and easier to sleep with men for money.

It wasn't long after that Smooth informed me and Dasha that we were going to travel to New Orleans for a little while to work. *After that night I had slept with my first john Smooth knew he had me wrapped around his finger.*

Dasha was excited about leaving for New Orleans. I was excited, too, since I had never travelled much before. We got up the following morning and hit the road. *Dasha and I talked the whole trip and it was so ever clear that I was beginning to conform and settle right into this new environment.* Dasha hadn't spent as much time with Smooth as I did and it was obvious.

She was becoming spectacle about why he was spending more time with me. To Dasha it seemed as if Smooth was trying to push her out of the picture. She was really starting to dislike Smooth and his controlling ways. I didn't see it as controlling I saw it as help.

Dasha smoked cigarettes at the time. Smooth planned to break that habit. He gave her four cigarettes for the whole ride to New Orleans, and she was so upset. He was already monitoring the food we ate and how our money was to be spent. She began to question why he was so adamant about holding our money. She was starting to believe that he was keeping the money all for himself.

In Smooth's defense he explained that he felt as though Dasha had a secret drug problem and was trying to hide it. I was certain that she had only smoked weed and popped pills from time to time. I tried to defend her, but Smooth didn't believe me.

In regards to Smooth keeping our money he said that Dasha and I didn't make enough money to even afford *his* lifestyle. Using our money for himself was impossible. He continued to reassure me that he was holding our money to go toward the dream. *Since he had the plan and knew the way it only made sense.*

Still with all this going on Dasha and I were still hopeful that the trip was going to bring in the money and Smooth promised us. Whenever I hit my first big break, I had some serious business to take care of. I figured it would take me three to four months to make the money I needed to get my family and I back on track.

After a close to ten hour drive we made it New Orleans safely. Instead of us going to his place he took us to a hotel in a nearby city called Metairie. I was expecting to go to his place since I had let him come into my place with open arms but Smooth didn't operate like that. He told me that I didn't deserve to see his place just yet.

Now I had to *earn* my way into to his place by meeting a quota every night at work. Smooth gave me a quota of a *thousand dollars* to meet before I could call him to come and pick me up from the club. My quota covered my living and travel expenses. Before I could send any money home I needed to take care of all that.

I could have been upset like Dasha but I wasn't.

Smooth had really been working on me in our private time. If anyone had told me that Smooth was trying to stab me in the back I wouldn't have believed them. It wasn't that I had even seen Smooth as my man. I was just beginning to believe the lie that he was a man that *finally cared.*

*When you're broken and lost someone could be harming you in the worst of ways but you won't see it like that. It's just like the woman who stays with her abusive boyfriend/husband. Although he abuses her she somehow still sees love. Although Smooth was **exploiting** me I still saw someone who cared.*

I would have still been at my 9-to-5 job if I had never met Smooth. I respected him for pushing me to move out from my comfort zone, even if it meant sacrifice. I believed what Smooth told me. I didn't want to be a *square* and live life **unfulfilled.** What better way to change my life than to have someone in my life who was willing to show me?

He hadn't changed what I was doing he had only given me a new perspective on why I did certain things. I was still promiscuous only now my promiscuity included a **price.**

*Aside from the new perspective, I was too blind to see that he was giving me a new identity. The new identity would include me needing someone around to affirm who I was on a daily basis. In the past my need of affirmation came from the men I dated. Now it was going to come from a **pimp.***

*I didn't care that he called himself a pimp either. I had dated and given myself to guys who had hurt me worse than he had. In my eyes he wasn't treating me any better or worse than any man I had known or dealt with. They just didn't carry the **label pimp.***

Instead it was dad, baby daddy, and boyfriend. They hadn't convinced me to become a stripper or sale sex for money but in my eyes their absence and their actions were just as bad if not worse. What had happened to me before I met my pimp was the very foundation that made his trap, **the game,** *attractive to me.*

Smooth had only raised his voice at me a couple of times and those moments I confused with passion. He called me bitch but the acronym made up for that. ***He was actually nicer than a lot of guys I had dealt with in the past. Most importantly he wasn't rejecting or abandoning me. He was encouraging me and motivating me to be more.***

The next day after resting from the drive Smooth came over and took us to Bourbon Street to start working. This street in Downtown New Orleans had a slew of strip clubs with a mixture of bars and little souvenir shops. Smooth already had the club picked out that we were going to work at.

On Bourbon Street there was a strip club to fit every need and every type of man or woman that strolled down that street. Smooth had informed us that New Orleans was known as a really popular convention spot. *Meaning a lot of men would be travelling from out of town looking for pleasure while out of town on business.*

New Orleans was also known as a party city where the people never slept. Which in Smooth eyes meant that we were going to meet our quota without any hesitation.

New Orleans was a total different ball game from what we had seen back home. Smooth hadn't really prepared us for it. We filled out an application, paid our tip out, and auditioned like before. We both got a yes from the manager to stay and dance. Then we were given a tour of the rest of the club.

The VIP section was huge and broken off into sections. One section was a room with big comfy chairs and couches. Another section of the club were three private

154

areas hidden behind satin- like curtains that had loveseats inside of them.

The two last VIP rooms had a full size bed inside of it. It was nothing like the previous club we had danced at before. The managers assumed Dasha and I knew about the things that went on behind the scenes. *But, at the club back home, the VIP section was nothing more than just a little corner in the club.*

At the last club I had never witnessed anyone turn tricks, exchange sex for money, inside of club. The manager went on to explain to us the rules inside of the club. He stressed to us that there was to be *NO* sexual activity going on. But, little did we know, the manager was basically saying, *"Do what you want, but don't get caught, and if you do, you're on your own."*

Strippers made some money on stage but mainly in the private areas. The stage seemed to be the place you promoted the product for sale. Any buyer that was interested would be waiting for you after you were done dancing on stage. It was so many girls dancing at the club it a couple of hours would pass before Dasha and I got back on the stage. So we sat back and observed for a little while.

The girls in New Orleans were more aggressive than the strippers back home. When they weren't on stage they were standing at the door of the club pulling men into the club dragging them to the *ATM* and off to the VIP section. Like clockwork they would head upstairs shower and do it all over again.

It was clear that the girls were exchanging sex for money but the managers had already blatantly told us that it was off limits for us to do. Dasha and I got a few dances that night but we never made it to the VIP section of the club.

We didn't leave the club each night until five *AM* the next morning. We never made our nightly quota. We seemed to be the only girls in the club that night that didn't make over a thousand dollars. We never exchanged sex for money inside of the club either and if the other girls weren't doing that their multiple showers and changing of clothes made Dasha and I assume otherwise.

Smooth picked us up and dropped us back off at the room without saying a word. He later texted and asked me what the problem was on why Dasha and I hadn't met our quota. I explained to him what the club was like and the activity that went on in there. He told me to do **WHATEVER** I had to do in the club the next time in order to meet my quota.

When he took us to work the next night he dropped us off with our tip out money and some condoms. One of the managers that night had pulled me over and told me that if Dasha and I wanted to make more money like the other girls I could have sex with him. If I did he would look out for us and make sure that we had clients come our way. If I didn't do it he would make sure that Dasha and I would continue to not make any money in the club.

He never sent us any customers. Dasha and I would continue to witness the other girls brag to us about leaving the club with well over three thousand dollars for the next few nights. It wasn't that Dasha and I wasn't attractive or that the product we had wasn't profitable. A night never passed that didn't include a guy telling us,
"You guys don't belong here."

Even the girls in the club had started interrogating us. One girl in particular kept asking me who my pimp was. She claimed she could tell that Dasha and I hadn't woke up one day and decided that we wanted to become strippers.

By the way we acted she could tell that someone was behind us being there. I told her about Smooth and she warned us to get away fast. I wasn't at all trying to hear

156

what this she was talking about. Smooth was going to help us like he promised.

We tried to be aggressive. Didn't work. We tried teaming up together. Didn't work. We tried getting high and drunk before work to loosen up our nervousness. Didn't work. Dasha and I were still making a few hundred dollars each night but that wasn't enough for Smooth to be satisfied with. He kept reinforcing to us that the quicker we started to meet our nightly quota the faster we could be done with this.

Smooth still hadn't let us see his place but we were seeing him every day. Once we made it to New Orleans Smooth started driving us around everywhere. When he dropped us off at the hotel every night after work he always took my car. I never seen his truck again until we moved to another hotel.

Aside from Smooth holding our money he was also holding our identification cards. He was holding it because girls at the clubs were thieves and he didn't want it to get stolen. It made sense, so I gave him my driver's license to hold.

After I shared with Smooth that I had told some of the girls at the club that I was in town with him he moved us to another club. He moved us from Bourbon Street all together. He said it was because we could make more money at this new spot. Smooth had told me not to tell any "squares" that I had a pimp.

When he moved us to another club he told us not to share with *anyone* that we had a pimp. At the new spot he told us that there would be more black men in the club and that we needed to be careful. If any dude who looked to be under fifty tried to talk with us we were to ask him if he was a pimp.

He continued to transition us into the game. Pimps had rules that they followed out of respect to the game. I'd later

157

find out that there was a whole book, and even movies about the rules to "the game". He told us to loosen up at this club and to focus more on turning tricks than dancing on stage.

Smooth told me to think about how important it was to take care of my kids. He promised that I would be able to start sending money home soon to my mom. When I told him that we needed to pay my rent soon, he told me that we would take care of it when it was time.

I had made well over enough to pay my rent and send money home. It wasn't the first of the month yet, but I was a little afraid that it wasn't going to get done.

He introduced us to a lady at the club whom he said was his cousin. She was going to be dancing as well, and we could go to her if we needed anything. When we were in the dressing room getting ready, she asked me if I had met his white *bitch* yet. I hadn't seen or heard him talk about any other woman.

Apparently, she had been with Smooth for years, and had the tendency to be mean and controlling since she had been around the longest. I wasn't worried about her, though. Smooth and I had a **business** to take care of and as long as she stayed in her lane I would stay in mine. His cousin bragged that Smooth was a really good guy and that I was lucky to have him in my life. *"He's different from other pimps in the game. You're lucky girl." She said.*

The new club had the same atmosphere as the last. The only difference was that the managers knew that each girl in the club was solely there to turn tricks inside of the VIP stalls. The club looked like a gambling shack on one floor, and the girls danced on the next floor. It wasn't set up like a normal strip club. There were stalls on both sides of the club wall. They looked like restroom stalls with swinging doors and seats inside of them.

The stage looked more like a runway stage for models

to walk down with a big mirror on the back wall. There were stools all around stage for the customers to sit on, and they picked out the girl they wanted for a private dance or something more. At the end of the two stages, there was a small round stage with a pole that they considered the main stage.

Until it was your turn to be on the main stage, you walked up and down the runway stage until a guy asked for a dance, or you went into one of the stalls for a private dance. The dancing, stripper poles, and music seemed like they were only there to create an illusion that exchanging sex for money wasn't all that bad. The atmosphere made it more acceptable.

No matter how much Smooth and I talked part of me still questioned just what was really going on. While part of me seemed to go along with everything, once I walked out of the dressing room every night my mind would always began to wander.

At my core, none of this was really who I was. Although I was sure that I didn't know I was anymore, like a drug I would **keep going back***. I had been trying to get my hands on anything that would help ease all that was going on inside of my head.*

I had seen some of girls including Smooth cousin snorting cocaine and asked to snort a line. She ended up telling Smooth about it and I got cursed out instead. Smooth kept insisting that if I couldn't do the work sober that I didn't need to do it.

When I mentioned us going back home he immediately shut that down and let me know that leaving wasn't going to be an option. I started thinking about how strange it was that I went from just wanting to make some extra cash to being a prostitute – *as my only source of* **income.**

The managers had already set the price that we were to charge. The stalls even had cameras inside so we couldn't lie about what was going on. The club took thirty percent of any additional work we did inside the stalls aside from dancing. Smooth hated that part but he kept taking us.

Dasha continued complaining and was ready to go back home. I kept telling her that it would get better for us. She hated the fact that Smooth restricted her smoking and he even made us wash our clothes by hand. I had never hand-washed clothes. I never even had to go to the laundromat unless our machines were broken at home.

My mother still did my laundry most of the time. It didn't bother me that much to wash my clothes by hand, as long as I had clean clothes. *"It's only temporary." I'd tell Dasha.*

I didn't have a job to go back home to and I needed stay focused and make money. *My life was in his hands.* Regardless of how complicated things seemed to be, Smooth always made sure that I called and checked on my boys. He got upset with me often, but I didn't care. I was trying my best to see the brighter side of it all.

My mom still didn't know that I was out of town but she knew that I was supposed to be working more to make money. To leave and go back home without a job or some money sounded **absurd** to me.

Dasha didn't have anything at stake like I did. She could go back to her regular scheduled program of living with friends for free. I couldn't do that. I had a family depending on me. Smooth had already made it clear that *I* couldn't leave.

What if Smooth was only doing all this for his benefit? What if I tried to leave and he didn't give me any money? What if I really was getting played for only his benefit? If Dasha accusations were true, and the girls advice from the club to leave Smooth were valid, then that would really make me a..... That reality was unbearable to accept.

So while I mentally kept trying to convince myself that

this had to work, I continued trying to convince Dasha as well. When I mentioned everything to Smooth about how I was feeling, he just kept telling me that I was doing the right thing.

Smooth thought it was crazy to depend on a check, because anything could happen with a regular job. A 9 to 5 wasn't security or a means of real stability to him but it had been for me.

He wanted me to see that I needed a hustle and a man on my side. So far, I couldn't see it, but I had hope. That's what kept all this going. I wanted to see how working for Smooth was so different from the job I left, but all he kept saying was that I had to stay down in order to see.

One night on the way to the hotel Smooth told us that we were to walk to the room with our heads down and not to make any eye contact with anyone. Dasha and I just laughed with confusion.

When we pulled up, there were two cars parked near our room, a black Hummer and a yellow Dodge Magnum. We still didn't know why he needed us to walk with our heads down, but we obeyed. Once we made it inside the room, I remembered that I left my soap in the car.

When I was getting back onto the elevator, a man inside spoke to me and said, "Hey my beautiful black queen what's your name?"

I didn't answer him, and when I tried to get off, he blocked the doorway. He kept asking me, "Just tell me your name queen, it's no harm in that."

As soon we turned the corner Smooth was coming towards us yelling for me to, "Get my ass back inside the room."

Smooth was pissed and he had never cursed me out the way he did that night. He kept pacing the floor and checking the window to see if the guy was outside. Smooth kept grabbing his pistol as if we had been threatened.

Dasha and I was totally blind sided. I just thought the guy in the elevator was giving me a compliment. I didn't see the harm in it. Smooth warned us to not leave the room or look out the window for any reason after he left.

Dasha had reached her limit with Smooth, and was ready for a change. She told me that if we hadn't promised each other to stick together, she would have left a long time ago. *I was feeling out of place as well but Smooth was interjecting on every doubt I shared with him.*

I didn't know anybody, Smooth had my car, and my money. I was still lying to my mom and I wasn't ready to face her or my boys. I continued to come up with different lies about where I was and why I couldn't come get the boys.

The day we were packing up to move Dasha and Smooth got into a really bad argument over cigarettes. Smooth had even raised his hand to slap her. I screamed and told him that if he touched her I was leaving too. He didn't hit her but it was clear that if I hadn't of said something Dasha would have met the back of Smooth's hand.

She asked to get dropped off at the bus station as we packed up our belongings. I tried to convince her to stay, but she made up her mind that she couldn't take it anymore. "Good. Pack your stuff. You're a distraction anyway." Smooth yelled.

As we packed our clothes into separate trash bags Dasha and I both cried because I wanted to leave, too. We both knew that he wasn't going to let me leave.

As soon as we walked out of the room more confrontation began. The same guy who corned me in the elevator and his friend was now trying to snatch Dasha and I up. They wanted us to leave Smooth and roll with them. *They were talking about how Smooth had been mistreating us and that we deserved to be treated like royalty.*

Smooth yelled back in his defense that they needed to mind their own business. Smooth kept yelling for Dasha and I to get into the truck. Dasha had made it in but I didn't. The guy had chased me around the truck and had finally gotten a hold of me.

Smooth kept hollering for him to let me go saying, "The game is a non- contact sport *P*, let my hoe go mane," but the guy wouldn't listen. I just stood there in total shock and fear still trying to get the door to open. Smooth finally realized that just talking wouldn't do so he pulled out his *pistol* and pointed it towards the guy to let me go.

He immediately let me go and ran off. I had barely got in the truck good before Smooth had pulled out of the parking lot furious about the whole situation. Dasha knew then that she had made the right decision to leave that day.

When we made it to the bus station, she apologized for leaving me but I had only wished that it could have been both of us leaving that day. I expected Smooth to at least pay for her bus ticket, but he didn't even give her money for food. *My heart was **crushed.***

Dasha almost changed her mind about leaving, but later told me that she didn't want to let Smooth win. She made some phone calls and one of her guy friends got her a ticket and a guy on the bus bought her some food. It would be a couple of weeks before I spoke with her to find out that she had made it home safe.

As we pulled out of the parking lot of the bus station, the same guy from the hotel pulled up to Dasha, but she refused to go with him. *After seeing how Smooth treated Dasha, I was grew scared of him and I was ready to leave.*

Even though I knew Smooth and I had a closer relationship that he and Dasha had, I still felt that at any moment he could treat me the same way. He still had my car, my money, and my driver's license. *I didn't want to leave any of it behind.*

163

I didn't have any friends to call on. My family was certainly out of the question. *Since I got myself in this mess I was going to get myself out somehow.*

I didn't work the night Dasha left because I refused to. I laid in bed and cried most of the night. I was in his territory and I had no idea where to start. I needed a new plan because this one wasn't the one for me.

Chapter 10

Flipping the Script

Have you ever received a promotion on the job or a new gig that offered you more money? You read through the job description and qualifications and you meet all requirements. You can go from making $20,000 a year to $50,000? You nailed the interview and they offer you the job right on the spot. Without hesitation, you accept the job without any further investigation.

However, there were some things the company failed to mention in the interview. They didn't mention the long work hours. You make more money, but you work so much that you never have time to spend it. The deadlines become more intense and you're always the last one to leave the office. You even have to lie for the company here and there, but your boss promises that it won't hurt you. The job itself doesn't even fit the job description you read about.

*It's **clear you've been lied to** and this new position can even jeopardize your freedom if you get caught in the lies your boss has convinced you to tell. **Yet you still stay.***

My new position didn't come with a disclaimer. If it had, it would have read something like:

*"**If you accept this offer, in return, I will exploit you. I will ruin the life you've always known and leave you more hopeless than ever before. I will strip from you the identity you've always had. I'm going to flip the script and you'll have no choice but to accept it. I'm going to pimp your pain and brokenness.**"*

When I went back to the club, I started talking to the ladies more to get a better understanding of the game, and what it took to get out of it. I tried to act cool around Smooth, but he could tell that something wasn't right.

All the ladies had negative things to say about Smooth. I wasn't the first girl that he had brought to the club for work. In New Orleans, at least the places he took me to Smooth was rather well known. It wasn't because of his rap songs or his other business endeavors that he had shared with me. *He was only known as a pimp.*

The girls weren't really concerned that I was trying to leave and go home. *Their solution was that I just needed a new pimp.*

"Girls didn't make it out. They always leave and come right back."

"You just get a new pimp instead."

"Things will get better you're just with the wrong one."

One girl had even called her pimp to let him know that I was looking to leave. He came up to the club to talk to me in person. He bought me a drink and paid for a dance.

Instead of dancing he only wanted to talk. He wanted to know how I got started in the game. When we were done talking, he asked if I had any money to pay a choosing fee if I wanted to be with another pimp. I didn't even know what that was.

He explained to me that it's an amount you pay a pimp upfront before you're able to join his stable. He went into more detail on how it was supposed to work.

Since I already had a pimp, the new guy would call Smooth and tell him that I *chose up,* meaning that I was leaving him to be with someone else. They would meet up so the new guy could get my belongings, and if Smooth decided that he wanted to keep my belongings, most do, I would just start over with the new guy. Most pimps had a set choosing fee that started at $1,000. With certain pimps

166

that fee went up.

He asked if I had ever paid Smooth a choosing fee. Smooth had asked me the first night if I had any cash on me but when I told him I didn't he changed the subject. I told him I had never given Smooth any money up front until after the first night of dancing and *he didn't call it a choosing fee.*

I was still under the impression that we were working towards helping out my family and investing the dream. He then told me that Smooth was my turnout pimp. *The turnout pimp was the guy who introduced you to the game.*

I went on to explain to him that I had kids back home, my own car, place and even a job when I met Smooth. He questioned me on why didn't Smooth and I bring my kids back to New Orleans with us.

I gave him the reason Smooth had given me. He only laughed and shook his head. He gave me his number and said if I was interested to call him by the end of the night and we could make it happen.

I went back down to the dressing room to get a little peace of mind about just how fast everything changed for me. **Smooth had really turned me out.**

The promise of us making money for family and our dreams would turn out to be a lie. I would never see any of the money that I made after it touched his hands. It was like everything was just being ripped away from me.

How could someone who I shared my pain with turn around and make my life worse? I thought he understood? I thought he wanted to help and not hurt me? I thought Smooth was real and different from other guys I had been with. No modelling gigs? Dasha is now gone? What happened to family comes first?

I had so many questions for Smooth I was at the point where I didn't even bother to ask him. I knew he would find a way to convince me to accept all of what was being told to me. I was ready to get back home.

I continued weighing my options that night on how I was going to get back home and away from Smooth. A guy that I had dated in the past came into the club. I contemplated asking him for help but quickly changed my mind. He had already asked me in the past if I was working for a pimp and I lied. I concluded that he wouldn't help me since I had lied the first time. He had also warned me that all pimps were up to no good.

A guy walked over to me and introduced himself and asked me my name. *I was still using Charisma at the time, but he said that he wasn't interested in my stage name.* He wanted to know my real name. I laughed and tried to walk away because I could tell that he was probably another slick talking pimp.

He grabbed my arm and pulled me close to him and told me that the club was way out of my league. He told me to look around the club at everyone else and then, look at myself.

It was obvious that I wasn't a stripper and that I should be doing something else. He told me to put on clothes and that he would set me up to do a photo shoot immediately.

"Yeah that's what the guy I'm with now is supposed to be helping me with. This is only temporary. Just save it." I said.

"What I'm saying is that this shouldn't even be on your to do list. Is this supposed to make you better? No. I know he told you it's supposed to help you make some fast cash." I nodded.

"I would never let someone you like set foot in a place like this. Just give me a week and I promise you won't regret it. If I can't change things for you in seven days I promise I will let you leave the same way you came." He said.

"How do I know your plan doesn't include me having to turn tricks or stripping too? I know what you pimps are

168

all about so just come clean now and tell me what it really is you want from me?" I said.

"What planet are you from girl? It's more than one way in this game to money than to turn some tricks? Who been teaching you the game? What's your P's name?"

"Smooth."

Smooth had misled me, and ran my friend off. I was just ready to go. This guy told me to give him a week and he also offered to send money to my mom since Smooth didn't. I wanted to go home at this point.

Brandon promised me if things didn't improve in a week, he would let me go home and take the money that I made with him. I told him that Smooth had all my belongings, including my car.

He offered to call for my things. He claimed to know Smooth and to his knowledge Smooth was soft, so he was sure that if I chose up, it wouldn't be a problem getting my belongings. I figured that I would stay with him for seven days. After that, I would tell him I wasn't satisfied and leave. *I had a plan.*

I gave him all the money I had and went down to the dressing room. I was so nervous but it seemed like the best move at that time and the only way to get away from Smooth without causing trouble. *Brandon could be like my protection I thought to myself.* I didn't want to be there when he called Smooth with the news that I had chose up.

I said a quick prayer, asking to make it home safe and sound. I didn't pray often, but when I felt I was in deep trouble. I went back to the floor and he told me that he called Smooth. He told me to work the rest of the night and I wouldn't have to see that club again after that night. *I was relieved.*

Twenty minutes later, Smooth walked in the club, spotted me and quickly walked toward me. I ran toward the dressing room because I knew he couldn't follow me in there. I knew he would be upset, but I was pissed with him, and didn't want to talk about it at this point.

He grabbed me before I was able to make it to the dressing room. I kept my head down and my eyes closed. I told him I didn't want to talk to him or see him. I kept thinking about what he could do to me if I made him mad like Dasha did. He begged me to look at him and asked me why I gave my money to Brandon.

"You don't even know him. We have a plan. We're a team remember?" He said.

"I really don't know you either. Look at how you've changed my life so fast. What the hell is this? What am I really doing here? Is this about my family or your family only? Dasha gave you all her money and you left her with nothing? I know it's only a matter of time before you do me the same way. I can't do it. Please just let me go." I demanded.

I went over to the bar to put my head down and began to cry. Brandon came to the other side of me and told me to get to the dressing room so we could roll out. Smooth was yelling and pulling me on one side and Brandon was yelling and pulling me on the other side, both trying to get me to leave the other.

They argued with each other and made a huge scene in the club. I yelled for both of them to let me go. The music was loud so Smooth started yelling into my ear, telling me that Brandon beat his women and he would do the same to me. *Smooth kept telling me that I wasn't leaving him that easily.*

He didn't care that I had given Brandon money. Brandon told me in my other ear that Smooth didn't like black women and that's why he had be working in this raggedy club. Smooth began apologizing for how he treated Dasha and promised me that he would never do me the same way. *I was different.*

170

Brandon wouldn't give up. He reminded me that Smooth had already proved himself to be a liar and a manipulator. He told me I needed to let Smooth go and come with him.

Security finally came and escorted me downstairs. The club had closed and everyone was being escorted out of the club, including Smooth and Brandon. *The owner called me into his office while he was counting the money from the night.* The managers and owners of the clubs know what's going on and as long as they make their profit they don't interfere.

The owner told the security guard to shut the door and he asked me to have a seat on his couch. He wanted to know why I was there. *"A girl like you should be in school, doing something with your life. You look so innocent."* He said.

I told him that I just wanted to get home and that Smooth had my car. Security called in and told him that both Brandon and Smooth were outside waiting for me. Neither one of them were leaving without me. I had a huge dilemma.

I had paid two pimps that night and I had to decide who I was going to go with. The owner told me that he knew both Smooth and Brandon, but he felt Brandon would be the best choice for me. But something didn't feel quite right.

I thought about the possibility that Brandon did hit his women. *That wasn't the life I wanted either. Smooth seemed sincere in his apology and although he had raised his hand at Dasha, he didn't hit her. He probably wouldn't hurt me. We did have a bond and got along rather well.*

I told the owner I was going to leave with Smooth. In a twisted way it meant something to me that Smooth was willing to fight for me. This was Smooth second time fighting for me. *No one had in the past.* Security instructed

171

Brandon to leave.

When I made it downstairs, Smooth was waiting with two of his friends and signaled for them to leave. One drove off in a Cadillac and the other drove off in his Navigator. Smooth and I left in my car. I looked out the window and remained silent for most of the ride.

Smooth turned the music down and told me to look at him, but I wouldn't do it. He grabbed me until I turned and looked at him. I looked in the backseat and all my belongings were there. *I couldn't believe that he was actually prepared to let me go.*

He told me we needed to talk and tears ran down my face again. I told him I was ready to go home. Things weren't going as he told me they would. My rent hadn't been paid and he hadn't sent anything to my family. I kept hearing that he didn't like black girls and that he had a white chick somewhere. *All that talk about the white man's dream and he was using my money to take care of a white girl? How ironic, I thought.*

He apologized for how things were going, but told me that he didn't want to run me off. He promised that he would explain to me later what was going on. I couldn't stop crying. I kept asking him to let me go home. I didn't know where he was taking me and when I asked him, he told me to just ride.

We ended up on Canal St. at the Westin Hotel. He pulled up to valet and took the keys out of the ignition, but told me to stay in the car until he came back with the room key.

My mom had called and sent text messages almost daily. She was fed up and wanted me to come home immediately. I kept telling her I was working more to get some extra money to pay my bills.

Smooth came back and told me to grab my bags and follow him to the elevators. The hotel was beautiful. *It was definitely an upgrade from the Super 8.*

We made it to the room and argued for hours about me wanting to leave. In the midst of the argument, he convinced me to stay. It didn't matter what I had said he wasn't trying to hear me going back home.

He apologized about how things had been going and promised that he was going to make things right. We came to an agreement that I would stay a few more days and after that we were going back to Texas.

That night we ordered room service, showered together, watched a movie and had sex. By the time I woke up the next morning, Smooth was already gone. When I called him, he told me to order room service if I was hungry and that he'd be back later to get me for work.

I talked to my mom again and told her I would be picking up the boys soon. I could tell how worried she was, but I tried my best to stay calm and ignore it, like everything was alright. My mom told me that there was an eviction notice on my apartment door when she went by to get clothes for my boys. I needed to either pay my rent or move my things.

My mom just couldn't understand what was happening with me. When I got pregnant with my first son my mom became my confidante. I used to share almost everything with her, especially when it came to relationships and my life issues. This time, it was different. I continued giving her the run around about things.

I informed Smooth about what was going on and he said that he would handle it. All he wanted me to do right now was chill since I had only been off one day since the first night I started dancing.

Instead of getting ready for work I watched movies and surfed the internet and people watch from the wonderful view my room had. The room sat right next to the Mississippi River.

Smooth came the next day to take me on a tour of downtown New Orleans. We walked along the shops on the Canal and over to the casino for Smooth to play some blackjack. Afterwards we had lunch at the local ***Popeye's Chicken.*** Smooth knew how much I loved chicken.

He continued creating this atmosphere of a new normal for me. I had just about brushed off and forgotten about the previous night's craziness. I was back questioning when I was going to be making some more money. If Smooth was pimping me it wasn't that bad. In these moments I felt more like his girlfriend than his ***hoe.***

*As a normal routine, for someone who is on a mission to breakdown and manipulate a person he was doing just that. When Smooth and I spent time together he made me feel like I was worthy and had value **in spite** of what I was doing for money. To him getting money the fast way better than a square who had sex for free.*

*He praised me for being a woman that was willing to see profitable value in **my body**. No more heartbreak stories to replay in my head because now the control was in my hands. The more we talked the more he twisted up what I was doing and made it seem more attractable.*

Smooth would most times make me feel like I could be more than the woman who got up daily and waited for a check every two weeks. Sitting in a cubicle doing the same thing every day while the rest of the world was living. Smooth gave me purpose and confirmed those deep feelings within me that I was made to do something great. *He had given me a **new identity.***

Although I didn't like what he had me doing, Smooth reassured me that the reward on the other side would be great, for me and my boys. He wasn't perfect nor was he the greatest guy, but he wasn't all bad either.

I didn't grow up with a lot of positive or healthy male role models. I had always desired to have a positive male influence in my life but it never happened. I always known what that was supposed to look like. By this time I had **lost** all hope of ever receiving that.

Most of the men I knew were abusers and manipulators just like Smooth. They took from me and left. They lied to me. Smooth had lied but he seemed to be fighting for me. *Although his fight wasn't really for me but the potential I had in making him a profit.*

He asked about my boys and had me call and talk to them while he was there. He seemed to genuinely care. My kids' fathers stayed less than ten miles away from us and we couldn't even get a phone call out of them. Smooth hadn't come through just yet but he had done more than I what I was used to. That counted for something.

It bothered me that I had let my kids down. **I never** *wanted them to be* **affected** *by my brokenness, insecurities, and ignorance. I had to make it up to them. Although this wasn't how I wanted to do things. Like Smooth said,* **"If you hustle your kids won't have to."**

Meaning, if I stayed focus and obeyed Smooth my boys wouldn't have to grow up and sell drugs like their uncle. They wouldn't fall prey to the things of this world because we'd be stable and established.

Aside from me being under the influence of drugs when we first met. Once the drugs wore off I continued to keep him around because *he was in some ways like guys* I was used to dealing with.

Only difference, Smooth seemed reluctant about wanting to help me. Since I was already in a bind and needed the help I saw him as the answer to my cry. The absence of a healthy male role model allowed me to set a very low standard when it came to the type of men I dealt with. *Smooth wasn't going to be the last.*

As soon as things had gotten back cool between Smooth and I he came over to the hotel with a camera to do my very first photo shoot. It was nothing at all close to the type of photoshoot that I envisioned for myself but it was better than being in the strip club.

Smooth had informed me that the photos were going to be used on an on-line website so I could work. Instead of me working inside of the strip clubs Smooth now wanted me to work from the hotel. *Turning tricks.* He took all my calls, and would forward me the information if someone was coming by the room. Prices were negotiated by Smooth.

For the next few days he had me getting dressed and waiting as if I was going to be receiving calls and working. Nothing was coming through. Smooth wasn't even answering his phone. He would only respond by text.

All I could do was think. So much was going through my head. It was hard because part of me wanted to obtain what Smooth had promised me.

The other part knew I needed to leave – knew this was not what my life was all about. I was being played and it hurt like hell. *I hated the fact that all he needed to do was show me a little attention, whisper lies in my ear, and I was content – for a minute. But it never lasted.*

He had been hyping me all up but then no action would follow it. After a few threatening text messages saying that I was going to leave the hotel room and tell someone what was going on, he quickly made his way back. I was furious and my bags were packed.

I didn't care for the pep talks anymore. It wasn't going to work this time. I asked Smooth for my car keys and I told him that I was leaving. He refused to give me my keys, so I ran to the door in an attempt to escape but he grabbed me and refused to let me leave. *I was on this roller coaster ride where one second I was all for it and the next I wasn't.*

He didn't care whether I made any money or not. At least that's what I thought. The whole point of me coming was to make some money. Now, I was just sitting in a hotel room, looking crazy every day. Upset one moment that I wasn't making any money. Then sad the next because the man whom I now had feelings for was playing games with me. I didn't like these mixed signals and emotions I was beginning to feel. *This was supposed to be a quick come up but it was only breaking me down more and more.*

We checked out of the hotel room to finally head back to Texas. Relief flooded over me. I drove my car, and followed along behind him in his Navigator.

We stopped at a store along the way, a woman and a little boy – he looked to be about three years old - got out of the vehicle. Smooth came over to my car in an attempt to explain but I completely brushed past Smooth to follow her in the store.

Smooth truck had really dark tent you had to really be paying attention to get a good look inside. I was just driving and thinking so much that I hadn't even noticed he had people in the car with him.

I acted like I wanted some snacks, and grabbed some stuff to get a better look at her. She saw me, and was sizing me up as well. I just laid whatever I had in my hand on the counter and walked to my car.

They both got into his Navigator and pulled out of the parking lot, and as I pulled behind to continue to follow, I could tell they were arguing. I wondered if this was the woman I kept hearing about. Was he with her on those nights he would leave me alone? Is this where my money was going? A part of me wanted answers. I was pissed off. I was hurt. Smooth had done me like every other guy had but this time it was worse.

Why was my family not as important as his? Why did he separate me from my sons, but she was able to be with hers – theirs? It was obvious that he was lying to both of us, but **why?** *Why did he come into my life with all these dreams*

177

and promises like he could turn my life into something great?

*My life was the total opposite of what I was promised. I had quit my job, so I had no guarantee of money coming in. My rent was still unpaid and I had to move out of my apartment. My family had moved my belongings while I was in New Orleans. I had no money to my name. **Just like that my life was completely wrecked and it felt like I was sitting in a bottomless pit.***

We made it to Houston and Smooth pulled up into a hotel parking lot. Smooth came over and told me we were staying to work a few days, and he went back to his truck and continued booking the rooms on his laptop.

After several minutes he came back, but the little boy had hopped out of the Navigator and almost got himself hit by a car. This completely upset his mother, and she stomped over to my car, screaming and cursing at Smooth. She demanded he book her a flight so she could go home. She kept calling Memphis her home confirming the **suspensions** in my head that they were a family.

Then her anger shifted towards me and she started screaming about Smooth having a new bitch. I wasn't concerned, though. Smooth was the only one I was upset with at this point. It was clear that she had no clue about me and she had been led there on a dream and a lie as well.

I grabbed the stripper outfits out of the car and gave them back to Smooth. I asked him to give me some money to leave and he refused saying that he wasn't going to let me leave. While he sat in the car with me trying to convince me to stay the girl came back over to my car and started making a scene.

She was pissed that I was there. Smooth sat there unable to finesse us both at the same time into staying. He stepped out of my car to calm the other girl down and I took the opportunity to get away. I had close to a full tank of gas. I prayed that would be enough to get me home and I sped off onto the highway.

I called my mom and apologized for my recent actions and, I told her I was finally coming home. Once I got there I would tell her the truth on what was going on.

My mom had thought that I was working at my job. When she told me about the notice on the door. I did tell her that I was out of town working with some friends but I hadn't told her that I quit my job. I was on a leave of absence and could return back.

When I had quit my job Smooth had asked me about my retirement plans and I shared with him that I had a 401k account. He had me call and cancel my plan and they ended up cutting me a check.

Before I got off the phone with my mom she informed me that my 401k check from my job had arrived. I didn't feel as bad anymore about leaving money behind with Smooth. *Just like that, most of it had all been replaced with my 401k check.*

I wasn't planning to catch feelings for Smooth but a part of me had fallen for him and I was disappointed that it all ended how it did. Not just him, though I had fallen for the promises he had made me, and the **dream** of something better.

Every other guy always wanted something from me. I was never enough. I fooled myself into thinking all I wanted was the extra money but that was not true at all. I wanted a partner, a helper, and a friend. I wanted my boys to have a dad. I wanted someone I could depend on.

I figured if I gave him my all, including my money, he would have my back. It lined up with what he had promised me. I was hurting inside and I felt so ashamed, but I **refused** to let it show. I was going to finish what Smooth had started--*with or without him.* **I had escaped physically but mentally I was trapped.**

179

*Since the beginning, people have fallen for the enemy's tricks simply by a conversation and a desire for more. If Eve fell for a serpent, snake, isn't it possible I could fall for slick-talking pimp name **Smooth**? The enemy's cleverness with words, and man's desire combined have ruled the nations ever since that day in the garden. Just check any history book. As for me, I was already on the edge, and I soon would find myself tumbling right off the cliff into **self-destructive** pattern I had never known before.*

Chapter 11

A New Normal

"A spirit of prostitution leads them astray." Hosea 4:12

    Anytime people hear the word **"prostitution"** *they always assume sex. Since they aren't exchanging sex for money many people often feel as though there is no way in which prostitution can be relatable to them in their life. But I would like to interject on that.*

    A Prostitute is not only defined as someone who exchanges sex for money. Prostitution is also defined as someone who uses their **gifts** *and* **talent** *for* **unworthy purposes**.

    In the bible, God asks the prophet Hosea to marry a promiscuous woman named Gomer. God told Hosea that his soon-to-be wife would be unfaithful to him by becoming a prostitute, but he needed to stay with her and remain faithful. God called out this noble man to marry a woman that totally contradicted who he was. **Why?**

    During this time, the people of Israel were unfaithful to God. God wanted to show them a life of purity and freedom but instead they desired a different kind of normal and freedom for their life.

    Hosea, being the obedient prophet he was, obeyed God and married Gomer in-spite of what she was known in the town as. By using someone well known in the town like Hosea, God's plan was to show the people of Israel the way in which He still loved them even **after** *turning their backs to him.*

    They engaged in prostitution, sex outside of marriage, they squandered their money, and just totally forgot about

181

the God who delivered them from slavery. They bowed down to wooden idols as if they were God yet He would still have mercy on them.

*This is also evident in our generation today. We no longer worship wooden idols though. Instead we worship money, people, false ideas of love, our pain, and even ourselves. Turn on the TV and you'll see where people will do just about anything to get what they want. Even if it doesn't please God or goes against their **own core beliefs.***

*You can't turn on the radio without a song talking about sex or money. Degrading women has become a social norm. It's no surprise to me that many young girls and women today are still trapped in the sex industry and don't want to get out. **They don't see hope.** They rather have the trick as their client than a dead-end job. A pimp as a confidante instead of a cheating spouse.*

Our society has created this world that parades perverted and unhealthy styles of living as normal.

*Today people tend to find more value in the size of a woman's butt than her true worth from **within.** It's even considered cool now to have more than one woman. Women don't even care about dating men who are married and being side chicks or mistresses.*

*During this time in my life my love for money and the need to mask my pain became greater than love for myself, my family and even God. **Just like the story in Hosea I would go on to live a life completely opposite of a life that pleases God.***

*You may not be prostituting your body like I did, but are you exchanging your gifts and talents to please people or God? Are you asking God to help you bring Him joy with the life He has given you? Or have you become like the Israelites and I living in destruction as your **new*** *normal?*

When I made it to town it was well past midnight. I went by the strip club to see Dasha. She had decided to keep stripping after leaving Smooth and I. I had called her while I was on the road and she was happy about being able to see me again. Dasha and Julie both greeted me with hugs and excited when I walked through the club doors that night.

I had met Julie at the club when Dasha and I first started working there. She was one of the few girls who was actually nice to Dasha and I in front and behind our backs. We ended up keeping in touch while I was gone, and she always had my back, giving me advice and helpful information.

Smooth didn't mind me talking to Julie because she was in the game too. I found out she had a pimp and when she seen I did too, after hitching a ride home from Smooth and I one night we became close. She had tried warning me about how things went in the game but on our initial introduction no one could tell me that Smooth wasn't just a guy trying to help a girl like me in need.

Smooth had lured me in, but it would be my own desire and brokenness that kept me chained to the game and the sex industry.

I ordered some food talked a little with Dasha and Julie then headed home to see my family. By the time I made it to my mom's everyone was asleep. My mom seemed at peace when she finally seen me later that morning, but it was obvious that there was some disconnect. I had left my children without any notice and they couldn't understand why.

When I came clean with my mom she was very disappointed in my actions, but still supported me. I explained it to her in much the same way Smooth pitched it

183

to me. *I would have more freedom, financial stability, and I would be able to take better care of the boys.* She wasn't convinced, but she could see that nothing was going to stop me from continuing down this uncharted path of destruction.

She left me with these words: "Chanel, I hear you loud and clear. Always look at the people who are doing what you're wanting to do and what they have. Is what they have what you want or even worth having? All the friends you have don't have a car or even a place of their own.

You've had both before being in this *"game,"* as you call it, and your little business partner or pimp has managed to make you lose your apartment. Will your car be next? I just want you to be smart about the situation. I will never let you take your sons with you while you're doing this kind of work. If you're going to continue on this way don't forget to take care of your family first."

I had my mom supporting me too. There was no turning back now.

Now that Smooth wasn't in my life, I was as determined as ever to accomplish what he promised the game had to offer. There was no way I could go back to my old job at this point, or any square job, for that matter. I had been *exposed.* I figured I could make it happen for my family without Smooth. My life in the sex industry continued. I couldn't just turn back now.

I told myself that I wasn't going to let the game, drugs, and alcohol ruin what life I had left. I would stack my money and go after my real dreams of being a model and someone with influence.

That was going to prove to be easier said than done. I would soon learn that with a shattered heart, no Godly vision, and no Godly purpose my temporary plan of being in the sex industry would in turn become my new normal.

I started dancing at different clubs, but I couldn't get

184

into it. I was always worried about the way I looked, but stripping brought out insecurities that I never had to face with my clothes on. I was comparing myself with the other ladies. I would get drunk and do things for attention rather than for money.

I thought that being away from Smooth would make things easier for me but it didn't. I was more out of control without him around. Now that things were beginning to feel more normal at times I missed not having Smooth around to motivate me.

Since I changed up my circle of friends, everybody was somehow connected to the game or the sex industry. Not everyone had a pimp, but everyone was sleeping with men for money. I only hung with girls who were strippers. Everyone was somehow being exploited. I knew women who claimed to have boyfriends but they were collecting their money every night just like a pimp.

It was the norm for women to date men who could help them pay their bills. It was better than dating for love. Now I knew the truth and I could stop wearing my heart on my sleeve. Being the nice girl had failed me.

I even changed the music I listened to. It was more Too Short, Pimp C, Smooth and Rick Ross. All that love stuff was thrown right out of the window. I was done chasing that façade of love that didn't really seem to exist.

I picked up a job at a local massage parlor where Julie and I started working together in the day time. I had found the ad in one of the adult newspapers at the club. I didn't learn until after the interview that I would in fact be turning tricks and the massages we only a cover up.

We continued dancing at night. Although I would go home feeling like crap, I kept going back. Back then I would say it was the money and the idea of me hustling on my own but it seemed like my pockets had holes in it. *Soon as I was getting the money it was leaving my hands for drugs and*

185

alcohol.

The parlor was owned by a lady who I will refer to as Madame. *She was basically a female pimp/trafficker.* She wanted two hundred dollars upfront at the start of the week and fifty percent of everything we made under her roof, including our tips.

She didn't care about us like she claimed to. I was losing all that I worked hard for to hand it over to her while she rode around in her BMW and lived in her big, fancy house with a hair salon in the back.

She said that she wanted to create a safe environment and give us an opportunity to learn new things. We did go through training to become massage therapist. She even said that she would pay for us to get our license but none of the girls working in there had their license. *Some had been with her for years.*

Underneath our scrub outfits was lingerie. Every customer wanted some type of sexual favor. I had only turned tricks a few times, but I was convinced that turning tricks was much easier and quicker. I didn't have to deal with competition, fighting, fake friends, and being seen by other people.

Madame had her own special list of clientele and not just anybody could come in for services. Most of the time she would either choose the guy we'd date or we'd stand up in a line up for him to choose. Either way she always tried to make sure that we all made something. It was less stressful than the club scene at night. I could do my services, get my money, and be done with it.

After befriending some of the ladies at the parlor I found out that a couple of them were living in a shelter while working at the parlor. *That talk with my mom always came up in my head, so it was easy for me to leave a situation and try something new.*

I kept searching for my big break. I had even done

some photo shoots since I had been home. I was still pressing toward becoming a model while drowning in the new life I lived.

I remember feeling so lost about my life in my private moments but I was desperate to keep that truth hidden. *As long as I was around other people who viewed the new life I lived as normal, I was okay.*

When someone came along who tried to challenge my new normal, I was uncomfortable. I can see now that God was sending people into my life to **remind** me of who I was, and that I was better than this. Back then I would be too busy judging the messengers.

Some of those people were in the club with me and seemed to be living a double life and it was rather difficult to stand on the encouraging words of hope that flowed from their mouth. I didn't want to live a double life like them.

I believed I had crossed a line and that there was no coming back over it. So while their words sounded good their life didn't reflect the words flowing from their mouth. *In my mind, I wondered if they really even believed the words they spoke to me.*

I could have went back to my old life but in my eyes it was my old life that led me to this place. I now had the answer to the mystery of my life. It was like a light bulb had went off in my head. *In reality no light had come on but rather **darkness** had finally prevailed. All those things that Smooth and I had spoken about were making more sense.*

I just didn't know what to do. People started contacting through social media networks, asking me if I would be interested in doing porn. I declined. Pimps were reaching out to me trying to convince me to join their stable. *Dangling more false promises.*

A lady I met through a photographer asked me to check out a few porn websites. One site was like humiliation porn and it seemed so intense and painful. I couldn't understand how the chicks could go through with it. I spoke to a lady who had actually did porn and she explained her experience to me. The scenes involved white guys who humiliated black women in a sexual way. I turned the offer down and never talked to the lady again.

I reconnected with a guy named Robert I had met previously, and I told him about what I had been doing. He was intrigued and wanted to link up and talk. We met at a strip club in Dallas for drinks and had a great time.

Robert and I started spending more time together. Like Smooth, he wanted to help me make some money and he claimed to know where I should work to make more money.

Robert lived in a beautiful high rise tri-level condo in north Dallas. Robert was a Muslim from the east coast, and was very family oriented. He had children of his and seemed to take very good care of them.

Dasha and I were still hanging out together again and ended up introducing her to Robert but she had bad vibes about him. She ended up hooking up with a photographer who had done some work for me. That would be the last time I'd hear from Dasha for a while.

I got a call from Robert to pack my bags and meet up with his chick who was working in Indiana. I had only spoken with her over the phone, and she seemed really cool. Leslie sounded very confident every time we talked. They even offered to give me money upfront before leaving to show me that he wasn't trying to keep my money for himself.

I didn't want to take money from them and not be able to pay them back and be in more debt. I did accept the offer to travel out to Indiana alone to work with Leslie though.

Back then, I saw the travelling aspect of the game as a perk. I never got to travel before.

They took care of my flight expense. I kissed my kids goodbye and left from my mom's house with Robert that night. Robert was supposed to get me to the airport, but his drinking habit would get in the way and totally ruin things that night. He pulled over twice to throw up and I ended up missing my flight. Robert was so drunk that he took me to the wrong airport.

Instead of flying out to Indiana to meet Leslie I waited to meet her until she came back to town. I continued working in the club and the parlor. I was also spending a lot of time with Robert and we were now having a sexual relationship.

It was finally time for me to meet Leslie, after the big airport mix up. She came back with another girl named Nicole. Leslie travelled often and when she came home, it was only for a couple of days at a time. Leslie was much nicer over the phone than in person. It became obvious very quickly that she was protective of Robert.

We immediately got to work. Leslie and Nicole were working out of hotels as prostitutes. She scheduled a few dates in Dallas for me near their condo and bought a room for us to work out of. We all made a few hundred dollars that night and the following morning got on the road. Our first stop was New Orleans.

Leslie and Nicole had already been there before, so they were confident that we would make money. Nicole was working for one of Robert's friends. Leslie was a regular to New Orleans and she already had appointments lined up. Leslie was in control of all the appointment setting.

We were in New Orleans for about four days. Leslie was busy, but Nicole and I were not. Nicole told me that Leslie ran off all of Roberts's other girls because she didn't want to share him. She saw Robert as her boyfriend. Nicole could tell that Robert liked me and she wished I had more experience so I could work alone. She felt Leslie was going to run me off, too but I didn't see Leslie as someone out to get me.

Nicole tried to warn me that Leslie was sneaky and greedy. Nicole didn't have any children, but she could see that I seriously wanted to make some cash for my family and she felt that I needed to know that with Leslie around, it was going to be impossible. I didn't want to believe her.

Nicole and I still weren't getting any calls. So Nicole created her own account and Leslie finally set up one for me as well. That's when we started receiving calls. We went down to Bourbon St. to get the long day of work off our minds.

I told Leslie that I wasn't there to step on her toes or get in between her and Robert's relationship. I only wanted to make money and build a better living for my family. Leslie and Robert were older and more experienced in this than me. *They lived a lavish lifestyle. High Rise condo, children in the best school, closet full of designer clothes, and Leslie kept a bankroll of money.*

I expected them to teach me what I needed to know to make it in the game. *My new world. My new normal.* Like a mom and dad, they were just supposed to help me find my way. Although Robert and I had shared sexual relations, I tried to keep that to myself because I felt I owed it to him, since he had trusted me to be around Leslie to help me out.

I asked Leslie about sending money to my mom and she told me to speak with Robert. Robert said that my expenses needed to be covered first and eventually, my mom would get money for my boys. The plan was to build something together as a team and the only way to do that was to keep the money together. *Handing my money over to people became an automatic for me.*

We left New Orleans and made it to Atlanta. We were headed to North Carolina to pick up Leslie's daughter and bring her to Texas for good. After partying and pouring out my heart to the girls after getting drunk one night Leslie and I began to connect. *Like me, Nicole and Leslie wanted better lives for themselves and were willing to get it by any means necessary.*

We partied and worked in Atlanta. I felt like I was on a vacation I had never been on before. I wasn't stuck behind some desk, thinking about how broke I was going to be when Friday came.

I kept my mind set on this as being about business and no pleasure was involved in what I was doing. Sex just was not at the top of the list of things that I liked to do but it always became the bridge I needed to cross in order to get what I wanted. Before the industry, it was a relationship. Now it was solely for the money.

Even though I had secretly battled with masturbation issues for a majority of my life I was never the type to try and embrace sex as something that I loved to do. In my eyes it was just something that I felt that I always had to do.

Not all dates I went on included intercourse. I got exposed to so many different things. In the beginning, I had no idea about people and their secret fetishes.

*Even though **I had never** had an interest in being a prostitute, I was beginning to feel a sense of freedom. I couldn't stay away, or maybe I did not want to. I was learning a lot about myself, and people, and the world in general.*

Leslie opened up to me and told me that she liked women. I told her of my previous experiences in high school with girls and how I learned the hard way that a man or woman was capable of hurting me just the same. That same night we would become intimate.

Nicole was upset and didn't like it at all, but it wasn't because she was jealous. She had seen this picture play out before with the other women that came and left. I tried my best to reassure Nicole that it wasn't going to end up bad like it did with the other women that Leslie ran off. My heart was not in this. *It was just business.* Leslie and I were just having a little fun.

We finally made it to North Carolina and Leslie knew I loved chicken, so she took me to a spot called Bojangles.

Leslie was beginning to grow on me and I was loving every minute of our bond and the trip. She made me feel special. I liked the fact that she paid attention to me and listened to me when I talked. With everything that was going on, I felt I had actually found a *friend* in both Leslie and Nicole. *Like Smooth there was always a ulterior motive.*

Leslie would eventually go on to ask me how Robert and I met. I was never a great liar, so I told her the truth. Our initial meeting was never about business and I actually had no knowledge of Robert being in the game. We had been intimate and spent time together in the past.

She didn't seem upset – and I did not expect her to be. We had been around each other for a while now, and I figured she could see that Robert and I had a connection of sorts, even though the main purpose was now business related.

We finally made it to pick up her daughter and immediately headed back to Texas. The ride back was mostly quiet and I assumed it was because her daughter was in the car but that was only partially the reason.

When we made back to Roberts condo she immediately yelled for him to follow her upstairs. All you could hear was screaming and yelling coming from their room. Then I heard a loud, *"Smack."*

Robert stormed back downstairs as Nicole and I were unpacking our things from the car to tell me what I had done wrong. I was *NEVER* to speak with Leslie about what we did in private. In her eyes Robert was her boyfriend not her pimp. At one point that was the truth but that had all

192

changed and at times she forgot. I apologized to Leslie, packed my bags and left.

The holidays were around the corner. My mom made sure to keep me up to date about my boys while I travelled. I called them every day, no matter what I was doing. I wanted to make sure I was home to be with my family. My family could see the change in me but felt powerless to say or do anything that would help me. *I had totally bought into my new normal.*

After thanksgiving was over I continued working with Robert and Leslie. Robert had explained to me the basis of his and Leslie's relationship. Leslie had even apologized for acting out of her feelings and asked me to come and work with her again. Leslie and I went back to Louisiana to work as prostitutes together.

Leslie and I had dated a guy together and made a substantial amount of money from the call. Leslie was the controlling type and always played the lead role in everything. I was cool with that to some degree. It was clear that she was more experienced and knew how to handle the tricks. *When we dated she was always the one who took care of the money.*

After the date, I asked Leslie if she could send money to my mom the same time she sent money to Robert. Even though she said that she would do it, when we made it to the store, she sent all the money to Robert instead. My mood instantly changed.

We got a room in Baton Rouge and she left me at the room to go meet some of her friends to smoke weed. She borrowed my car and left me at the room. I called Robert, but it was obvious he was drunk and in his careless frame of mind. I hung up the phone with him, and decided that when Leslie got back, I was leaving to go back home.

Leslie held all the money when we worked. It was a requirement since I was the new chick. Even though she understood my situation, she wasn't going to break the bond between her and Robert. My feelings were hurt and I felt foolish once again. We had talked and shared personal and intimate things while on our way to Louisiana.

I thought we had gotten past the previous incident between Robert and I but it was clear that Leslie only wanted to get back at me. She wasn't trying to help me make a better living for my boys and I like we had discussed.

She was trying to let it be known that she was in control. When she returned back it was like Leslie was a whole new person. She wasn't the same girl that I had just drove hours with talking about everything under the sun.

After gathering my things, I went to the gas station up the street and a guy in a Dodge Ram pulled up next to me and called out my work name, Charisma. He said he recognized me from the pictures online.

I was on the phone arguing with Robert, but ended the call immediately. I needed to make some money to get home and this could be my only chance. We chatted for a little while and he told me his name was Pete. He was a regular of Leslie's and he asked me if I was one of the new chicks. *I told him that I was.*

He offered to let me stay at his place overnight since it was raining. He insisted that I shouldn't be driving back to Texas in that kind of weather. I just wanted to make the money so I stayed. We first stopped at his office where he owned a construction company. He showed me around and we talked for a little while and stopped at a local bar for drinks. I declined the drinks and watched him drink a glass instead.

Afterwards, I followed Pete to his house, and he let me shower. We watched a movie together and talked a little more. Things were going too smooth and I grew a little nervous, so I sent my mom his address just in case. He

194

claimed that he only wanted to help me out but something kept telling me that it was going to cost me.

The cost turned out to be an excruciating encounter, lasting far longer than I thought I could bear. When it was finally over, I cleaned myself up, and cried myself to sleep blaming myself for accepting a friendly offer from a trick to let me stay the night.

To him it was nothing, I was just another hoe. That night he did things to me as if I deserved it. Because I was a prostitute I deserved to be treated any kind of way. My request to stop didn't matter. I didn't matter anymore. I was devastated that night and I remember feeling so helpless. I wasn't prepared for all of this.

When the morning came, I woke him and told him I was ready to leave. Once again, he had different plans. Instead of paying me, he wanted to book me a room at a motel to work. He was going to send guys over and I would split the money 50/50 with him.

I played it all cool and acted as if I was down. I followed him over to the room and checked in. Once I seen his truck was out of sight I left and changed my number right away. I called my mom to send me some cash to come back home.

During the drive home I pondered on what my next move was going to be. I had done a few photo shoots but I didn't know what to do with my photos. I had only posted them on social media and gotten likes and comments. But that wasn't brining in any money. I needed direction and protection. I felt like things would have been different if I would have just stayed working with Leslie. I wouldn't have gotten raped. I wouldn't be driving back home unaccomplished again.

I made a phone to a guy I befriended through Myspace who lived in Miami. He was in the game too and had sent me his number to talk but I had never called until then. He had seen much success from the game. We had chatted online a few times and he had seen that I was dancing and wanted to get to know more about me.

I was openly sharing explicit photos and even began to change my lingo. I started sounding more like someone who was in the game and on social media I quickly began to attract others to my page who were in the life. From their pictures and postings I was able to see more about the game. **At least the image that is paraded to the world that glamorizes the life.**

I decided to finally call him. He immediately remembered who I was and I began explaining to him what had went on. Kevin explained that I needed to make things right between Smooth and I. I had let Smooth down by leaving and then trying to make things work with someone new.

"Smooth is your turnout for a reason. Smooth was trying to be way more than a business partner. The team is your family. If you want to be blessed by the game you gotta play by its rule. So he lied to you. What person hasn't lied? He lied you got away yet you're still in the game. Apparently, he was right about something." Kevin said.

He didn't end the call without first inviting me out to Miami. The offer was open for me to come down anytime I was ready. After the conversation with Kevin, I cried for a little while, thinking about how I could have messed up something good with someone by giving up so easily. What if Smooth was going to be the family I always dreamed about?

This just illustrates the level of manipulation that goes on in the game. My mind was swimming with confusion. Did I really let Smooth down?

Smooth had reached out to me several times but I never responded. That was all going to change.

I had made it home just in time for Christmas and was

really disappointed in myself. All the money from my 401k was gone. The money I'd made was gone. I couldn't make Christmas happen for my kids that year. Instead my mom and Jason came together. Jason had come back around to check on us and once I told him what was going on he immediately decided to help us out.

Jason never tried to convince me to leave the industry. My mom did a few times but I continued undermining her attempts to help. When Jason started coming around all he wanted like always was sex. It hurt because we had history and he knew my heart but none of that mattered anymore. *I was just a hoe now and there was no turning back.*

I reconnected with my friend, Faith, and we decided to go out Christmas night. She had done a total 180. She gave up dancing, and was planning to go to school to work in the dental industry. She hated how much my life had changed, and the road I was on. It was all too familiar for her.

She connected and related to me because in so many ways, our lives were similar. We always gave each other advice, and although she had realized that nothing she could say was going to stop me from moving forward, she supported me and stayed in my corner. When Faith went through things in the past, she would call me. I was now calling on her.

That night, we went out to a couple of spots and popped Ecstasy pills together. I didn't have friends who partied sober. We all needed some form of a boost. We ended up at an afterhours spot and it was like a big high school reunion. My mind kept wandering back to Smooth. I hadn't spoken to him since I left him in Houston, but I had a lot of things I wanted to say and get off my chest.

I had never looked at the situation as if I was letting Smooth down, or he needed me. I figured he would have something to say to me as well. High on ecstasy I gathered up some false courage and called him. When he answered, I immediately started rumbling about how I felt.

I felt so lost and unsure about everything. I was jobless with not a clue of what to do with myself. He always told me that he had my back. I had put my trust in his words and he failed me. On top of that I had shared so much of myself with him that no man had ever seen of me. My feelings were hurt. This wasn't supposed to be my life and although it was true that I had gotten away I couldn't stay away.

He responded back saying, I was too impatient. I wanted things to happen overnight and it didn't work that way. After about thirty minutes of back and forth he convinced me to come back. I looked over at Faith, took a deep breath, and hung up the phone. I told Faith I was going to go back to him, and begged her not to judge me. I drove her back to her place, and then went home to pack my bags.

Smooth sent me the address to a place he had gotten in Metairie. When the morning came I kissed my family goodbye and got on the road. I told my mom I was leaving town to meet some friends for work.

*Being home was only making things worse for me. I had really believed that I was striving to make a better living for my children. I wanted to be able to raise them in an environment different from what I had experienced growing up. **I hated leaving them behind but I knew that once everything got better I would rescue them.***

When I got there, I was glad to see the place was a house and not a hotel. A few of his friends were there, along with the chick that was with him when I left. I didn't want to stick around for introductions. I was exhausted and just wanted to lie down. Smooth greeted me with a hug, gave me a tour of the house, and then escorted me to my room.

He was going on and on about things being much better

now. He was telling me my boys could move to New Orleans with me if I actually stayed this time. He promised we would work on finding me my own place. He also told me there was another chick that would be coming soon, but he was sure we would be cool around each other.

We were going to be sharing a room together once she came. He offered to let me come up to the living room with everyone and chill, but I stayed in my room to rest and to call my mom.

The white chick came to my room and introduced herself as Megan. She apologized about the first time we had unofficially met. Smooth hadn't told her about me and it caught off guard. She assured me that I would see a much better side of Smooth and her this time. Smooth liked to keep everything discreet between his women. I decided to keep it that way.

The first few days back, I just stayed in the house. Being around Megan's son made me miss my boys even more. Sometimes I avoided him because it didn't seem right to give someone else's child affection and attention when my boys weren't there.

Whenever she seen me looking down and out thinking about my boys she always encouraged me that I had made the right decision by coming back to Smooth. She always tried to say that she understood how I felt but I couldn't tell how. She had her son I didn't.

It was clear that Megan was not just in it for the money where Smooth was concerned. She had a strong love for him, and so did her son. I liked Smooth a lot, but I didn't like him enough to stick around no matter what happened. Smooth promised me a better life, with more money for me and my boys. *I wanted him to live up to his promises.*

Before I ever agreed to come back to Smooth I made it clear to him that it had to work this time. The strip club wasn't going to get it. He was going to have to show me another way to get money. He was supposed to hook me up with a photographer for a photo shoot, but that never happened. I had even showed him the photos I had taken since we hadn't been around each other. But he insisted that I wait on my modeling career and keep my focus on stacking my money.

I started working out of one of the hotels down the street from the house while he posted ads for me on backpage. Money was rolling in then one of his friend's chicks got busted in a sting by the cops, so he pulled the ad off the site.

I chilled at home with Smooth until things cooled down and I got to know Megan and her son more. I still refused to set foot in a strip club, and for a little while Smooth was cool with that. While we chilled at the house during the day I continued to surf the internet posting my pictures on website to get modelling gigs in the adult entertainment industry.

Megan worked the strip clubs and she had regular clientele. I expected Megan to be upset at the fact that I hadn't worked since the bust but she never said a word. She still went to work faithfully every day and night at the club.

New Years was around the corner and Smooth planned to bring it in big. He went shopping for us and got new outfits, shoes, Mani's, and Pedi's. That was the first time Smooth had ever treated me to something new. *He was taking us out in public and needed to make sure that we looked good just in case he recruited someone new.*

He reserved a VIP section for us at a nice club in New Orleans, and ordered bottle service for us. He even got a bag of Ecstasy pills for everybody. Smooth normally did not allow any drugs in the house except for weed. But because it was a holiday, and I wasn't going to take the pill alone, he made an exception.

We all got dressed up, popped a pill, and headed downtown to a spot called Republic. It was a regular club, but Smooth mentioned that he and his other pimp partners wanted to find potential women there. The club played a variety of music.

Once the pill kicked in, I was relaxed and didn't even care about where we were or who we were around. Initially, I expected for people to look at us funny. But everyone was nice. We blended in right with the crowd. When we were finally seated in our VIP section, people treated us like we were celebrities.

Chicks kept coming over to our section, taking pictures with Smooth. Smooth *loved* all of the attention. He slipped the girls his number at the same time that he took pictures with them. Telling those same lies saying that he could hook them up with modelling opportunities. He had business cards and everything that night. We took shots and had a great time.

Then as Megan and I are in the restroom she decides to pour her heart out to me. She tells about her rough childhood and many other things that occurred in her life. Smooth was the only father that her son had known.

She apologized again for how rude she had been with me in the beginning. Now that things were looking up for her, she felt the need to reassure me that if I stayed consistent, things would work out for me. As long as I was willing to put in the time, the money would always come. I told her how Smooth and I met and how quickly my life had changed.

I even shared with her about the fact that I didn't think it was fair that her son could be around and my boys couldn't. Megan told me how she didn't have family like I did. She really didn't want her son around while she was working.

She had come to Smooth with her son, so it wasn't an option for him to go anywhere else. She didn't like that her son had to experience all of this. By the time the conversation was over we were both in tears.

Did I need to love Smooth in order to stay around this time, or did I already have some sort of love for him that was bringing me back to him? I was totally lost, but I wasn't going to let it ruin my night or my high. I texted my mom and the boys to tell them Happy New Year.

We partied some more and then headed back to the house. I went into my room to lie down, but Smooth called me into their room. He wanted a threesome, but that wasn't about to happen. I had been with women before, but I didn't have any interest in her like that. I played around with Smooth for a little then drifted off to sleep in his arms.

A few days, later Smooth told me that the new chick, Tameka, was finally coming. Tameka had her own car also, and was very distant and quiet in the beginning. She completely ignored Megan, like they had met before or something. She wore glasses and was a little thicker than me. I expected us to hit it off, but since she was so quiet, it just didn't seem possible.

Smooth had me back working at the hotel again turning tricks. I had went ahead and posted the photos I had on a website where models posted pictures to get called back for real gigs too. Smooth didn't like that, but I was determined to get the modeling thing going.

I had finally got a call back and did a one day gameshow on Playboy TV that I got paid for. I thought that Smooth would be happy that I was making money but he was upset that I wasn't making money the way that a *hoe* was supposed.

After the New Year, Megan told me numerous times her life was going to be much more than this, but I couldn't understand it then. She seemed so content and happy. I couldn't imagine her leaving Smooth anytime soon, unless she was stashing cash behind his back. I chuckled at the thought because she showed him much *loyalty.*

Tameka and I talked more when Smooth had me go back to the strip club and work with her. Tameka had made it clear she did not want to work on the internet. She said she would rather make her money at the club, even if the money was slow.

She was a black girl, but she sure did not possess a black girl's rhythm. I always teased her saying she was a white girl trapped in a black girl's body. I could tell she was fresh in the game, but she was not as insecure as I was. *My insecurity always showed on my face and in my attitude.*

Smooth put me back in the club, thinking I may have been more comfortable if I had someone there working with me. Tameka was just as lost as I was when it came to working in the club, though. Smooth never gave us extra money to buy drinks so, we always danced sober until we made money or someone offered to buy us a drink.

She didn't want to be there alone. She begged me to stay and give it one more chance. She had left Smooth once and had come back. This time, she said, she planned to stay for good. *She believed that all things happened for a reason, and there had to be a reason that we both came back to Smooth.*

She also threatened to tell Smooth about my plans to leave. He would surely find a way to force me to stay. She believed that Smooth was eventually going to bring my boys to New Orleans. Part of me believed but I was too anxious to be as patient as Smooth wanted me to be.

Smooth smoked weed and slept the days away. He always asked about my boys, but I wasn't convinced that he was trying to get them with me any quicker.

When I mentioned to my mom about bringing the boys to New Orleans, she was completely against it and refused. I decided to stay in New Orleans and Tameka was happy about that, since she wouldn't be working alone.

As we grew closer she began to open up more. Tameka held a bachelor's degree and was in a very well-known sorority. She didn't come from a dysfunctional home life, and even had two parents at home. This **"game"** was far off from what she imagined her life would be. She had high hopes that Smooth's plans would work out for her good. This time she was sticking around to see his promises fulfilled in her life.

She went on and on sharing different things with me. Then she shares with me that Smooth hit her when they were working in California, which was part of the reason why she left the first time.

She made me promise to never mention it to Smooth, He had never hit me, but he had raised his hand at Dasha, and now I was hearing that he hit Tameka. I thanked her for being honest with me, but I knew that was my sign to ***get away.***

From the little knowledge I had obtained about the game, Smooth was no longer pimping. This was not the life of the game. Smooth always told me that no one ever got hurt physically. *Then again, maybe this was the game and everyone else just left the harsh details out.*

He let Tameka and I work at the casino a few nights, but Tameka was really nervous about it since she'd worked at a casino before and ended up in a jail cell. I led the way because I didn't want to go back to the strip club.

One night, this guy started popping up everywhere we went in the casino, as if he was checking us out. He was dressed real flashy, Gucci attire, but he was an older guy. I assumed that he was interested in dating one, or even both of us. He was on his phone as he followed us around the casino. He ended the call, and made his way over to us.

Tameka walked away and acted as if she was playing the slot machine. If he was an undercover, she didn't want to get caught. He introduced himself as Jay, and we started talking about random stuff. A few seconds turned into minutes. Those minutes turned into hours. Jay and I talked so long Tameka ended up going to sleep on the slot machines.

In the middle of our conversation, he told me that he could tell I had so much potential to be a really good hoe, but I had to get my *game tight*. He admired how I was eager to get to the money and make a better life for me and my boys. I couldn't believe that I had mistaken a pimp for a potential trick. *I learned that night that pimps come in all ages, colors, backgrounds and swag.*

Jay and I exchanged numbers, and we talked on the phone most of the night. He was on his way to Miami for the Super Bowl and he wanted me to go. A few days earlier Leslie had just reached out and wanted me to go work with her in New Orleans. I had considered going to work with

Leslie again but I thought about it and remembered how things didn't work out between us.

I decided to go down to Miami with Jay instead. I got caught up in the thrill. A new scene. The beach. More money. Celebrities. Better opportunities.

Megan was leaving for Atlanta to get her plastic surgery done, and Smooth had to leave the house before the trick came over to pick her up. As soon as they drove off, I grabbed my things and met up with Jay downtown.

Chapter 12

Making My Bed in Hell

It's sometimes hard to see and understand that you're living in darkness when everyone around you is engaging in the same things as you.

It's more difficult when you recognize that you're lost and in a dark place but decide to continue to blend in because you don't believe or see any hope. I was sold out. The game was now my new reality. Yet like other men I had dated Smooth had let me down again.

Instead of walking away there was another pimp waiting to pick up right where Smooth left off. A Choosey Susie is a woman who keeps switching pimps in the game. In the game, that was my label. Yet nobody ever explains why she switches up.

Maybe it was the bait and switch that most pimps used to sway the women and girls into their house. The lies they tell versus the truth she is exposed to that keeps her on the run. Maybe it's the shame and embarrassment that keeps her running to a different pimp rather than going back home.

Maybe she doesn't have a home to run to and the unknown seems better than what she's already accustomed to. Maybe she was just sold a dream that turned out to be a nightmare and she runs, hoping that one day, the dream will come true.

What if she ran because of the things she witnessed in these households and she knew if she stayed, it would only be a matter of time before she was next in line to receive the exact same treatment? What if she felt bad for those who stayed in the house and had a heart to want to help them, but couldn't even help herself, so she ran away?

207

She's a lost girl on the run who's looking for freedom, but doesn't know where to start. So instead, she makes her bed in hell.

Have you too ever made your bed in hell? A relationship or lifestyle isn't good for you but you can't stay away?

After I left Smooth and made my way to Miami I went down this path of trying to find where I fit in, in the game. I still wanted to give my boys what I thought they deserved. A better life and a dad. Only now my passion had been misplaced. My brokenness got in the way of what was most important.

This was my life now, and I wasn't going back to the old me. I couldn't. **I was sold a dream and I bought it.** *I was at a point where I embraced the false promise and fell for the glamorized images that the game portrays to the world and was now going to go after it by any means necessary.*

My old life and the game was all that I had ever been exposed to back then. My old life had failed me and since I had took such a big leap of leaving everything behind this had to work for me. The lies and half-truths that had been fed to me I was starting to believe.

I'd given up on finding love my way. It had failed me too. I didn't need a boyfriend who would mistreat me anymore. Instead, I could have a pimp who had money and some direction. Sure, he had other women, but at least I knew them.

I looked at a pimp as my boss who managed my money. I saw him as a source of protection. He was to teach me the way of life and survival that no one else had done. I was already used to having toxic people in my life.

It wasn't like I had picked the best fathers for my sons in the past or dated innocent guys. Just about every dude I

208

had dealt with during this time of my life was a criminal or an ex-convict of some sort. I still *leaned* on the promise that at least a pimp wanted to help us.

I was too blind and too ashamed to face the reality of what was actually going on. So, the game became a new *hiding place* for me. But on this journey of mine I would discover what being a pimp and belonging to a pimp really meant.

Life with Jay- The Sexual Abuser

Jay didn't want me to work immediately. Instead he took time to get to know me better. I followed him to the West Bank, and he asked me to park my car at this very sleazy motel and get in the truck with him. He drove a navy blue Range Rover that was all decked inside and out. I had never been in a Range Rover before, but I knew they were more expensive than the Navigator that Smooth drove. *I was already coming up.*

Jay and I went to the movies and it was pretty silent on the way there. Smooth and Tameka called and texted me multiple times. Smooth was begging me to come back home, and Tameka was upset that I put her in the middle of my escape.

I powered my phone off, and went into the movies. Inside, Jay treated me more like we were on a date. He held my hand and kissed me passionately. He kept telling me how sexy and beautiful I was, and how he hadn't had a black girl on his team in a while.

He said he was going to have sex with me every day, no matter what. He laughed as he said it, so I took it as a joke unaware of what I really getting myself into. Smooth and I only had sex a few times. *I wanted it to stay about business but with Jay that was all about to change.* He never asked for a choosing fee and said that I had probably given all my money to Smooth anyway.

After the movie he took me back to the motel and got

us a room. That night he recorded us as I gave him sexual favors that I really didn't want to do. I contemplated answering Smooth's call but I felt too foolish to turn back around and go to him so I stayed. Not knowing that I wasn't just about to become Jay's new hoe but I was in fact on my way to becoming his new *black sex slave.*

The next morning I followed Jay back downtown to meet up with the other girls. He introduced me to two white girls named Sasha and Rachel. Sasha was the oldest and she had been with Jay the longest. They were both excited to meet me.

We loaded their things into the truck, and he took Rachel with him and put Sasha in the car with me. Sasha drove my car, and I rode on the passenger. I really didn't like driving, so I didn't mind one of the other girls driving my car.

Sasha asked me twenty-one questions. Did Jay and I spend the night together? How many kids did I have? Was jay my first pimp? How long had I been in the game? Even though I felt like I was on trial being interrogated, I answered her questions and asked some of my own.

Sasha grew up in a gang and was all over the place before she met Jay. He helped her get on her feet, and in her eyes, he had saved her life. Although she was a prostitute now for a living, she lived well in her eyes. She no longer lived a violent life and she finally had stability and a real family. She got to travel to amazing places all over the world, and the way she saw it, Jay was a great guy. Aside from being a pimp, Jay also owned a clothing store back in Chicago.

He took very good care of his children. Sasha let me know that my kids wouldn't have to worry about anything as long as I was with Jay. She knew all about pimps and their false promises, but she was convinced that Jay was nothing like them.

Jay planned a new life for me in Chicago with him, as long as I followed his instructions and did what was asked

210

of me. My own condo, luxury car, and a good school for my boys. *Sasha was confident that my desire for stability and success was attainable working with Jay.* After a few stops, Sasha got in the car with Jay and Rachel got in the car with me. Rachel didn't ask me twenty-one questions like Sasha.

Rachel was nineteen years old. She was Amish, but somehow had met Jay, and he had changed her life completely. She told me how she'd made so many mistakes when she first started working for Jay, but she had never been happier.

In the beginning, she didn't speak to her family, but eventually got back in contact with them and even went to visit them. She always came back to Jay, though. He was her family now.

Pimps like have their girls feeding the newbies with any information they needed to hear to make her feel comfortable about being with a pimp.

I rode in the car with Jay the rest of the way to Florida. Jay wanted me to loosen up and talk more since I had shut down after that long night at the motel. I just wanted to clear my mind, but I kept going over different scenarios in my head about how this could turn out for me if it went bad.

Jay acted like what happened the previous night at the motel was normal for me. Maybe he thought I was turned on by it. I wasn't. *I wanted out.*

For the remainder of the ride to Florida he'd ask me questions about my life from childhood to present day. He would sing to me and try all kinds of stuff to make the trip fun. Let Jay tell it, I was riding with a millionaire and I needed to appreciate the fact that he allowed me to be in his presence.

He got upset when I did not seem appreciative, and since I could not just tell him how I was feeling, I had to let my guard down again. It was too late to turn back now but as soon as I had decided to embrace the game the more the truth would be revealed.

Our first stop when we got to Florida was Tampa. It was around 3 a.m. and because I had come empty-handed, the time had come for me to finally make some money. I picked up my first date as soon as I hit the casino floor and I met my quota right away. Immediately, I thought that was a sign that maybe I had made the right decision coming to Florida.

When I got back to the room, Jay had Rachel there with him. His plan was to have her join us, but I could see that she wasn't interested. I tried to talk Jay out of Rachel joining us, but she insisted that I let Jay have his way. I never looked at him the same after what he had done to Rachel that night.

I couldn't stop apologizing to her about the incident because I sat there as a helpless witness, even though she kept reassuring me that everything was alright. She opened up to me more after that and began to tell me more things that she had endured while being with Jay. It was to the point where they now acted as if they enjoyed the things that Jay were putting them through. They felt obligated to.

*We took risks every day, not knowing what would happen to us if one of our tricks harmed us. When in reality, all along, we were being sexually **abused** by the man who claimed he was there to **protect us.***

Jay was living up to his promise that he would have me every night. No matter if I came home with zero dollars or a thousand he wanted my body. Jay normally had the girls on a routine scheduled of who was to spend alone time with him. Now that I was there he instead wanted to only have me. Unless he forced one or both of them to join us.

The girls were giving me a hard time about it and I was forced to work alone many nights because of the jealousy it brought. When we made it to Miami, instead of getting separate rooms, we had one room with double beds. I wanted Sasha and Rachel to see that I wasn't their problem, but that Jay was.

The girl's only saw that I got more time with Jay though. I didn't even want the extra attention because it wasn't attention at all but **unwanted** sex. I would even tell him I was on my cycle longer to keep him away from me. He didn't care. He was very creative about getting what he wanted from me. I cried in the shower most nights thinking about how I was going to escape all this.

Jay had even let me send money to my mom for the boys and took us shopping frequently thinking it would make me feel better. I didn't care. I was tired of going through what I went through behind closed doors with Jay.

I had even tried confronting him about it in front of the other girls thinking it would put an end to it. They ended up being mad at me because they felt that I should appreciate my time with Jay in spite of what was going on. They worshipped the ground Jay walked on.

One night, Sasha and I grabbed dinner at an Italian restaurant on Lincoln Rd. A guy came up to us and told us we could make major bucks in Naples, Florida. He talked to us as if he knew what we did for a living. We never stood on the corner or anything like that.

We picked up our dates from the local bars and blending with the tourist crowds. When you're in the game it's as if you have a little invisible radar on you for others in the game to notice you by. *Tricks know a working girl when they see one and vice versa.* Traffickers/Pimps know working girls/women.

When he went over his client list, Sasha was sold. She contacted Jay and told him we were headed to Naples. I didn't want to go because I could tell he was more interested in Sasha, and it seemed like a waste of time for me but I decided to go anyway since it would relieve me of duties to Jay for a night. He acted all devastated, and texted me multiple times saying he missed me and couldn't wait for my return. *I began thinking of my escape.*

When we made it to Naples Sasha went on a couple of dates immediately. I ended up getting into an argument with of her tricks for making a racial comment towards me. I wasn't going to accept money from someone like that no matter how much he was going to charge me. Instead of working with her that night I stayed back at the hotel responding to text from Jay all night.

The next morning the guy who invited us to Naples took us shopping and we headed back to Miami. He wanted us to stay and work but he ended up admitting to Sasha that he wanted a cut of the money from the clients he gave her. Jay wasn't up for that and instructed to come back to Miami immediately.

When we made it back to Miami Jay surprised us with news that he had another girl coming to work with us. She was a black girl named Lisa who he had picked up from one of the rough areas of Miami. Jay described her as a ***diamond in the rough.***

I was relieved that he was getting someone who could take my place because I was done being his little black slave girl. He had been threatening me that he was going to replace me but once I came back from Naples he tried to go right back to how things had been.

Lisa hadn't made it to hotel with us because she hadn't paid her choosing fee just yet. He finally brought Lisa to stay with us. For a few days, she wouldn't talk to me, and I was cool with that. When she finally did talk to me, we realized we had more in common than I expected. We were both from Texas, we both had children and both felt out of place.

She had met a guy online, and he bought a ticket to Miami for her. *Like me, she was enticed by the promises of a better life, and she had never been out of Texas so the experience was worth it to her.* Once she made it to Miami, he had her turning tricks, but things went sour with them and he kicked her out with nothing. She had been trying to work on her own and then she met Jay and decided to go with him.

Lisa was tough, and a little rough around the edges. She was very outspoken. I was getting tired of the mind games from Jay and the competitiveness from the girls. I thought having Lisa there would have made a difference. It didn't Jay was now beginning to do things to cause Lisa and I to now have issues. He didn't want us to get along but it was too late.

Amidst all the *chaos,* Lisa and I still managed to bond. Lisa and I talked about driving back to Texas together since this *"game"* wasn't what either one of us expected it to be. One night, Jay gave Lisa an ultimatum to either come home with her quota or leave. *She chose to leave.*

I was already out working when she called me with the news that she had left for good. A couple of days later when Jay was out and left my keys behind, I packed up my things and left. I hooked up with Lisa and we had made decided that we were going to drive back to Texas together and leave all this behind.

Jay wasn't surprised that I left and he had a lot to say about it. He said I was weak and that I was a renegade, a prostitute without a pimp. He told me I wasn't going to get anywhere in the game.

"You're trying to save hoes and you can't even save yourself. The game isn't about making friends. Get out your feeling and come get this money," said Jay.

I wasn't sure that I wanted to anymore. The journey was supposed to end at this point. We were supposed to make some money and head back to Texas, then those *plans changed.*

Lisa had started talking to this guy who was in the porn industry. She had been spending time with him while she was still with Jay. She told me that I could come and crash at his place until I figured everything out.

They were exclusive and she didn't have to work anymore. He had promised to take care of her. Then suddenly, all that changed. He wanted her to work and told her that she couldn't come back to his place until she made some money. He turned out to be a pimp too.

We went over to his place to grab her belongings, but he wouldn't let her into the apartment and never answered his phone. She never saw him or her belongings again. All she had was her ID and the clothes on her back. I told her we would replace her clothes and that she could wear mine in the meantime.

We found us a nice cheap motel on Biscayne to stay in while we worked and gathered us up some money to head back to Texas. Lisa and I worked on South Beach for the next couple of nights. We were beginning to enjoy ourselves and questioned whether or not we were both really ready to head back to Texas so soon.

The Super Bowl was going to be in Miami that year and we both were anticipating on making lots of money that weekend.

The closer it got to the super bowl the more Miami began to be swarmed by pimps and their working girls. It really only seemed to be tricks, working girls, and pimps on the streets at night. When we went out to work we made sure to not make any eye contact with them acting as if we were still with a pimp to avoid getting snatched up.

This one guy walked alongside me up and down Washington and Collins, whispering stuff in my ear. *Macking. Pursuing a hoe.* He had been chasing me since I had been with Jay. When I was mad at Jay, I strolled down Washington to clear my mind and he would always come

216

along side of me. Lisa and I were coming back from work one night and to my surprise, the guy who was all in my ear was staying at the same hotel as us. He rushed over to my room and beat on the door for us to open it. Lisa told me not to open the door, but I opened it away.

His name was Dre and he was from Memphis. He wanted me on his team. He had given me the run down on his background and told me about the girl he already had. He had fed me the same promises the last pimps had given me. *Yet in my mind the idea of having a pimp or man around continued to bring me comfort.*

I couldn't do this by myself. I didn't want to. Money management was always an issue for me and I liked the idea that the pimp was holding my money and investing it in something when I couldn't. If I had it, I spent it. Living paycheck to paycheck was all I knew.

As long as I did a good job at work and I didn't have to worry about being laid off or fired, I knew what to expect every two weeks. It was different now. I never knew what I was going to make or if I was going to make any money those nights.

I wasn't having the best luck with a pimp, but I wasn't ready to give up and be on my own either. **The game had a hold on me mentally.** I yearned for some direction and stability that being with a pimp was supposed to bring.

Dre was struggling financially at the time but had big hopes of coming up real soon. He wanted me to be the girl by his side that helped him to accomplish that alongside the bottom chick that he had. I never paid him any money but I did entertain him with a lie that the possibility was there just in case we needed him for something.

Lisa was upset because she didn't want to be controlled by a pimp. But, we had promised to never leave each other. She listened to me complain about my problems and trusted me 100 percent, even when I didn't trust myself. Dre was

217

always a phone call away so if we needed anything, we could call him.

Life with Kevin the User

Lisa and I continued working and partying on South Beach. One night I spotted a blue *Bentley Coupe* that kept circling around Ocean Dr. It looked familiar but I couldn't quite place where I had seen it before. Then it hit me. It was Kevin--the guy I had spoken to from Myspace. I yelled out to him and he told us to get in. Lisa was excited because she had never been in a Bentley. I had never been in one either, *but I played it cool.*

It didn't take long for him to remember who I was. We exchanged numbers again and he asked me out to dinner. He let us out, and immediately Lisa wanted to know how to be down with him. I made it clear to her that he was a pimp, but she didn't care. She was convinced that if he rode in a Bentley, he lived lavish, and she **wanted in.**

I had only seen pictures of him on Myspace but so far, he checked out as the real deal. Lisa had a different attitude than normal once we crossed paths with Kevin. She was determined to let her guard down if it meant being with Kevin.

Kevin and I went out to dinner at a steakhouse for our date, which was really an interview to find out if I could be a part of his team without causing issues in the house. More established pimps don't just allow any and every woman or girl into their home. *Because pimps have their own strategy of manipulation they normally play the romance or getting to "know you" role in the beginning.*

Kevin had played college basketball and had plans of making it to the NBA until he got shot. After dropping out of school he turned to selling drugs and then pimping. He went on to tell explain to me how his household worked making it clear that he was nothing like other pimps and

218

never hit his women. By the time dinner was over I had told him my story and my plans.

He wanted Lisa and I to come and work for him whenever we both were ready to pay a choosing fee of a thousand dollars. The weather would turn for the worst and instead of us being able to go work at the beach we decided to go to the casino so we didn't have to club hop in the rain. After leaving the casino on a date my car would break down on side of road and I'd end up calling Dre instead to help us once we made it back to the room.

I was waiting to receive my tax refund and when it finally came Lisa and I decided that instead of going to Texas we were going to go with Kevin. I paid some bills, sent money home, went shopping, and chose up with Kevin.

Kevin and the three girls he had working for him at the time stayed in a high rise condo in Downtown Miami. We all got along really well and Kevin immediately put us to work with his two highest paid working girls. Things were going alright until I realized that Kevin had a drug problem.

Since he held our money we depended on him for everything. His drug problem would keep him in bed and sick most of the time. While we were all supposed to be out hustling Kevin was high or sleep. I was over it and ready to make moves. All of the girls had begun living separate lives aside from the game and were planning to leave him soon. I wasn't going to stay around to see all that happen.

Kevin had even convinced me that I needed to work back in the strip club because it was safer than picking up tricks at bars. I had already made it clear that I would do anything besides work in the strip club.

His girls had been known to make ten thousand dollars a night at the strip club and he believed that I had potential to make it happen too. I knew I didn't have the strip club hustle like that. He was determined to prove otherwise.

219

Life with Heartless Kenny

Lisa and I were going back and forth from the strip club to club hopping on South Beach for work. One night, we were working on South Beach and *a guy called out my real name.* I turned and glanced, but kept walking because the only person who would know me was Jay and Dre. It didn't sound like either one of them. To my surprise, it was Kenny. He was surprised to see me, but he had heard the news that I ran away from Smooth. *Since somebody had did all the hard work and I had fell, he wanted me on his team now.*

I was trying to get settled in with Kevin and I knew Lisa wasn't going for another move. Kevin called me to pick up his Benz and drive it back home since he got pulled over. I was the only one in the house with a valid ID and clear record. I exchanged numbers with Kenny and went on my way.

Kenny kept reaching out to me asking me to leave Kevin for him. Kenny wanted me to work for him badly. He didn't feel Kevin needed me and Lisa. Let Kenny tell it, Kevin had all that he needed and wanted and all he was doing was collecting our money to pay for his lavish lifestyle.

Kenny said Kevin would find a way to make us leave empty-handed. I didn't want to believe that about Kevin. But, Kenny was sure that we were getting played. I left with Kenny and I felt bad for breaking our loyalty to Kevin. But, he was right. Kevin didn't call or come looking for us.

Kenny immediately introduced Lisa and I to his two girls. A veteran black girl who had been in the game for years and his white girl. She taught me some things and was very well-known. When we walked down the strip together, instead of pimps chasing us, they moved out of

220

the way and bowed at her feet. She had much respect in the game and I was glad to be working alongside her.

Lisa followed me with Kenny and continued telling me that she had bad vibes about it all. I kept encouraging her with the same hope that was given to me. *In due time things would get better.*

While I worked with Kenny's black girl Lisa worked with the other girl. One night after Lisa and her received a call to go on a date at a nearby hotel they never returned. We finally got the news that their call was a sting and both of them were in jail.

Kenny got out his girl immediately and left Lisa in there over the weekend. I was pissed that he had done her like that but because she hadn't made any money he refused to get her out.

When Lisa got out, we immediately went to get her. We drove to a hotel in an area I had never been before. It wasn't the place we had been staying so I knew something wasn't right about it. We got Lisa soap to shower and told her that we were coming back to pick her up.

When we made it back to our hotel, Kenny said he was firing her. I refused to get out of the car. I told him I was going back to pick up Lisa. *I couldn't just leave her behind like that with nothing. It didn't feel right.* He refused to get out of the car and let me go back, so we sat there arguing.

Then things turned violent and we had a little throw down in the car. I had never been hit by a man before. Without even thinking I picked up my phone and pressed the number nine. He slapped me one more time, grabbed his pistol and jumped out of the car. We were done for sure and I never spoke to him again.

I went back into the hotel and tried to get my things, but the girls had already turned on me. They wouldn't let me get my things. Kenny instructed the girls to take what he brought me out of my bag first then they threw my things in the hallway.

I grabbed my things and went back to get Lisa. She had already called Kevin and he was waiting to meet up with us. Kevin greeted me with a tight, affectionate hug and apologized for slipping. He asked me to never leave him and told me that the next time I had problems, I should come talk to him.

Kevin made me feel like he really cared about us. To show me how sorry he was for his recent behavior, when we made it back to the condo *I was greeted by an English bulldog.* No man had ever gotten me such a sweet gift.

So when he told Lisa and I that we were going to be working at the strip club with the others girls in the house I was down. Lisa was really excited about going to work at the strip club.

She even offered to give me some pointers on how to get VIP clients and work the pole. I had already made up my mind that if I was going to work at Coco's, I needed a pill and some alcohol.

Kevin didn't rush to put me in the club because he didn't want me to use that as an excuse to leave again. So Lisa and I journeyed back to the beach one more night. It was Friday and it was normally jumping.

Some guys in a white SUV flagged us down. At first, Lisa waved, but then she immediately turned away. Since she had been to jail, she had her guard up even more.

The guys drove off and then came back around. I told them to get out and follow us to the club. But one guy made it known that they wanted the 'other fun.' We just walked away. Less than five minutes later, they had us pinned to the ground, yelling that we were under arrest for solicitation. Granted we were there for that but we hadn't offered them **anything.**

We hadn't even discussed sex, but they were convinced we were prostitutes. They called us everything but children

222

of God. Since it was Super Bowl weekend, the more prostitutes they got off the streets, the better. They were doing a round up.

We were getting booked and Lisa had just got out of jail. She was furious. I apologized a million times, but it was neither one of our faults. We weren't even dressed up that night. We both had on pants and a jacket. It was the one of the coldest winters in Florida that year. They took us to the precinct first and took pictures of us and all of our tattoos, if we had any. I didn't know whether to be mad or sad.

I just tried my best not to think about it. I had never been to jail for anything in my life. I rarely even got traffic tickets. Most of the other girls were upset and were clearly ready to work, regardless of the weather. They finally took us down to the jail for our actual booking. It was a horrible experience.

If you tried to talk back and defend yourself that made your stay even worse. They replaced our shoes with jail flip flops, but if you talked trash, they left you barefooted. The holding cells for booking were terrible.

The place was filled with other women who had committed other crimes, such as driving under the influence or without insurance. Some of the women threw up on the floors. The toilets were in the center of the cell so if someone used it, we saw it and smelled it.

They even snatched girls' wigs off their head, but I was determined not to waste the $600 wig I had just bought. I explained to them that it was securely glued to my head. They pulled and tugged at it, but it didn't bulge. They wanted to embarrass us. The officers were yelling these are the nasty "hoes."

After the cops handcuffed us they claim that they were looking for underage working girls but not once did I see them treat any of the girls like victims. We all were treated like criminals that night.

It was well over a few hundred or more of us that got booked that one night. They finally let us use the phone. We both called Kevin, but his phone continued to go to voicemail. I panicked because we didn't have anyone else to contact.

We used up all of our calls to contact Kevin and I started to worry that we weren't getting out. I didn't want to stay there another minute longer. It sunk in that I was actually in jail.

They moved us again to anther cell. They kept all of the prostitutes together between two cells. We were allowed to use the phone again. I called my mom and got her voicemail. I called my granny and had her call my mom until she picked up.

My mom finally answered and I gave her Kevin's number to call, until he answered to bail us out. My mom finally got in touch with Kevin. By the time I called, he was already in contact with a bondsman.

Some of these women had been in the game since their teens. Some started out with their boyfriends, who later turned out to be their pimps. Some ran away from home and a pimp rescued them from homelessness.

I had never been around so many working girls at one time. Some of the women got settled because they knew their pimp wasn't going to bail them out, it was routine to stay once you got caught. Most of the girls had been to jail before, so they knew we'd be released no later than Monday.

I didn't think I would make it until Monday. The food was terrible and I had only been drinking apple juice. They gave us small blue mats and a thin sheet to sleep on, the lights went out for the night and we all slept on the hard floor.

We went before the judge via satellite and then we were

224

taken upstairs to the actual cells with beds and TVs. They gave us orange suits to wear. We took showers and they separated me and Lisa. When I talked to Kevin, he told me that our bond was paid and that we would be out shortly. Only one girl had been released before all of us since she had her money with her. Most of the women were repeat offenders and had to do their time.

I met a girl from New York who was sure that her current dude wasn't going to bail her out. The guards gave her a real bad time, and even called her a man, but she didn't let it bother her. A renegade was there serving six months. The chicks with pimps debated with her on reasons why it was better to have a pimp. Women tried to recruit others to join their stable once they were free.

I thought about how fast my life had changed. I went from having my own fully furnished place and a decent, boring job to a jail cell with a fourteen-inch TV and twin bed.

They called us one by one to be released. It seemed like forever. Morning came again and I was still locked up. When we finally got to see the other women, I looked for Lisa. She was already gone.

When the guards changed shifts, the new guards were much nicer than the last crew. Most of us stayed longer than expected. I was on the verge of giving up that I was leaving anytime soon. *I just fell back asleep to avoid the humiliation of my reality.*

My name was finally called and I still had to wait over three hours to be released. Nobody was waiting on me and my car was still in the garage at the beach. I found out that I was only a few blocks away from the condo, so I took a cab back to the condo.

Kevin's uncle was coming out, so he paid for my cab fare. Everyone who was awake greeted me, including my favorite dog. I headed straight to the shower to scrub the

225

jail smell off of me. Kevin was happy to see me. He took me to pick up my car. He asked me to give the strip club another chance, and promised that things would be different this time.

He always kept pressure on me, but the motivation to execute just wasn't strong since my mind was always somewhere else. I was totally lost. I wasn't sure what I wanted out of this life anymore. *I wanted to be comfortable, but I never found comfort.*

The first couple of nights, we didn't even have to audition. I was relieved after a few drinks and an X pill. I went into a totally different zone under the influence. Depending on my mood, that could be good or bad. I realized that I worked better sober.

The drugs made me slack off but it felt good to be high. I was introduced to cocaine one night, but I didn't like it. One of the girls in the house did it and said that it made her less intimidated of the other girls.

Amateur night had finally come. Lisa and I were to finally go ahead and audition. Lisa was more nervous than I was. I couldn't understand why since this was what she always wanted from the start. Lisa had been telling me that she danced back in Texas but that night she acted as if it was her very first time.

She just kept saying that she needed to prove herself to Kevin and she didn't want to let him down another night. She felt like Kevin had only taken her in because of me. To her, Kevin showed that he wanted me there, but she didn't feel like he wanted her there. This was her night to prove herself to him.

I went on stage first to get my set over with and encourage Lisa to not back down. When I looked around for Lisa, she was gone. I went into the dressing room, VIP sections, and restroom, but she wasn't there. I finally went to check my bag and my keys and my clothes were gone. I called her cell phone a million times and she never answered. I called Kevin and told him. He was hopeful that she would return. *I popped a pill to ease my mind.*

The owner of the club suggested that I file a police report since I was unsure of her intentions. It just wasn't like her to just drive my car without asking. It wasn't like her to just up and leave. I was paranoid. I called her until the phone either went dead or she turned it off. I ended up putting on my clothes and not even working that night.

Everyone had something to say or some advice to give. All of a sudden, it turned into an intervention just for me. I was cool with a girl who danced, but wasn't in the game. She didn't have any kids, a pimp, or boyfriend. Her and a group of girls pulled me to the side and told me that the game wasn't for a mother. The game was always, always only going to be about the pimp.

All the money I made had stayed with each pimp I had but they told me that I had to pay my quota and expense first. In my eyes it made sense to pay the pimp. They had the direction and the plan that I didn't have. I had normalized and justified what was going. They didn't understand because they weren't in "the game." I had been totally **brainwashed.**

A person is considered to be brainwashed when they start to believe in an ideology and **refuses** *to believe any new argument against their ideology. Even though things seemed to all be going wrong I believed in the game. I embraced it. I was purposed for this.*

They warned me that if I stayed with a pimp, I may never see my children again. They offered to help me get out if I really wanted to but I was afraid that they were going to take me down a crazy path just to use me too.

Another woman interjected and told them that all pimps weren't bad. Her body had been totally constructed to perfection by plastic surgery, her kids were in private school and she was able to see her children whenever she wanted. She even had her own place paid for because of her pimp. She admitted that the game wasn't all good, but for her, it wasn't all bad either. She looked like she was as old as my mom, but her body looked like it belonged to a twenty-five-year-old.

My night was getting worse by the minute. My car was gone and the truth was coming out. I didn't know what to do. Kevin's main chick saw me getting lectured and pulled me over to the side to talk. She tried to be discreet and stay out of the way at work because she didn't want people to know that she had a pimp.

We sat down in the dressing room and talked. She had plans to leave the game soon. She was going to move back to Memphis and go to college.

She kept telling me that things weren't what they seemed to be and that I needed to find my way back home to my kids. She asked if I had sex with Kevin, but I only knew of one person who had—and it wasn't me. I left that night with her. I should have just gone to the house, but I had her drop me off at South Beach instead.

I would never see Kevin and the girls again and my life continued to crumble.

Chapter 13

A Prodigal Daughter

Jesus continued: There was a man who had two sons. The younger one said to his father, 'Father, give me my share of the estate.' So he divided his property between them.

Not long after that, the younger son got together all he had, set off for a distant country and there squandered his wealth in wild living.
After he spent everything, there was a severe famine in that whole country, and he began to be in need. So he went and hired himself out to a citizen of that country, who sent him to his fields to feed pigs. He longed to fill his stomach with the pods that the pigs were eating, but no one gave him anything. Luke 15: 11-17

I wanted to be down so bad it's sickening still sometimes when I read this. I was so lost behind the lies and deceit of this cold, wicked world. I was scared to go back to where all the pain started because it only led me to run away again. So I continued trying to make my bed in hell. I was desperately trying to accept who I was becoming. A hoe was all I would ever amount to being.

One of the most humbling lessons I've learned is that you can know that you're here to do something great in this world but have no plan or direction of how to get there. If you don't seek God for the answer you're subject to falling into the enemy's trap...

Whose plan are you following? Yours? Gods? Or mans?

Life with Con Artist Magic

Lisa never picked me up that night. My car hadn't been found. Everybody was living double lives. Kevin's girls were sneaking off and meeting up with men they didn't charge for sex because they actually liked them and had built relationships with them. Kevin wasn't attentive to his household and everything was out of place. From the outside, everything seemed like it was all good. ***Fancy condo, lavish cars, the finest food, lots of money and expensive clothes.***

I was being played by everybody—even Lisa. I was never mad at her because a piece of me felt like it was all my fault that things were going wrong for her. She followed me everywhere. I figured I let her down and she was paying me back by taking my car. I ran into Kenny's chick and I sat down and talked with them as they ate breakfast.

They were willing to take me back without Lisa, but I wasn't cool with Kenny putting his hands on me. She could tell that I was high, but I reassured her that I was okay and in control. She encouraged me not to give up. She reminded me that my kids always come first and whoever I worked for needed to understand that.

It sounded good, but that didn't seem like the truth to me anymore. *It was all about the pimp and my survival.* I wasn't in the mood to work that night and after breakfast I went down and walked on the beach until the sun came up.

I was still wandering around South Beach when a gold hummer pulled up alongside of me. In the morning, pimps would just ride around looking for girls to pick up. When this hummer pulled up I just knew it was a pimp trying to get me to choose up. I yelled for him to just leave me alone.

A guy in the passenger seat smiled and shouted, "I wouldn't ask you for anything because if you were mine you'd willing give me your money without me having to ask for it."

As I got in the cab he yelled out his number and told me to call him real quick. I jumped in the cab and dialed the number. He picked up on the first ring and I just told him the truth.

I was tired of all the lies being told to me. Everybody is claiming that they want to help me make my life better for my boys and I. Once I get with them it was a total different story. I had just about lost everything. This wasn't the life I had envisioned for my family. I was tired of being toyed with.

No one could even keep a calm household amongst the girls' jealousy and competition. I was looking forward to the help and stability but I wasn't receiving that. I wanted to go back home, but part of me was still afraid to return home with nothing.

I had never been this low before. I didn't know how I was going to explain everything. I couldn't even understand myself. I was drowned with guilt. I had never felt so weak-minded and powerless.

Magic listened without saying a word. He asked me where I was going and when I got out of the cab at Kevin's condo, Magic had switched cars and was there waiting in a Benz right behind my cab.

I was hesitant to go at first, but he made it clear that he was only going to take me to breakfast and that he would bring me back afterwards.

Magic wore really big flashy rings and a diamond crusted necklace that had his face on it. His whole mouth was full of diamonds. He stood about 5'7 and was very stocky. He was a rapper but like most pimps their *"legit"* businesses are used to clean the dirty money they have.

231

Magic told me that he was more than a pimp. He said he would protect and teach me and not just lead me on with false promises. He was from Dallas, Texas and claimed that his veteran chicks lived in Texas with their children in their own houses.

He even had a nanny set up for the girls with kids in Texas while they worked out of town. He had children with some of the women, and one of his girls was pregnant when I met her. He had over ten girls working for him at the time. *I was number **eleven.***

After breakfast with Magic, he took me back to a hotel instead. When I got in the room, he patted me down and asked me to pull my pants down. He said that he needed to check to see if I had any money hidden on me. He thought I had been working that previous night but I was just wandering around the beach thinking.

He pulled on my wig and everything to see if it could come off. I hadn't heard of women hiding money in their private area or their hair. He took my cell phone and my coin purse, and said that I wouldn't need those things anymore.

He told my name was now ***Sexy Black***. He could tell that I was high off of something and he told me to lay down and get some rest and he'd be back for me later.

"Please don't make this difficult for yourself and try to run off. You don't want to see Daddy's bad side do you?" He said.

Magic never got loud with me or used physical force to keep me in his presence but something in me just told me to obey his commands if I didn't want to experience another side of him. He laid out the ground rules to follow to avoid his not so good side and I obeyed every last command.

So, I shook my head no and went to sleep.

After I woke up and the pill wore off, he came and took me to another room at the same hotel where the other girls

232

were. He told me that I wasn't to tell the other girls my real name. Since I had never experienced having a real pimp, he was going to show me what it really meant to be ten toes down.

I didn't have any clothes other than what I had on my back. He refused to let me get my things promising that we would go and buy me stuff.

The girls seemed happy to have a new chick in the house and each introduced themselves by their pet names. A couple of the girls had seen me on the beach the night before and were excited that their daddy had found me. "She's pretty daddy. I'm glad you brought her home."

While they got ready for work Magic took me back to his room and explained to me what I was going to be doing. Magic told me that his girls didn't have sex when they worked. They only had sex with him. Instead of them being called prostitutes or hookers, he referred to them as *"Magic's Thieves."*

Magic explained what the girls did as the "perfect exchange." They were coming to date you to take advantage of our precious jewels. "So why not get him before he gets you?"

The first time I went out with one of his girls, I was so nervous. I didn't think I had what it took to do what the other girls did. What if he saw me? What if he had a gun or a knife? He's stronger than me and with one hit it would be over for me.

To them, it was like taking candy from a candy store. I just watched and assisted with the easy stuff like searching the jeans or watching the door. I was too scared to do anything else.

I had to make a lot of money in order to leave and that didn't seem possible. He wanted $20,000. I just couldn't rob a man like that. I could give my body over because I had always done that for a majority of my life stealing was going to take some getting used to.

Magic let me work with other girls to get more training and learn other ways to rob the tricks. Instead of learning the men and the new rules of the game, I got to know the women more. Instead of working they would share their stories with me.

We worked twenty-four hours a day straight because things were so slow. There were many nights I made no money and I wasn't even trying to. Talking more to the girls and stealing moments alone to think as I walked the streets felt better to plot and rob people.

Magic was pissed when he found out I wasn't really working and he would make me feel guilty about my decision to not make any money. He would bring up my kids saying, *"Remember their why you're doing this in the first place. I'm just here to help and guide you."*

So many times I wanted to scream back "you liar this isn't for my kids this is about you." Out of fear and knowing saying such a thing would get beat I'd say, "Okay daddy you're right. I'll try harder next time." *Magic even had me write out a list my personal goals to carry around with me as I worked so I stay focused.*

If I could make the $20,000 in the next two week he promised he would let me go home to see my boy's. I would never reach the 20,000 and the promise of me going to see my children would continue to be dangled over my head causing me to become someone I didn't want to be. *Magic's thief.*

I got huge blisters on my feet from walking the streets for hours and I figured that would get me a day off. Instead, I still had to work. Magic said it was part of being broken in and that I would eventually get used it. I put cold towels in my boots to bear the pain. After working in Miami, he took us to out Orlando to work.

In Orlando, we stayed in a two-story five bedroom house in a gated golf course community. The security guards knew Magic as a rapper. When we came through the gates each morning security would ask how the promoting at the club went. We never went near a club. *Instead we walked the blade every night, street, called Orange Blossom Trail.*

At the house all of the doors had key locks on them from the inside so no one could leave. Nobody seemed to want to leave. It was just we were one big happy family at times.

We normally had at least one day off during the week, like Tuesday or Wednesday. On our off days he would take us out to eat and then we'd go home and get high. The refrigerator stayed empty and I stayed hungry.

When one of girls eventually was able to go shopping, we ate stuff like noodles, bologna, frozen pizza and fish sticks. I hated bologna and fish sticks but since that was my only choice of food, I ate it.

The girls claimed that they had made over $100,000 by robbing tricks a piece each year. A couple of the girls had been with Magic for over ten years and were preparing to retire.

A lot of the things that I desired to have none of the girls didn't have it. The ones that did have money of their own, stability, and their own homes they had been with him the longest.

Magic always said that I would be the exception and could obtain what I wanted well before ten years. I'd eventually see that was just another way for him to keep me hopeful.

The girls always encouraged me that I would get better with time on doing things his way, but Magic needed to *mold me first.* When I begin to make enough money to satisfy Magic, he gave me a new phone.

I checked my voicemail and found out that my car had been picked up and was sitting at the pound waiting for me. Magic refused to let me get my car and added the possibility of a new one to his list of promises. "No real pimp will let a chick have her own car unless she earned it." He said.

I immediately called my mom and updated her. Magic and the girls had given me so much information to justify why I was there. I tried to explain it all to my mom, but she couldn't understand what was going on.

One day, I was calling her telling her I was going to leave and the next day, I was saying that all was well and that I would be back once I had my money stacked.

Magic and I spent a lot of alone time together. In those moments I was very open and honest with him about a lot of things. *He was really comforting the broken lost girl in me. I actually began to see him as a dad in a weird way. He was teaching me discipline and instilling things in me like no one else had ever done.*

Magic and I bonded on such a deep level and I didn't care what was going **I wanted nothing more but to please him.**

One of his girls named Almond and I went to work in Miami together and he left the others in Orlando. He said that he wanted to spend more time with each of us and that she could also show me the ropes of the game.

Almond didn't like me much at first and she always gave me a hard time when I tried to be friendly. She often left me behind when we worked together. I wasn't too fond of her either because I thought she was stealing my stash to make herself look better to Magic.

She was instructed to hold my money because I was the new girl. I never complained to Magic about it since it all ended up in one pocket. He was the type of guy who paid attention to a lot of what was going on. He sensed my issues and addressed them without me saying anything most of the time. *He constantly reminded me of my purpose for being there.*

Magic had deep bonds in different ways with all of the girls in the house. Almond was upset with Magic one day because he had been spending more time with me and not paying her any attention. She decides to light a cigarette in the no smoking hotel room. ***Life in Magic's household changed for me instantly.***

Almond was only about 110 pounds, and Magic was closer to 200 pounds. As soon as she lit the cigarette, he jumped across the bed and smashed her face into the ground, stomping her with his foot. I had never seen anything like that in my life. She cried out, saying she was sorry. But he just stomped her harder and smiled while he was doing it.

I was scared for my life and I knew I needed to get out fast, but he continued to make sure that I didn't work alone. Magic and his entourage was always near when we worked at night. While we worked they rode around acting as if they were there to protect us. *I know today that it was to make sure nobody tried to escape.*

He later apologized for me having to witnessing that, and promised me I would never experience that as long as I stayed in my place and didn't act out of character.

I had gotten close with one of the girls in the house. When we made it back to Orlando I shared with her the things that happened in Miami and she spilled out the truth.

She warned me that if I stayed, I would definitely be next in line. There wasn't a chick that Magic had that he didn't beat on. She made it clear that the bond between Magic and I wasn't that deep to keep me from getting beat like everyone else. I wasn't going to stick around for that time.

Apparently everyone was receiving beatings when I wasn't around. But in front of me they were parading around as if Magic was just the most perfect guy to be with. The longer I stayed the more things began to come out into *the light*.

Oprah was a beautiful, 35-year-old woman that worked for him. At times, it seemed like she liked me. Other days, not so much. One night, Magic told the girls I was ready to work on my own. Oprah felt differently and she spoke up about it. She didn't think I was ready to be on my own just yet.

As we were loading the car to leave, Magic reached into the car and pulled Oprah out of the car from the window. I cried as we watched him punch and drag her, slamming her body against the garage. She begged and yelled for him to stop, but he wouldn't.

That same grin came across his face with every blow to her face. I couldn't stop the tears from rolling down my face. *When you're with Magic you have **no opinion** of your own. That was one of his many rules.*

He tapped on the window and asked me to roll it down. He kissed me on the cheek and told me to make him proud. The ride was silent until one of girls finally spoke and told me not to worry because it was Oprah's fault that she got in trouble. One of the girls reassured me that I would never have to experience that because I was special to Magic and everyone could see that.

In reality I wasn't special I was just a newbie. Most newbies in the house get the best treatment and aren't exposed to the realities of the game so they won't try and run off. Magic believed that I was going to be there with him for good.

When we made it to the track that night, I called my mom to tell her what was going on. As I talked to my mom, Magic had pulled up and yelled for me to get off the phone and get to work. He asked me if I was making plans to leave him. *I lied, and I told him that I was talking to my family to tell them good night.*

He told me not to worry about things I saw and to stay focused on making my money. As long as I stayed the same, nothing would change for me. I tried to run off with two of my tricks that night, but I was so scared and nervous that I frightened them away. They both backed out and dropped me back off.

Oprah still had to work the night Magic beat her. She was light-skinned so it was very obvious that she had been beaten. The pain eventually got too bad for her and Magic let her go to the hospital. I grew quiet and distant around the girls because I was beginning to see more and more that the game was more about being **trapped** than living a care-free life and making lots of money.

Sexy was always open and honest with me. Although she didn't want to leave, when I confided in her about my plans to leave, she supported me all the way. She knew the other girls hid the truth from me to keep me around and, more importantly, because of their loyalty to Magic.

The girls warned me that Sexy was a liar and she liked to run chicks off, but it didn't bother me. I didn't want to stick around much longer anyway. I believed her and had witnessed it with my own eyes now.

After coming home with little from being unable to steal from men Magic tells me that it's time for me to be molded. He was tired of me making money my way and he wanted me to start stealing like the rest of the girls. *I knew molded meant my first beating was on the way and I wasn't about to stick around for it.*

Magic initially told me that I would work in Dallas within the next few weeks when I first got with him, but weeks turned into months. Then one night Joy went to him complaining because I had been telling everyone I was

239

going back to Texas soon to see my boys, like Magic had been promising me in our alone time together. He told Joy that he had to lie to me about seeing my children to keep me cool so I wouldn't try to run off.

*I found out that each chick was required to be away from their family for a year, **no questions asked**. Magic had gathered that if a chick stayed away from her family for at least a year, she would be too attached to him because of the beatings and manipulation she'd receive she would no longer desire to even want to visit her family. Out of the eleven of us he had eight women around to prove that his plan worked.*

Magic had only ten girls when I was there but he often bragged about pimping on hundreds of others along the way. Some chicks hadn't seen their children in years, and some didn't care to see their family at all anymore. ***I couldn't imagine not ever seeing my boys again. I had left them but I was sure that I would return one day.***

The women continued to get beat regularly in the house in their private time with Magic. *The only reason I didn't receive those beatings is because I would manage to get away before my time had come.* I heard the stories behind the scars on the other girls. I always assumed that the scars were from childhood.

I never thought they were from Magic. I started paying attention more and I began to hear Magic tell the girls whenever they got out of line, *"that's fifty licks for you."* If they talked back or did anything out of line the number would increase.

Sexy wanted to show me what the results to the licks looked like. She pulled me over to the side one evening and lifted up the back of her skirt. She had this huge open wound on the back of her thigh. It was fresh and she told me that her quality time that everyone was so jealous of

240

consisted of her receiving licks. *It didn't bother her it was all part of the game. She was numb to it all.*

I grew more and more scared for my life each day, but I tried my best to stay calm and not let it show. I decided to cooperate and do as I was told at all times. *It was easier that way.* It kept me out of the fire with Magic. The more I tried to stay calm, the nicer Magic seemed to get, as if he knew I was planning to leave.

Sexy brought along another girl named Blonde. She wasn't feeling the atmosphere as well, so Almond, Blonde and I planned to escape together. Almond began to see that I genuinely wasn't after her or trying to compete and she opened up to me.

We were going to get a ride to the bus station and all go our separate ways back to our family. Almond and Blonde wanted to work a few more nights before they left town so that we didn't leave broke, but I refused to work. With Magic and his entourage patrolling, I couldn't see how they were going to make it out. Magic had a group of men ranging from the age of 18-35 follow us and him around everywhere we went. Like most well-known rappers are known to have an entourage, he called them is *goon squad.*

Almond told me that the day he stomped her face, she had actually got a room and was going to leave, but changed her mind and decided to stay. She hadn't seen her son in eight months. Magic promised she would see him soon. Like me, he had kept the promise dangling over her head with a debt to pay that she hadn't reached yet.

She admitted to lying to me in the beginning because of her loyalty to him, but she could no longer keep lying. She told me that the beatings I saw on her and Oprah were nothing compared to the beatings they received when they didn't meet their quota or when they upset Magic.

Magic split us up and some of the girls went back to Orlando while some of us stayed in Miami. Magic loved to get his feet rubbed and he sometimes slept the whole day away. I liked those days because if gave us a free day of rest.

In Miami, we had more freedom since we stayed in a hotel. Magic always got separate rooms from us. While he spent time with Sexy, my mom purchased my ticket and I took a cab to the bus station. Almond and Blonde stayed back to work and then leave. The greyhound was the only way I could travel without any identification.

Magic finally got word that I was leaving and he chirped me. The phone that he had given me was a boost mobile phone and instead of contacting us by calling us he would instead chirp us. So it was like having a walkie talkie. When his chirp came through I didn't have to pick it up. He could just start talking.

As he started talking he began to call off, "4 7 0 4 Norr." Magic had my driver's licenses and he had met with Kevin to pick up the remainder of my personal belongings.

He went to ask me, "How far do you really think you can go when I have all the information that I need to come and find you? Sexy Black, I thought you promised that you wouldn't bring this side of me out?"

"Why are you running away from me? Don't you see that you were made for this? Oh I wish I would have gotten you sooner in life." Magic continued going on and on.

I was so nervous, but I finally responded and told him how terrified I was of him and that I was leaving the game for good. He always had the right answers to get anybody to believe in him, but I just couldn't do it anymore.

I cried and he continued to ask for a chance to explain. He told me how much of a loser I was if I went back home to my family with nothing accomplished.

He told me that I had no job, no car, nor a place of my own to come home to if I went back. "Your sons are going to be so disappointed in you if you go back now like this.

242

I'm really trying to help you but I think you really don't know what real help looks like." He said.

When I finally made it to Orlando, the girls and the goons were waiting for me at the station. I had on pajamas and my eyes were swollen from crying, but Magic *insisted* that I still work.

We stopped by the hotel that they had been working out of to let me clean myself up from all the crying I was doing. As I sat in the room trying to process all that was going on and share with the girls why I was trying to leave, they each began to share with me how they ended up in the game.

Everybody story was different but not none of them had planned or wanted to be there. They just couldn't see themselves leaving at that point. What could they go back to? Some had no families. Some had neglected their family. Some had been neglected by their family. *In spite of the beatings and the work we did it was better than living a square life to them and returning back to places that had hurt them.*

Pimps drilled it in us how horrible of a life squares had it. Jobs with little to no pay. Families that hurt you as a child. Square women had it bad because they wanted love and to be appreciated by men while all men wanted was sex. Pimps had drilled in us that we had somehow surpassed squares because we were getting money instead.

It didn't help the situation at all being that I was one of those women who was once a square and was now in the game because I had experienced all of what the pimps had talked about. *I understood and even respected the fact that they didn't want to leave the game, but I promised them that one day, I hoped to get out for their sake and my own.*

Something on the inside of me still *believed* there had to be more to live than this. I just didn't know what but I was determined to keep searching. I couldn't see myself going back to my kids and telling them that this is all life is about.

I had only been in the game about eight months and I knew just how much it had changed me in so little time. I could only imagine how changed a person could be after three years or more in the game. It was because of them I got to see what my destination would be if I stayed in the game. Although they gave up on escaping, *I would never give up.*

In Magic's eyes we belonged to him for good. The quality time, long talks and sex with Magic normally worked to keep me hopeful.

Pimps had done what no other men in my past had done. They made me feel important and valued even while I was doing what some may see as the most **detestable.**

Magic would tell me things like, "No matter what you do for a living you are valued. Never define yourself by the price tag a trick or anybody tries to put on you. You're true value is priceless. No one can afford it."

If you were with someone for years who talked to you this way and treated you half way decent wouldn't you stick around? Especially if your background is one of brokenness? In so little time I was trapped. I knew my wifeys had kids with this man, knew his family, and shared so many moments with him one little lost girl wasn't going to be enough to convince everyone to leave that day.

Even while our situation seemed hopeless God was working it ALL out.

But this time, nothing could change my mind. I needed to find a way to leave. Almond contacted me and told me that Magic beat and raped her, but he let her leave and go back home. Her face was so bruised up that she cried every time she saw it.

She was disappointed that I hadn't made it out yet, but she was glad that I didn't stay with her and Blonde to experience what they had gone through. Blonde came back with Magic, but her happy spirit was gone. She was quiet, and it was obvious the black eye she now had scared her straight.

Magic took us all back to Miami for our off day and gave us money to go shopping and ride scooters on the beach. The day almost felt normal, but another one of the girls was fed up.

The last I remember is seeing Magic and his crew watching a video of her and I could hear her pleading for her life. The trip was bittersweet for a girl named Raven because her family was there and she wanted to see them.

The hotel room was about five minutes from her parents' house, but she hadn't seen them in years. Magic told her that she would be able to see them but when the time came, he changed his mind.

Raven was one of his favorite girls. She loved him to death and if she couldn't convince him to let her see her family, then the conversation I had heard between him and Joy was true. I was never going to see my family or Texas again if I didn't leave him soon.

Life with Flashy Duke

It was the Saturday before Easter of 2010. We worked on the beach that night instead of on Biscayne Blvd. I sat down and tried to figure out where I went wrong.

There was so much more I could be doing, and I didn't understand why my life had to be so ugly in order for me to travel to such beautiful places. I had so many mixed emotions and thoughts about everything.

It was about 7 a.m. when we moved to downtown to the after-hours spot, where all the drunk and high people hung out after partying at the beach. It was a strip club called Gold Rush where the pimps hung out right across the street. I had been there before with Ray.

On the morning of Easter, my mom sent me a picture of the boys dressed in their Easter suits. I was saddened again. I was supposed to get my babies out of the hood. I wasn't looking for a boyfriend anymore. I didn't want to be someone's sex toy.

I called my boys and told them that I loved them. I was so tired. I just stood there, hoping someone would rescue me. The other girls continued to walk around and pick up dates. The police patrolled and tried to shut us down but, nobody moved.

A girl walked up to me and asked what was I doing there. I told her I was working, just like the other girls she saw. She was new to Miami, but had previously worked in Vegas. She was actually about to leave, but saw me and refused to leave until I left with her.

Some of Magic's girls came over to check and make sure I was alright. They joked to see if I was trying to recruit her to come home with us.

We continued to talk and I told her that I just wanted to go home to my boys. I was tired of playing these pimp and hoe games. It never turned out to be what the pimp claimed it would be. *The truth always came out and I didn't want to be a part of any more crazy households.*

Ashley promised, like everyone, that if I came with her and didn't like it, she would put me on the first bus back to Texas. I didn't know anybody but the pimps I had out there. I was sure I didn't want to return to them so if this didn't work and she was lying about sending me home, I was going to be stuck.

I explained to her that if she was expecting me to have cash, I didn't. Magic had us drop off our money to him before we went downtown. She didn't care. She pulled out credit cards and said we could go shopping after we got some rest. A chick was waiting for us in an alley in a silver Mercedes. She introduced herself as Tammy and asked me if I was one of Magic's girls.

She was very familiar with him and his whole operation, and told me I was lucky to get away from him. By this time, Magic was upset and was calling me back to back. At first it was all sweet with apologies.

Once I told him this time I wasn't coming back no matter what he said. He got upset and told me that he should have just whooped my ass and if he ever saw me again, he was going to do just that. It was obvious that he had been drinking and was around a crowd because ten minutes later, he called and begged me to come back.

Tammy told me to turn my phone off so we could talk. She was counting big bundles of cash as she drove us to the destination. It was all in a Louis Vuitton bag and it looked to be about well over ten grand. Ashley told me that I was about to meet her boyfriend and what to expect when I got there. Tammy explained that the house, cars and everything that I saw from this point on belonged to her and her dude.

Ashley was only visiting. They argued about who was going to have me and Tammy said that once I saw the truth, I was definitely going to choose her dude. I asked Tammy if I didn't want to stay if she would pay for my ticket home and she agreed.

Tammy phoned her dude and told him that she was bringing a girl home, and he asked for cash. She explained to him that I didn't have cash, but if he just saw me, she was sure he wasn't going to turn me away.

We made it to a mansion in a city called Weston. This was nothing compared to Magic's home. Magic home in Orlando was only furnished in two rooms. The living room and the bedroom they let me sleep in. The other rooms only had floor mattresses and a futon downstairs in the living room.

The home had a circular driveway, a fountain in the yard, luxury cars and a backyard pool. There was also a spiral staircase on the inside. Tammy told me to sit on the staircase and wait for her dude to come. He introduced himself as Duke and asked me to stand up and turn around.

He told me that he liked me, but he couldn't disrespect the game and let me in his home free of charge. Magic had already called him and gave him nothing but bad news about me. *He had told him that I was just another Choose Susie in the game that like to run away and wasn't stable.*

He also told him that I didn't make him a lot of money but that he wanted me in spite of all of that. He showed me to my room and the bathroom, and told me to freshen up because I was going to the casino to work.

Duke dropped me off at the casino. He said I was different from most since Tammy liked me. All his chicks had their own places and didn't even know where he lived. He told me that he didn't like drama and preferred to keep everybody away from each other. He knew that I had two boys. As long as I played my cards right, he would send for my boys to come. The same old lies.

He felt it was best for me to be settled first. Even though they couldn't come move with me immediately, he promised that he would let them come down and visit and let me take them to Disney World.

Duke felt that it only took one or two girls on his team to get to the top. It seemed to me that Duke was already at the top. Sunday was their day off and since I was new to the household, they didn't want me to feel out of place. After picking me up from the casino we picked up their personal boat and set sail… *The day was so beautiful.*

We ate dinner at a restaurant off the beach and Tammy talked to me more about why she liked me. She could tell that I wasn't the jealous type nor did I seem to like drama. I didn't act like the type of chick who was looking for a boyfriend instead of a pimp. She could tell that I was hungry for the game and to make money.

She knew all about the long nights of walking and working the street and trying to rob tricks that weren't even worth it. She could tell I was tired and drained. They took me to the mall the following day to get clothes. Shopping was an every other day thing in their household.

After grabbing a few things from the mall Tammy let me grab some more clothes out of her closet. Tammy's closet was just like being at the mall because she had every high end label you could think of. Some designers I had never even heard of. Clothes still with tags on them and shoes unworn. Red bottoms and all.

They didn't believe in me having to wear the same clothes twice. The first few days after Easter, we slept in and relaxed around the house. They would come in the room and tell me to get dressed, but they never took me anywhere. I was tired from all the restless nights I had so I took advantage of their slowness to put me to work.

My blisters on my feet still hadn't went away from walking and wearing worn heels and boots. I needed to make some cash, but I wasn't about to complain about the rest I was receiving.

I had a room and bathroom to myself. They offered me the kitchen and went grocery shopping for me. I was accustomed to eating as much as I pleased but that all changed after being with Magic.

I felt spoiled at Duke's house so when I did work, I tried my best to let go of any fear or doubt I had because I felt he had rescued me. I owed him and Tammy so much. I had lost everything and nobody believed my story. Tammy believed me and she even let me drive her Mercedes alone. They trusted me to go to the mall by myself with cash.

Although I was still in the game, it was beginning to feel like something I could be proud of.

When Tammy and I went out to work, I never had to take my clothes off. Tammy worked fast. We worked about three hours most nights. Tammy's skills were so tight sometimes we didn't even have to get out of the car to make our money. More illegal activities. Tammy hated being called a prostitute or hoe. She was a veteran in the game. Her bank account and lifestyle status was proof that she deserved respect in the game.

Duke make it clear to me that everything they had was because of Tammy's hard work and no one else. They had personal barbers, stylists' maids and shopped at on the high-end designer stores. *When we shopped at stores in BAL Harbor Mall like Gucci, Duke and Tammy we're greeted on first name basis with the staff.*

They were treated like celebrities. Duke was a rapper by day. Being in the music industry was a way to cover their money trail. *Duke was what you would call a CEO pimp.* He had several other ventures outside of pimping and the music industry. He had plans of making it big in the music industry and leave pimping for good one day.

Things were starting to look up for me. Money was consistent. Duke was letting me send money home. I could do things again on my own. Duke was actually setting my money aside.

A couple of weeks had passed and Tammy came in the room to tell that we were going to Atlanta to get their son and work some events there. When we made it to the airport, they refused to let me board the plane without my license.

Magic still had my ID, Social card, and birth certificate and was refusing to give it back. Duke and Tammy kept the luggage and gave me cash for a cab, a bus ticket and food.

I finally made it to Atlanta and the bus station was directly across the street from Magic City strip club. It was late at night and although I tried to call Tammy and Duke, I wasn't getting an answer.

A white Range Rover pulled over next to me and my phone rang at the same time. It was Duke. They were asleep and he apologized for having me wait.

We pulled up to these high-rise condos in downtown Atlanta. When we arrived, their son was in the living room watching cartoons. I showered and went to bed.

The following day, Duke was already gone and Tammy walked in with groceries. I asked her what she thought about me asking Duke to go home and visit my family. I didn't get the response I was expecting. Tammy and I had made $10,000 working in just one night. *I knew for a fact money wasn't the issue.*

She couldn't understand why I wanted to leave after all they had exposed me to. They had lavish things but it wasn't enough. I still missed my kids. It was unfair that they were with their son and I wasn't with my mine.

I went downstairs and called my mom and asked if she would purchase my ticket. She was joyful and confused at the same time. Tammy came out and explained that she wasn't trying to be hard on me, but I had to understand that I couldn't compare myself to them.

Where I was at in my life, they had already been. She told me that I needed stay down. She told me about the time she had to go to jail, the times they lived in hotels and times they had other struggles. In her eyes, I was lucky to have met them and be in their presence.

I should have been thankful that they were willing to share their home and wealth with me. My situation could have stayed the same with Magic or turned out worse, but instead I was with Duke and her.

I understood what they had done for me, but I could never be comfortable the way I wanted to since my boys weren't there with me.

Plus the game just wasn't what it was promised to be. It still felt as though the game was just toiling with my emotions and insecurities.

We went over to Duke's mom's house and I met his sister and other relatives. I don't think his family knew exactly what he did, but they welcomed me and were really nice. I messaged my mom to purchase my ticket again.

Duke pulled up in a red Lamborghini and took me for a spin and to talk. He was upset that I wanted to leave. He told me to call my mom and have her bring the boys down to Florida so we could go to Disney World.

I knew my mom wasn't going for that. He told me that the white Range Rover belonged to the girl who had left previously and if I acted right that or something even nicer could be mine. I told him my ticket was paid for and all I needed was a ride to the bus station.

He was upset that I booked my ticket and that I put my mom in the middle of our business. In his eyes, I belonged to him and I made my own money. I didn't need my mom buying my ticket as if we didn't have the money to get it ourselves. "You ain't ready to grow up. Run back to your mom like you always do." Duke said.

He felt that he had failed and that I didn't trust him since I didn't give him a chance to live up to the promises he made to me. I told him I would come back, but that I needed to see my children and family. He asked me to cancel the ticket again and again, but I refused.

Tammy and Duke refused to take me to the bus station, so I asked his cousin to take me. His mom tried to convince to stay too but I missed my family. Duke left without saying goodbye, but later texted me telling me to have a safe trip and to come back soon.

I had to leave my luggage behind, which included all of the clothes they gave me. It was all the new stuff they got me but by this time the game had taught me not to be attached to clothes anymore. I left with only the clothes on my back and money to eat with. I was finally on my way back home. Nothing else mattered.

Chapter 14

Running Reckless

I've always been a runner. I changed relationships frequently. I changed jobs a lot. Now I was switching from pimp to pimp. It's like I was always looking for something and I'd tell myself that I had found what I was looking for.

Then shortly after receiving what I thought I wanted I'd find something wrong and move on. It became a life pattern for me and now it was evident in my destruction.

Besides the pain and low self-esteem that I suppressed for so long, I now had hidden shame to go along with that. You can't just go back to living a normal life after being a prostitute. I couldn't. At least I had never seen it done.

I had completely lost my way and didn't see a way out. The game had a hold of me and even though I had experienced some horrible things, I couldn't stop trying find satisfaction in the game.

It wouldn't be until I surrendered my life to Christ that the satisfaction that I was looking for from people, jobs, and the game could only be found **in God.**

After almost twenty-four hours of travelling on the bus, I finally made it to Texas. I waited for my mom at the station downtown. She finally pulled up and got out of the car to hug me. She was looking for my luggage, but all I had was a blanket that I had purchased on the ride back home. We had a lot of catching up to do.

The boys were at the YMCA when she picked me up. When we picked them up it was a whole new emptiness that I had never felt before. My children looked at my mom as their primary caregiver *and I dreaded the day I would hear my babies call her mama instead of me.*

I didn't have contact with any of my old friends other than Amber from Brinks. I sat at home during the day with my youngest son and just thought about what my life should have been. I couldn't apply for jobs without my Driver's license. My social security card and birth certificate were still with Magic and of course he claimed that he lost them.

I didn't know anybody with transportation other than my mom. My mother even questioned why I came back if I wasn't going to enjoy my time home. *I kept focusing on everything that was wrong with my situation and I couldn't find any peace.*

My kids were treating me so differently and I just didn't know how to deal with it. I needed *some real help* but asking for help was just out of my vocabulary.

I had really *underestimated the depths* of how much being in the game was affecting me. *I had normalized it.* I had changed the way I talk, dressed, and carried myself. It was like I had totally became a brand new person. I was more reckless than I had ever been in my entire life.

My mom assumed that it could all just be swept under a rug. I could live at home with her forever and find me a little part time job. She figured I could just get over it and simply move on. She didn't open up to many people about what was going on because she was embarrassed about it all.

She didn't want to be judged by people so she started carrying on her own little lie to minimize what I was going through. Everyone just knew that I was working out of town.

After sharing more with my mom about what I had gone through, she suggested that I just stay home in my room and do nothing. At least she knew her daughter was safe. No matter what my mom said and how much she tried to convince me, being home and doing nothing wasn't okay for me. I just couldn't give it up.

I called Duke and he told me I could come back anytime, but I couldn't come back empty- handed. There was no way I could make money being at home.

I got in contact with my old friend Amber and went out to the club with her. *I wasn't ready to deal with my reality so I resorted right back to my old ways of coping.* I didn't have anyone around me at that time who had my best interest at heart and everyone was really just entertained by this drastic change I had made.

Many assumed that I just didn't care anymore but that wasn't the case. I had allowed people to manipulate me so bad to the point that I couldn't break free. I didn't want to break free.

I had got in contact with Smooth and Tameka, purchased a ticket and went out to New Orleans to meet up with them again. I wanted to be around people who understood the game and the new me. My plan was to work and then head out of town to Florida

He picked me up from the bus station in New Orleans. By this time, Smooth had the *BMW* that he always talked about getting. Tameka was still around, but Megan had left shortly after I did.

The house was gone and they were living in hotels at this point. Tameka was hesitant about opening up to me this time because she didn't want to get attached and watch me leave again. In Tameka's eyes, Smooth was not manipulating us. She truly believed that he wasn't going to let her down. At least that was the lie she had told me.

Smooth was still talking about becoming a well-known rapper and if he ever made it, we would never have to worry about anything since we stayed around when things were hard. Smooth was pretty good at rapping but at the time, he wasn't doing much recording or any shows. *He was still pimping. He still was manipulating. He was even mismanaging money.*

Tameka still danced and Smooth let me go down to Bourbon Street to pick up dates. Everything was going smoothly until there was a small altercation between me and some tricks. Tameka was afraid to work at the club after the incident and Smooth didn't want me to get caught up and catch a case.

The following morning, we got on the road and headed to Florida. We had more than enough cash at this point to leave. I was ready to go back to Florida because I had fallen in love with the place

It was on my list to move there one day permanently *if I ever got out of the game.* Although the work I did was hell, waking up near the beach and walking along the sand was so quiet and refreshing. No matter what I was going through, the peace I got from moments I stole just to walk near the ocean was priceless.

Smooth knew that Duke would be looking for me to come back to him if he saw me in Florida. He asked for Duke's number to tell him that I chose up, but I refused. Duke didn't get out much and I wasn't concerned about seeing him like I was Magic. Magic was the type of pimp that would snatch you up if he had to in public. But not Duke he was too cool and arrogant for all of that.

Tameka always made me promise to never leave them again. I always told her I would stay as long as it seemed like we were making progress. I couldn't promise her that I was going to stay because I had become so accustomed to running. As soon as something didn't go right, I would be on my way. I still didn't feel as though I had control over my life, so my protection was to run.

We finally made it to Miami and the first few weeks, he tried to get me in the strip club with Tameka, but I wouldn't do it. I told him about Fountain Bleu Hotel and the luck I had there many nights. So I worked on South Beach instead.

One particular night, I was leaving a room after a date, I noticed a lady lying in the hallway. I checked to see if she was sleep or hurt and she woke up and assumed I was trying to help her. My first intentions were really to check out the Rolex she had on her wrist but I continued to just play it cool.

She insisted I go with her to the desk to get a key to her room. She was a reporter from New York who was in Miami celebrating her birthday. She had stayed out and gotten drunk, and fell out at the door of her room.

She kept asking me if I had ever been in a magazine or modeled before. She asked what I did for a living and I was ashamed to tell her. I kept changing the subject and she assumed I was a stripper. I let her think that.

She gave me her number and invited me to come to her birthday party later that night. She also asked me to call her if I ever came to New York. She kept telling me I was so beautiful and that I needed to do more with my life. *Was it really more to life than this? If it was I couldn't see it anymore.*

She walked me down to Smooth's car and as soon as the door opened, my reality set right back in. *I had given up my life and was really a prostitute, a call girl, thief, and an escort. I didn't even have to get high or drunk in order to work anymore.*

Smooth always had a tendency to get moody when money was slow or if things didn't go his way. I walked in on Smooth and Tameka having an argument. He raised his hand up to hit her and she screamed for him to stop. I left the room and went back down to the lobby to think. Later that night, Smooth instructed Tameka and me to work the beach.

I showed Tameka around Washington, Collins, and Ocean Drive. We walked around for a couple of hours with no luck. We went inside Delano Hotel to see if we could find some tricks to date.

As we were leaving, Tammy spotted me and forced her taxi driver to stop. She ran up and asked me what I was doing back in Miami and why I hadn't contacted them. I explained to her what was going in and we exchanged numbers.

Tameka called Smooth and told him that I had been spotted out and that she thought I was going to leave them again. She tried to get us to leave the beach, but I refused because I wanted to make some money. We headed down to a spot on Ocean Dr. to get some drinks and catch a date.

Tammy was there and she pulled me over to talk again. She didn't understand why I went back to someone other than Duke. I explained to her my need to make money and the fact that I didn't know how to start on my own at home.

The only option I saw was to contact Smooth and go to New Orleans. *Because I had been introduced to the game by a pimp, it was instilled in me that I was to never work without one. I became very co-dependent on pimps. Just how they wanted it.*

She told me that Duke was going to call me and come pick me up when the night was over. When Tammy found a date and was on her way to make some money, she called me to leave with her, but I refused. I told her I was staying with the other girls. Shortly after Tameka and I had got a date and was on our way to make some money.

After the date was over Duke called and I answered the phone. At first Tameka wasn't paying me any attention because she was focused on getting us to our new location. When she realized that I wasn't talking to Smooth and heard I was on the phone with Duke, she stopped the car in the middle of the road and yelled at me to get out.

When I told her to come and leave Smooth too, she refused. She told me I'd never be satisfied and, from the looks of my situation, I was going to keep running. She told me I'd never get anything accomplished by leaving.

I split the money from the date with her and got out of the car. Duke came minutes later and picked me up in his Bentley Coupe. He dropped me back off at the beach to work with Tammy.

They were now living in a high rise condo in Aventura right off the beach. The view from the condo master bedroom and living room was amazing. The room they had set up for guest faced the buildings and the busy street. I could lounge on the balcony in the morning and late at night. It was so peaceful, even with all the traffic.

I texted and reminded Tameka about our conversations of wanting to get out of the game, but feeling stuck. She told me that she hoped that I would one day escape for good and be able to get back to my boys. Along though I kept going back I always talked about leaving for good I just didn't know how to. Every time I went home it was harder than I had expected it to be.

Initially it started off as me wanting to find a way to make money for my family. The longer I stayed in the game the more evident it became that I had more issues that needed to be dealt with rather than making more money. I was lost girl who needed to be saved.

Duke had been trying to contact Smooth for my belongings, but said that Smooth was claiming I didn't have anything. I spoke with Smooth secretly on my own and he told me he wasn't going to give me my things back unless I came back to him.

I found an expired ID and I had the papers to show proof that my birth certificate was coming but now it was back in the possession of a pimp. Magic had my information and now Smooth had it, too.

This one particular night Duke decided to let me work alone. I didn't really like to work alone because I had a few bad experiences with tricks and it just seemed safer to not work alone. All that talk about pimps being our protectors were lies too. *Many times the women and girls in the game hide behind the lies because it sounds better than the sick truth we put up with.*

All of my dates that night had one thing in common: they all asked me to get out of the game and get my life together. They each shared that they hoped I would get out the game and one day find my true purpose in life.

One of the guys had even decided to not date me that night and even tried to pray with me instead. He opened up to me and started sharing with me how he had come to a place of purchasing girls for sex. It totally spooked me out that each encounter I had that night encouraged me to leave and go back home. They all seemed very genuine and sure that my life had more meaning than this.

I didn't know exactly what I wanted to do with my life anymore, but I knew that I couldn't keep running away from my real issues. Back then all I saw was the game and going back to my old way of living. I didn't really want either. I wanted something new.

I called Duke and Tammy to see when I could come to the house, but no one answered. He sent me a text and told me to work on Biscayne. I was shocked because Duke had told me that I would never have to go work on Biscayne again. Duke had finally answered the phone and it was really loud where he was.

When I asked if I could come to the condo to shower first, he said no and told me to keep working. I called Tammy and she told me Duke was drunk and out with his pimp friends. She asked to pick me up because she felt it was unfair that I was still working while the other girls had already went in. I was upset that Duke had played me, but I looked at the situation as my opportunity to leave.

Instead of sending the money home to my mom, I found a way to the bus station, changed my number, and headed back to Texas.

I hadn't identified as a victim of sex trafficking and no one around saw what was going on as a cry for help. I wanted to erase it all and start fresh, but it would be much more difficult to do than I imagined.

I was determined not to leave home again. I got my license, social security card and birth certificate in less than a month after I was home. I was offered a job at Carter Blood Care. My kids were slowly coming around and life was slowly starting to turn around.

I tried dating a few times, but each guy either tried to manipulate me by trying to make me get back in the game or provide them with knowledge on how to get money in the game and turn women out.

The guys I dated didn't consider themselves to be pimps, but their actions fit the description well. They wanted women who were willing to give them cash and were okay with them having other women.

It bothered me to have to settle, but I actually believed that I had to in order to be happy at this point. *No one would take an ex hoe serious.*

I stayed away from jobs that required background checks until I had the extra money to fix the situation from Miami. I didn't really want to work at my old job but once I began to see that the idea of something new was untouchable, so I applied for my old job that I had quit when I got with Smooth.

They offered me a position and I accepted. I went for the drug test and background check and passed them both. The pay was more than my temporary job at Carter.

My social life continued to be a wreck. I was still going to the strip clubs, and tricks always tried to get me to leave the club for money. Sometimes I refused, but when I needed the money, I went. I found myself leaving the club with men for money, popping pills, trying other drugs, and drinking again.

I had moved back home, got my old job back, and got a new car. I was trying to start over, but my past just wouldn't die. ***I was going through a spiritual battle and fighting it with the wrong weapons.***

The case I had pending in Miami came up after working about five months at my job. I was devastated that people would find out at work. Mainly my boss.

When I went on interviews and was asked about the gap in my work history I would lie and tell the interviewer that I took off work to take care of my sickly father who had died recently. My lie had backfired.

I had tried to give the normal life another try but it wasn't working. When my case popped up, it devastated me. *Thoughts raced through my mind that I had made a wrong choice on coming home.*

I got back in touch with Dasha and she was in need of some cash to get her boyfriend out of jail. I didn't have any cash to spare at the time, but I knew of some places we could go to and make fast cash. We went out to one of the strip clubs in Dallas. We hadn't even been there an hour before some tricks approached us looking for fun.

While we were standing outside the club, I heard somebody yelling Sexy Black. *My heart dropped.* I looked back, but I didn't recognize the car. Then the voice said, *"Don't make me get out this car and snatch you up bitch. Get over here."*

It was Magic. I hadn't seen him since I ran away on Easter in Miami. I was terrified but I stayed calm. He asked me to leave with him to talk, but I refused.

"I'm not in the game anymore."

I explained I was with my friend and couldn't leave her and my car. He demanded that I get in the car and have Dasha follow us in my car. I obeyed. We stopped at the store and I introduced him to Dasha.

Dasha found Magic attractive and said she was cool with chilling with him since he had weed. I had already told her some things about Magic and how things were while I was with him in Miami.

I only told her part of the story because I knew that if anybody really knew the truth they would think I was crazy. They would want answers that I couldn't even explain myself so I did just what my pimps taught me to do.

Dress the game up with beautiful lies to cover the dirty truth.

She knew he was a pimp, but she didn't care. I started having second thoughts and I told him that I would just leave with Dasha instead and hook up with him later. He slammed me against the wall, grabbed my neck and whispered in my ear, "You either leave with me by choice, or take the beating I owe you for running away the first time."

I got back in the car with Magic. Dasha followed us and parked my car in a hotel parking lot and got in the car with us. Magic called Oprah and told her that Sexy Black was back and he needed to drop me off with her. I interrupted him and told him I wasn't going to work tonight. "I'm only out tonight to help a friend. I gotta go to work in the morning."

He laughed and said, "Once you belong to Magic, you're always mine. You were made for this and going back to your old life and square job is pointless. You got real money to make."

"No man will ever love you the way you want to be loved because he'll never understand you. I can sum up

264

your life for you right now. You will find a little truck driver who'll pay all the bills and half-way love your boys.

You'll live paycheck to paycheck for the rest of your life in the hood. He'll cheat on you probably with a friend or some trash from the hood and out of revenge. He will half ass love your boys because they aren't his blood. Why go back to that life?" Magic said.

All I could think about were the beatings I saw and heard about. I didn't want to be subject to his beatings. He told me to stop worrying about how he treated the other girls. He swore he'd never treat me like that.

He took my phone and car keys and told me to get in the car with Oprah. I remember looking up in the sky, thinking to myself, *"Lord, help me."*

Oprah was so happy to see me and complimented me from head to toe. She was glad that I was back with my boys and had a new car and job.

She informed me that two of the girls had lost custody of their kids for missing court dates. I felt really bad that things were still not going well for everyone but I knew it wasn't much I could say to help them. I myself was still trapped mentally behind the game.

Oprah and I met up with the others girls. We parked the car and walked the streets of Dallas. I had never walked the streets in my hometown and I didn't want to either. I wasn't feeling it all. The girls were pissed and looking at me all crazy. I called Magic to let him know I didn't want to do this anymore.

He said, "God united us for a reason. You sealed the deal by bringing your friend along. I like her. She made up for you running away from me last time."

Magic told me that Dasha had made the decision to be his girl and that I would never see her again. He had already booked me a flight to Atlantic City since he didn't trust me to work in Texas. *"You're my hoe for life."* He disconnected the call.

I wasn't going to quit my job again. I was frustrated and the girls could see it. They contacted Magic and told him I wasn't working. I wanted to go home. Oprah was the peacekeeper in the group. She tried to keep me calm and insisted that Magic was probably going to let me go once I made some money.

I wasn't convinced since he told me that he had booked my flight and I believed him. I called Magic again and we argued over my decision to leave.

Pimps would always say that it's our choice whether we want to stay but I had yet to meet a pimp who would just allow me to walk right out of the door with threats to hurt me, false promises that things will get better, or insisting that I pay him more money first.

We were all in the car and I handed the phone to his bottom chick. He told her to give me my car keys and leave me right where I was. In my clutch, I had my debit card and a little cash. This was the first and only time Magic didn't search my things.

Texas wasn't anything like Florida, so there weren't many taxi cabs. I walked to the store and asked a guy for a ride to help me find my car. He didn't speak much English but shook his head yes to let me in the truck. While we were on the freeway, he unbuckled his jeans and he grabbed my head.

I swung the door open and he slowed down. He apologized and stopped. I shut the door and told him to take the next exit. He dropped me off in a hotel parking lot and I ran into the lobby until I saw his truck leave. After about five minutes, he finally pulled off and a taxi van pulled up to drop off some people. I got in the taxi and he took me to my car and I headed back home.

Magic still had my cell phone and when I made it home I called Magic's phone to see if he would let me talk to Dasha. She called me back and said everything was good and that she was going to be able to go home later.

I went to go see her when she made it home. I felt so bad and apologized for getting her involved in this. She didn't get to keep any of the money she made. Dasha and I didn't talk much after that.

I still hadn't got any calls back from other jobs. Time was running out for me to come up with paperwork that I needed. I felt like maybe I needed to return back since nothing else was coming through. I didn't want to admit it, but seeing Magic that night and replaying what he had told me in my head made me feel like I had some unfinished business to deal with in the game.

I ran into Leslie one night while I was out at the strip club. We had started talking more on a regular basis and going out together. Leslie and I got along perfectly fine and since Robert was no longer a conflict of interest, we never really had any other problems. Leslie needed to go to North Carolina to go to court, but she didn't have the funds for a flight. She asked me to drive her.

I was off on weekends and I had already taken the following Monday off. Her court date was set for Friday. My mom agreed to watch the boys and I assured her that I would return in three days. I left home with only a small sack of clothes. I guess I wanted her to believe that since I left the little clothes that I had left, she would know I was going to return.

On the way to North Carolina, I filled Leslie in on my journey and she did the same. We both had experienced major loss from the game. *I told Leslie that my job was in possible jeopardy now and I didn't know what I was going to once they fired me or found out.*

We made it too late to North Carolina and she missed

her court appearance. It was the CIAA weekend in North Carolina so we decided to stay and have fun. Leslie did nothing but escort work, so she posted pictures up on Backpage to make some money while we were away.

I was okay with working a little on the side for extra cash, but I didn't want to go back full time. Our reunion would be the time to get things back right. A few calls came through, but there wasn't much work there for us.

Being in North Carolina without the control of a pimp, actually felt good. I contacted my mom to check on the kids, and she kept reminding me to have fun and reiterating the fact that I also needed to return home Monday.

Whether my mom agreed with my decisions or not, she always had my back and looked out for my babies. I know she didn't like me being away from my kids. When we talked, it was as though she wanted me to explore the world. I'm sure she wanted me to explore life in a much more positive and safe way, but this was all I knew.

Some guys at the hotel had been trying to get Leslie's attention and one morning, they succeeded. She introduced me to David, Jacob and Joe, who were in North Carolina promoting for *Extreme Entertainment.* David was the CEO of the label and Jacob had recently been released from federal prison. He served a 20-year sentence. Joe was an up and coming model.

Leslie wanted me to get acquainted with David so she invited him to our room. The more we talked, the more I was able to gather that he wasn't at all interested in paying me for my services. He was a pimp. I told him that I had already been a part of that and I didn't want to go back to someone's household to find out all the talk was a lie.

"Chill. I'm not here for all that. I just want to have a good time and get to know you." He said.

He gave Leslie and me shirts to promote his new entertainment company and we hopped in the jeep with

268

them for the rest of the day. We went to the mall, a few urban stores in the hood, and a family festival for the CIAA. David never talked anymore about the game. He was a gentleman the whole day, paying for everything and complimenting me.

Leslie had changed her mind about going back to Texas and wanted me to go with her to Jersey to make some money for a little while. Since I was already on the verge of losing my job, and I was too embarrassed to tell my boss what happened, I decided to follow them back to Jersey.

I disappointed my mom when I told her the news, but I was on the verge of being out of a job again and back to being broke. So I ran from my issues again and got back in the game.

David had a really laid back personality. He didn't drink or do any drugs. We exchanged pictures of our families and I shared my feelings about the guilt I had about being away from my kids and working in the sex industry.

David's friend Joe was an adult entertainment model and had done some porn videos. I had mentioned my interest to David and I told him that I would consider it one day if the money was right. They told me that I needed an audition tape and with David's connections in Jersey, he pull some strings if I was really serious about it.

After being introduced to the life of sex as my hustle, I kept my mind open about different ways to increase my income. I still wanted to model and since I had done sex work it seemed right for me to transition into the adult entertainment industry.

When we made to New Jersey, David had me list all my monthly bills and obligations and told me to set up an account immediately to keep that money separate from everything else. He was serious about helping me get my life in order. The first step was to make sure that my kids and my bills were taken care of.

I sent money home and I was able to pay my car note. I could shop and do things without always having to check in. As long as I gave him some money he hardly ever complained.

When we had our quality time together, we either went to his main chick's condo or one of his condos in Orange, New Jersey. He kept things fun and exciting whenever we spent time together. He took me to the movies, out to dinner and I even went with him to pick out his Porsche. He took me riding on his motorcycles and he stayed buying me nice things.

One night when we worked in Atlantic City, I was playing chess at the casino, and I heard someone say, "Sexy Black!"

It was Magic again. I got up and ran to the restroom. I thought running to the restroom was going to stop him from coming after me but it didn't. He walked in that restroom like he owned the whole casino.

No one said a word or tried to stop him. He claimed that he only wanted to talk to me. His talk turned into him holding me hostage in the casino hallway for three long hours. He was drunk and really acting out.

The girls that worked for him kept walking by telling Magic to leave me alone but he ignored them. He was dropping money out of his pocket and spilling his drink everywhere. His speech was slurred and everything.

He kept grabbing me by my neck saying,
"Bitch I wanna just take you to the room beat your ass and rape you. You keep embarrassing me. Running off with these other niggas. You're mine bitch and I should have never let you get away."

People walked by and acted as though it was normal to witness this. No one tried to help and security walked by several times. Leslie and I had even befriended a guy while we were there but once he saw that I was tied up with a pimp he ran off and we never seen him again.

"You're in my territory now. I can drag your ass out of here and no one would stop me. I run this shit." He said.

I cried and yelled for him to let me go, but he refused. He grabbed my bag took my money and my phone. He went through my pictures and found pictures of David and me. That made him more upset.

I had lied and told him that I didn't have a pimp and I was just working with Leslie. The only way he would leave without me was if I let him take my things. He took my phone and I had to promise him that I would gather my things and come with him the next day. He finally gave up and let me go.

David was sick that weekend and wasn't able to come to the city with me. He was sleep when Leslie called, but once he got the word, he got on the road and brought his goons with him. Like Magic, David had his own entourage when he needed them.

The next night, we all went back to the casino to surprise Magic. David had us go ahead of them and when David walked up, Magic had me by my arm, trying to get me to leave with him.

David walked up and asked Magic what he was doing and Magic responded by saying, "Talking to my bitch."

The next thing I know, they were fighting. The goons broke it up and then security came. We all flooded the scene. We headed back to David's crib and Magic called all night, arguing and requesting that they meet up again. David never entertained Magic again after that night. I would have another run in with him when I moved back to Texas. *Every time Magic saw me he tried to snatch me up and force me to leave with him. Somehow I would manage to escape.*

The holidays were coming back around and David had already told me that I wasn't going home for Thanksgiving. I spent Thanksgiving with David and his other girl that worked for him. David had already promised me that he was going to let me go home for Christmas instead.

I booked my flight in advance so he couldn't change his mind. The only thing I had to worry about money for gifts. By the time Christmas rolled around the calls were really slow. We were lucky if we got one or two calls. David told me that he wouldn't let me down, even if money was slow. I was afraid he was going to use that as the excuse to keep me there.

I still had an ad posted on this website for modelling gigs in the adult entertainment industry. I got an email from this booking manager asking me to come out and star in my first porn video. I told David about it and he suggested that I not do it.

The booking manager kept reaching out to me and pressuring me to take this opportunity. I had spoken with him before in the past and I had shared with him that I was wanting to get myself out there and be known.

He kept encouraging me that this video could be the one to help me get calls from major production companies in California. If I did it I could be on the road to stardom.

The gig was for a humiliation scene that involved white guys mistreating black girls. It was supposed to be like a fetish video shoot but once I got there it began to feel more like a hate crime video.

I had completed all my STD testing and decided that I was going to move forward with the shoot. I needed the money. I had never dreamed of being a porn star but at the rate I was going it sounded better. One of the girls I worked with drove me to the pill man first before she dropped me off.

She was going to stay at first but once I made it there the booking manager told me that no one but me was allowed upstairs. I got dressed, popped my pill, and called David. Once I made it on set and those lights hit my eyes I completely zoned out. All I remember was the production manager telling me that the only way that I would get paid was if I finished the whole video shoot.

Even if I didn't finish it they would still use whatever footage they had and make their profit from it. The first two scenes were oral sex and it was like they wanted to slowly prepare me for the hell I was about to endure for the next few hours.

Nothing on the video beat the pain I already felt inside. It didn't amount to the humiliation and shame I had already felt. The after effect of the video shoot would nearly kill me. All my emotions had surfaced and I was on the brink of a mental breakdown. I didn't work the next couple days because I still hadn't fully recovered from it all.

I had a lot of stuff going on in my head and I needed something to help me clear it. The girl I worked with at the time gave me a Xanax and ecstasy. I took them both. We drank and smoke that whole day.

I just wanted to erase it all from my head. I was hallucinating and everything. I had even called my mom and asked her what my name was. I just kept asking her, "Please tell me my name. What are my kid's name? Where do I live?"

The girl who I had gotten high with ran off back to her room. I started wandering down the hotel hallway beating on doors and everything. I contacted David and started asking him, "Why am I here? Was I really only created for this? I really thought I was supposed to be somebody and doing something with my life. What is wrong with me? Help me please!!"

He hung up in my face and I'd never forget that message he sent me that night.

"I can't help you. You need God."

No pimp had ever been so honest with me before in all of my life. He could have used that moment to plant more lies and deceit into my life but instead he spoke truth to me. I did need God. But I didn't even know where to start.

I made it home and I spent the night with my family. Then Leslie and I headed out of town to work. We needed to make money for Christmas shopping and David was expecting for me to come back with money for the new Porsche. Christmas was so great that year. I was able to finally buy my boys and all my family members something for Christmas.

Leslie and I had discussed coming back to Texas for good. I hadn't broke the news to David yet, but he already knew my feelings about wanting more out of life. When I came back from Texas after Christmas, he had an expensive watch waiting for me that valued over two grand.

We brought in the New Year together in his home town of North Carolina. His entertainment company hosted a really New Year's party and it was all packed out. Everyone had a great time and Leslie had even came down to celebrate with us.

When we got back to Jersey, Leslie and I continued to work together. Leslie invited me to go out to the strip club with her to meet Joe after work one night. I didn't think I needed to ask David if it was cool or not. I had already made my quota and he normally never questioned where I was anyway.

David showed up to the club, snatched my drink out my hand, and pushed me outside to the car. I had never seen this side of David. I didn't know whether to be scared or just laugh. He had me sit outside in the car until he was done inside the club. It was freezing outside, but he didn't care. He finally made it back to the car and he drove 90 miles per hour all the way back to the condo, yelling and screaming at me.

He punched me in my face and snatched my wig so hard that he split it. He held my head in his lap, pressing on it the whole ride back. Because I didn't tell him I was going to the club or give him any money yet, he figured that I went out to try and find a new pimp.

When we made it inside of the condo, he took my watch back. Then he took his belt off and beat me until he got tired. I kicked, screamed and cried, but it only made him angrier. After it was over, he apologized, had sex with me and went to bed.

The next morning, he gave me my watch back. I had a black scar under one of my eyes. I put make-up over it, fixed my wig and got back to work. I was planning to leave town with Leslie for work temporarily, but after that beating, it was the confirmation that I needed to leave.

The only thing I needed to go back to Jersey for was my court date for a prostitution charge I had got from a sting operation. Leslie was happy that things ended between David and me, but I wasn't so sure that I could trust her anymore either. We did a two-girl show before we left Jersey and after we left our room to get on the road, I noticed that my watch was gone. We went back to the hotel and it was gone. I felt like Leslie had stolen it. She was just too nonchalant about it.

When we arrived in Atlanta, I found out that her sister-in-law was a jeweler. Before we made it to Atlanta, we worked in Baltimore. When I looked at her laptop, I found her pricing the watch online. She denied stealing my watch and said that I was overthinking everything. I didn't know who to trust anymore. I couldn't even trust myself.

When we finally made it back to Texas one my childhood friends contacted me and said that she wanted to go and make some money with me. Leslie and I had already planned to take our trip to Killeen, El Paso, and Phoenix.

My friend was on board and we met her at her mother's house to drop off her kids. She came back to the car with some disturbing news to share with me.

"My mom said the Holy Spirit spoke and told her that you need to get away from Leslie or she is going to be the death of you." She said.

When Wanda and I were alone, I told her that I wanted out. She told me that I was better than this. Although she had chosen to come along, she wasn't going to make this permanent. She promised herself that this would be her only time.

She went with us to Killeen and it was extremely slow. None of us were getting calls. I needed to pay for my attorney and David wanted new rims for the Porsche. I got a text from a girl who said that she liked my pictures and she wanted to know if I would let her come work with me.

She'd just had a baby and her boyfriend was going to watch the baby while she worked. Leslie saw it as a way to try and make more money. I just wanted to help her and the baby. We picked her up before we headed to El Paso and Arizona. We made it to El Paso and we still didn't get any calls. It was never liked that when we visited before. It was like we had this strike of bad luck all of a sudden.

Our last stop was Arizona. My friend Wanda was fed up and ready to go home. When we made it to Arizona, we just chilled in the room. Wanda made plans to leave since things weren't moving for her. She took it as a sign from God that she wasn't supposed to be there.

Ebony was drinking and losing it. We had to let her go,

too. I took her to the bus station, gave her some cash and a blanket for the ride, and said my goodbyes. It was back to being Leslie and I.

I ended up receiving an outbound call to come to a hotel near the airport, but Leslie didn't want to go because she didn't like dealing with black clients unless they were older. It was obvious that these guys weren't older, but I was desperate and she was, too. So, we went.

When we got there, it was three guys but one of them was distant because he was on an important call. It seemed like he was on the call forever.

Leslie was getting restless. The guy finally got off the call poured out all the money in a duffel bag onto the bed to get our attention. He was boss man out of the crew. He paid Leslie and I for an overnight stay. We were both relived to finally be getting some money.

Boss man and I quickly hit it off. We stayed up for a majority of the night just talking. He wanted to know my story or how I ended up on an escort website. The next morning they took us to breakfast.

Boss man helped me locate an attorney and he gave me the money to pay for the attorney, as long as I promised him that I wouldn't go back to my pimp. I had even received a call from a video production company in California to shoot again. After talking with boss man I decided to decline on the offer and never went.

He said that he had something better and would make me more money sooner. He wanted me to transport drugs to New Orleans, but after getting to know me, he felt that he was put in my life to get me back home to my boys--*for real this time.*

He couldn't understand how someone as sweet as me could end up in the game and with such harmful friends. *He just keep telling me, "This is not you. I really hate this and want you to get out for good."*

277

We kicked it in Arizona a few more days until he got the call to make his next drop. Once he got the call we exchanged numbers and went our separate ways. I decided not to go back to Jersey. I continued working in the industry and travelling out of town with Leslie.

Boss man and I continued to stay in contact for a while. I had started doing research on opening up my own wig boutique. Leslie and I had planned on being business partners but once my IPhone came up missing I was done chasing dreams with her.

I was convinced that maybe the shop would work for me alone. I talked to my mom about it and everything. I had a new plan and for once, it didn't involve a pimp. As soon as I had decided to leave it all behind for once I got a call from where it all started. Smooth.

I was so ashamed of myself for picking up his call and leaving town I told no one that I left. I didn't make it a week out there with him. He used the same bait and switch trick on me. This time I hid my money and when we made it to the gas station to load up I looked him dead in his eye and told him that I was leaving for good this time. Not just Smooth but the game.

I waved him and Tameka good bye. I sent him a long text letting him know that I was going to do whatever it took to NEVER pay a pimp again. I didn't hear back from Smooth again until over a year later.

He contacted me on Twitter, and three days he was found dead in his home in Houston.

*There will be times in life where God won't rescue us from situations. God knows something that we don't know or seem to realize when we're trapped in bondage: WE HAVE THE POWER WITHIN US TO LEAVE. With all the brokenness I carried into the game I walked away with the same brokenness and some. But there was something on the other side of this choice I had made: **REDEMPTION**.*

Part Three

She Came to Herself

Part Three
Introduction

The love I once longed for was untouchable and expired. I was unworthy of it and somehow my life had turned for the worst. I tried to make myself believe that it was the money that kept me but it wasn't.

I had exchanged my mask somewhere along the way. Before Smooth came into my life my confidence and my identity was built on accomplishments, materials, and a job. **Now I had nothing.** So I held on to the game and its rules for dear life. Then the game and its rules *failed me.*

I learned our identity **can't** be rooted in material possessions or even a certain way of life. What if those things fail you then what will you do? Be depressed all your life or go on this crazy journey of trying to find yourself through a job or a relationship only to end up feeling emptier?

I didn't know who I was without the **security of things.** A job. A title. Money. Material things. They were the mask that was keeping me all together. Once those were taken away from me I didn't know who I was anymore. Instead of healing and dealing with my issues they became the driving force in my life.

As I journeyed through life there was always this small still voice inside of me trying to tell me not to do a lot of the things I had done. Back then I didn't know that small still voice was God. I argued with that voice on numerous occasions. God had tried to tell me many times to not take certain paths that I had chosen.

Every time, I threw my sin out there as the reason to ignore the voice to walk away from the game. I couldn't understand how I could be so low and still be given a chance to try again. The further I seemed to drift away the *more God continue to woo me closer to him and use whoever he had to help me to see that there was a better life ahead of me.*

*No matter how far I ran, someone always left me with a little hope. Somebody always encouraged me to never give up. For every lie that was fed to me today I know and believe God sent someone to speak truth to me **but I didn't have the faith to believe it**. Even while some preyed on me, Jesus had already prayed for me.*

"Simon, Simon, Satan has asked to sift you all as wheat. But I have prayed for you Simon that your faith may not fail. And when you have turned back, strengthen your brothers". Luke 22:31, 32

God already knows that his sheep will go astray. Even when I wasn't thinking about God, He was thinking about me. God feels that same way about you too.

Chapter 15

Lost Girl Embraces God's Grace

*When he came to his senses, he said, 'How many of my father's hired servants have food to spare, and here I am **starving** to death! I will set out and go back to my father and say to him: Father, I have sinned against heaven and against you. I am no longer **worthy** to be called your son; make me like one of your hired servants.' So he got up and went to his father.*

But while he was still a long way off, *his father saw and was filled with compassion for him; he ran to his son, threw his arms around him and kissed him.*

The son said to him, 'Father, I have sinned against heaven and against you. I am no longer worthy to be called your son.'

But the father said to his servants, 'Quick! Bring the best robe and put it on him. Put a ring on his finger and sandals on his feet. Bring the fattened calf and kill it. Let's have a feast and celebrate. For this son of mine was dead and is alive again; he was lost and is found.' So they began to celebrate. Luke 15:17-24

I always thought that life was either good or bad. You're either on the right side or the wrong side of life. To an extent that is true. But what about life for those of us who've done some bad things but still desire another chance to embrace the goodness of life?

*I would tell that person, have you embraced **God's grace?***

After leaving the game for good in May 2011 I returned home. Like my previous attempts of coming back home I was determined to get my life back on track. I did. Well, in a way. I got a legit job. Three to be exact. I was working at two call centers and Marshalls.

I got my sons back and I even got us our own place again after staying back with my mom for a few months. Things were finally beginning to turn around for my family and me. My boys and I were restoring our relationship.

The turnaround didn't include my problems with men to change. I still found myself in and out of broken relationships. Now I had this whore like mentality that I embraced. I continued to attract men who were similar to the pimps I had. *Manipulators and only seeking personal gain.*

Because I had this shameful past I now **believed** more than anything that I had to date any guy that would have me if I wanted to be in a serious relationship regardless of how he treated me. They knew they weren't good for me and would feed the lie I had told myself, *I didn't deserve to fight for or have anything better.*

It got so bad that I found myself dating this guy who would lead me to sitting in a court room about to literally lose my life through the prison system for being affiliated with him. I was trying to be his down chick and it backfired in a major way. All I can say is **BUT GOD.**

After the jury finished discussing what I shared on the witness stand, the detective came out and told me that the jury decided to let me off. Their only request was that I NEVER talk to that guy again and that I'd focus only on my kids and restoring my life back. I changed my number. I stopped writing and responding to his letters from jail. I started spending more time with my family.

I still didn't give up dating, I couldn't. As messy as my life was I felt it was still important for me to have a man around. The next guy I got with really seemed to be different. He seemed to accept my past instead of using it as a tool like other men I had dealt with in the past. He accepted my sons and everything but then things started to change.

People were all in our business and kept bringing my past up to him and he couldn't handle it anymore. He began to drill me all the time and he would ask me this question, "Where was God when all of this was happening in your life?" Next it was, "Why don't you go to church?"

Before I got with him I had attempted suicide while in the relationship that almost got me incarcerated. I remember thinking that night in my closet with that gun to my head, "God where are you? Why me?" I had never shared the guilt that I felt for my actions with anyone until after my suicide attempt.

I had just been released from court and I went to work trying to act normal and I broke down to one of my co-workers. She was always really positive and talked a lot about God and something in me told me to pass her a note that said, "If someone felt like they sold their soul to the devil and decided that they wanted it back, could they receive it back?"

Immediately she responded and told me about a man named Jesus and how He had died for someone like me. She shared God's grace and mercy with me and sent me the salvation prayer. That day at work I prayed, repented, and asked for forgiveness.

So when my boyfriend at the time asked me about God I knew I was in good standing with God when it came to my salvation. I just wasn't trying to attend church nor was I trying to talk about my past all the time. I wanted it to just go away but it didn't. It wouldn't.

I was working on Sundays at the time and I had begun telling myself that once I got my schedule changed I would find me a church home. A few weeks later my schedule changed at work. It totally blew my mind and I was nervous about actually finding a church home. In my mind I thought church was for people who *strived to be perfect.*

My life outwardly still didn't quite reflect what I thought God expected of me. I was still clubbing, drinking, and shacking up with my boyfriend. I thought God was after the righteous people but I was *so wrong.*
Jesus came into the world to seek and save the lost.

On mother's day of 2012 I got baptized and made a public declaration that I was giving my life to Christ and not looking back. By June, my boyfriend and I had broken up. He didn't even make it to church with me to get baptized and things between us continued to go downhill.

Initially I was supposed to use that time to get myself in order and wait on my boyfriend. He had some personal issues that he needed to deal with as well. But the wait wouldn't last very long.

I was getting involved in different ministries. My boys and I started going to church on regular basis. A lady at church brought me a study bible and I started reading it. The Word of God was really touching some deep parts of me that I wasn't ready to confront.

I would still go to party sometimes but I started getting convicted in my spirit about it. I tried drinking the feeling away but it wasn't working. I was still trying to hold on to other ways of escaping, *God was showing me more and more that my old ways of escaping wasn't going to work this time.*

For the next three months my life would only consist of church and work. I stopped clubbing and I put down the alcohol. I had even given up men and was finally learning how to be comfortable single.

I let go off all my old friends and I started making new church friends. We were doing bible studies at their house.

Talking on the phone all the time about God this and God that. I thought I had really found some new friends who understood the new path I was trying to take.

Before long the patterns of my past was back at my door. I assumed that because my new friends had been *"Christians"* most of their life that they were somehow better for me. Since they didn't have a dark past like mine I assumed they didn't have the same struggles as me. I was so wrong.

One of my new friends had a house warming party. There was alcohol. There was smoking. There were these discussions that wasn't at all about God. I had seen a side of my friends that night was very familiar to me. One of the guys from my church had been making eye contact with me and flirting. I blew it off at first.

When the party was over he stayed around at my friend's house and walked me to the car. We stayed outside talking for the longest and the next thing you know I had a one night stand with this man.

Since we went to church together I tried to carry it on and use the relationship as *my cover up*. I didn't want to be alone. He had made all these promises that we would make things right and get married one day. *It was a total mess.*

I was still afraid that love would never find me. More than anything he didn't seem to be bothered by my past. Every Sunday my conviction would get stronger and stronger and it seemed as if every sermon was centered on my life.

I would ask him if the service affected him and he'd say, "That's just because you're new to this and you have a baby conscious. Don't worry about it. We're good *all* Christians live like this." I remember thinking, why *go to church then if we don't even try to live like the Word of God?*

Then I started having these dreams about someone confessing to me that they had HIV. I couldn't see the persons face in my dream but I knew it was a guy. I had missed my period but I was scared to go to the doctor because I was afraid the guy in my dream was going to be this guy I was dating.

I just knew that God was finally punishing me for all the bad things I had done. My mistakes often had a way of catching up with me and I knew they would be worse now that I was supposed to a *Real Christian.*

After talking to my Sunday school teacher about it and praying the voice of God was clear to me. I broke it off with him and told him that I wanted to take my journey with Christ as a Christian serious.

He didn't take the break up well and I expected that because it was so sudden. He laughed and said, "I'm losing my benefits because you wanna try to be like Jesus now? Come on, just be you Chanel nobody is perfect."

Since the beginning I always thought the desire I had was to be loved. I thought being loved meant that I needed it to come from someone else. When the love from a man wasn't good enough I thought love from my kids was going to be enough but it wasn't.

Then my desire to be loved turned into a love for money. *I was so focused on trying to change the outer parts of me I was missing the bigger picture. God was drawing me closer so He could heal me and **change my heart.** Little did I know I would be on my way to discovering that even in all of my mess God would still have an expected end for me. A good one.*

One evening my mom calls me into the kitchen to talk. One of my old high school friends was in the hospital and it wasn't looking so good for him. It was my old friend Derrick.

287

We talked and met from time to time when I was working in the sex industry. I had even came home once and went to see him while he was in the hospital. He had told me it was for alcohol poison that time.

After a while I started to feel like he was only communicating with me to be noisy like everyone else who tried to come back into my life. He always wanted to ask me questions about the industry and it just didn't sit well with me.

I had made the decision to never talk with him again. It wasn't just him, I didn't want to deal with *anybody* from my past. He had been contacting my mom and everything but I would never make the phone call. I put all that aside and made my way to the hospital with my mom.

Immediately when I walked through the doors of his room I knew *this was my wake up call*. I asked everyone to leave the room so that Derrick and I could talk. I dropped to my knees and begin to pray. Derrick didn't need to say anything and he just started crying.

Like me, Derrick had a desire to be loved too and at the age of 24 his chase to discover that *love came to an end.* He only lived about a week after I went to go see him. I had learned something that day and unlike many other lessons I wasn't about to ignore this one.

Derrick had been in church all of his life. If anybody deserved to live simply because they went to church it would have been Derrick.

He wasn't perfect by far but he was someone I knew that in spite of anything that he went through he praised God. In high school he would always try to talk to me about God and I wouldn't listen. I was too busy judging Derrick.

I knew with everything in me that should have been me lying there in that hospital bed. From all the crap I had done *death* should have been my destiny. I had been a horrible mother. I had given my body to men. *I had turned my back on God, family, and myself.*

Yet, God still graced me with His mercy instead. There was no way I was going to take this chance to live again for granted.

I made it to the doctors and the results came back and confirmed that I didn't have any STD's but that I was going to be a mother again.

I wanted to be embarrassed and truth be told at first I really was. Then a memory of Derrick lying in his hospital bed, a replay of Lil Wayne's 'How to Love' video, and hearing Bishop Jakes say, "You're pregnant with Destiny", somehow I knew this time my journey was never going to be the same.

I began to take off the mask and allow God to truly take control of my life. Somewhere in the midst of all the chaos I found new life and a new song. My heart had been made new. My path had been made straight. The lover, friend, sister, brother, and confidante had been there all long, within me.

I didn't need a man I needed Jesus.

I didn't need to make a million dollars I needed faith.

I didn't need a pimp I just needed to surrender to God and allow Him to order my steps.

I didn't need to be Super Woman and cover up my pain. I needed to speak up and be the woman God had called me to be.

I didn't need some high paying job or a degree to make my life have prosperity and meaning. I needed to know that my true identity was in Christ and in Him I have all that I need to live a fulfilling life.

In my infliction God still had purpose. My lost journey had been covered in God's grace. Instead of looking at my sin and using that as an excuse to not try again I laid my issues at the altar and decided to embrace God's amazing grace.

I gave birth to a healthy baby girl in May of 2013. My relationship with my boys has been fully restored and they've forgiven me. *My mom and I worked out our issues. I forgave my dad and every other man I allowed to mistreat me. I forgave myself for my poor decisions.* **Forgiving myself has been the hardest part.**

I would be a liar if I told you that my life in Christ has no struggles. It does. Today, instead of escaping I've decided to make an effort to live a life I don't have to escape from. That's hard work but it's worth it.

God honored my desire and has given me many opportunities to get in front of the camera and be an inspiration to others.

Only this time it's for meaningful purposes. I didn't became an attorney but I do still get to witness seeing many lives being changed. At the end of the day that's all that matters to me.

Once lost now found. Once blind now I see. Through it all it's safe to say that God was still leading the way.
Signed,

Lost Girl Saved By Grace

But where sin increased, **grace** *increased all the more, so that, just as sin reigned in death, so also grace might reign through righteousness to bring eternal life through Jesus Christ our Lord. Romans 5:20, 21*

To my Readers

Thank you for taking out the time to read my book. I was very nervous about taking my life story public because I know how cruel people can be. I pray that if you made it this far that reading my book has challenged you in some way to step back and take a look at your own life. A lot of times we don't like to talk about or deal with what's really hurting us. I pray that if there is anything in you that you've tried to cover up and not deal with that you take out the time to deal and heal from those issues. I know life can put strains on us to always be in this mode of having it all together. Sometimes we must fall apart in order to reach a place of freedom that we're all out here chasing. If you feel like you're alone you're not. I don't want to sound cliché but I must share the truth with you, Jesus is truly the way.

Acknowledgements

I must first give all honor to God. When it's all said and done no matter what I thought I was seeking after in this world, ultimately I know today that it was you all along that I was longing for. I'm grateful that I was able to live long enough here on earth to finally embrace what true unconditional love from a father is really like.

To my oldest son Semaj, my King, I love you. I thank God every day for restoring our lives and bringing us back together. I'm ready for the new chapters God has in store for us.

To my youngest son Raylon, You're so much stronger than I was at your age. I pray that you will continue to grow into the King God created you to be. Thank you also for your forgiveness and warm embrace after such a rocky start.

To my little Princess Destiny. It's because of the trials that I've faced you won't have to go through or shed the tears I've have. The first and only man you've ever praised and worshiped is Jesus Christ. Because of that I can rest in peace. I thank God that after all my silly wrong turns he gave me one more chance to become someone's mom again.

To my family I thank you for your patience and unconditional love. Even when you guys couldn't understand my journey you still never left my side. I'm grateful for that.

To my sisters of Woman of Purpose thank you so much for accepting me for me. I can finally say that I know what sisterhood feels like.

To my sisters of We are Cherished. God really blessed me when he allowed me to walk through Cherished Doors that day. I know a lot of times you guys say I inspire you but the truth is you inspire me. I watch and read about you guys going through so much yet no matter what you still find your way back through Cherished Doors. As I take my chance to finally come out of my cocoon I look to my left and right and I see that I'm not alone. Keep flying.

Ms. Lynn thank you for always believing in me.

Dennis my first official mentor thank you so much for not wasting time and believing in me.

Raheem thank you for challenging me to put my thoughts paper instead of only sharing in between phone calls at work.

To ALL of those who contributed to my growth in anyway thank you so much!!!!!

The Story Continues...........

It's one thing to be saved by Grace.

It's a total different story living in

Grace!